Never Say Die

MELANIE DAVIES &
LYNNE BARRETT-LEE

Never
Say
Die

A young girl.
A horrific accident.
A love that captured
her heart.

harper
true

n order to
nd places
have been changed

HarperTrue

an imprint of HarperCollins*Publishers*
77–85 Fulham Palace Road,
Hammersmith, London V6 8JB

www.harpercollins.co.uk

First published by HarperTrue in 2009

1

© Melanie Davies and Lynne Barrett-Lee

Melanie Davies and Lynne Barrett-Lee assert the moral right
to be identified as the authors of this work

A CIP catalogue record of this book
is available from the British Library

ISBN 978-0-00-731752-3

Printed and bound in Great Britain by
Clays Ltd, St Ives plc

Mixed Sources
Product group from well-managed
forests and other controlled sources
www.fsc.org Cert no. SW-COC-1806
© 1996 Forest Stewardship Council
FSC

FSC is a non-profit international organization established to promote the
responsible management of the world's forests. Products carrying the FSC
label are independently certified to assure consumers that they come
from forests that are managed to meet the social, economic and
ecological needs of present and future generations.

Find out more about HarperCollins and the environment at
www.harpercollins.co.uk/green

foreword

by Dame Tanni Grey-Thompson DBE

I first met Mel in the mid-1980s, when we were both competing in South Wales. Right from the start, it felt as though I had known her for years. She is one of the very few people I've ever met who can talk more than me! She is always positive, no matter what may be happening in her own life, and it really seems that nothing will stand in her way, mostly because Mel just won't let it. She always shows an infectious optimism, confidence and gritty determination, even in the face of seemingly insurmountable adversity. It is that incredible stubbornness that is evident in everything she does and makes everyone around her think that they should be doing more.

For some, this book may be an uncomfortable read at times. Melanie certainly pulls no punches in describing in detail the everyday problems encountered by many wheelchair users. It is also an uplifting experience, a bit like meeting Melanie herself. It takes twenty years and a lot of heartache until she feels she has control of her life when she launches the TREAT Trust charity.

Time and again throughout the book you will find yourself wondering what else fate can throw at Melanie, and although she has had to deal with more than most, there are parts that made me laugh out loud as a fellow wheelchair user because I understand some of the experience. And what could be better than a fairytale ending to rival that of any Mills & Boon romance?

Dame Tanni Grey-Thompson DBE
November 2008

part one

chapter 1

I don't know how long it was before I fully woke up, but when I did everything felt different. My eyes opened and for a moment it seemed that I must have been hit on the head. There was no pain at all but a face loomed above me. A manly face. Rugged. Unfamiliar. Concerned. I wanted him to save me, but straight away I noticed that there was worry in his expression and sadness in his eyes. He asked me a question but I didn't really hear it. I felt terrified. Why was he looking at me that way? Then he asked me again, and this time I did hear: 'Can you move your feet for me, sweetheart?' I had no choice but to answer with a question of my own, because I didn't understand what was happening. Where were they? Where were my feet and my legs? Where was the rest of my body?

He was far too old to be my boyfriend. Not only that, he was too short as well. More seriously, though, he was also too wild. He'd been in trouble with the police, he was long-term unemployed and he was unquestionably Not Good Enough for me. In summary, he was all the things that inflame anxious parents when their naïve and impressionable fourteen-year-old daughters get involved with unsuitable nineteen-year-old boys. But I was fifteen by now, and I knew better.

I was also a very good actress, as my drama teacher had often commented upon. I was good in my role as a tough biker's girlfriend, without any need for the sort of parental concern that might impede my swaggering exterior. Yes, I loved my mum and dad – cherished them more than anything else in the world, truth be known – but to show my devotion just wouldn't have been cool.

And my parents knew just how to deal with me. They'd been through all the stages wise parents go through and opted for what seemed the most sensible option. Having voiced their opinions and found me less than receptive, they did what was probably the best thing to do: apart from ensuring we were chaperoned wherever possible, they kept their disapproval on a non-confrontational level and simply waited for me to do what they trusted I would. Grow out of it – out of *him* – if left to do so.

And they'd been right to feel confident. We'd been together almost a year. I was fifteen now, and through a combination of both time and circumstance I was beginning to do exactly that. Not for any of the reasons my parents had cited. Just because I was beginning to feel the first real stirrings of … well, of not needing him any more, I suppose.

Which, in hindsight, is often the way these things work. Older guy takes younger girl under his wing, gives her attention and confidence and a proper sense of self, and so, by whichever law governs such things, makes himself redundant in the process.

But for the moment, at least, we were still together. Still a couple, despite my knowing, even then, that this state of affairs wasn't permanent. Something testified by a still livid scar across my biceps – the result of the removal of a DIY tattoo, which my parents had organised at hideous expense.

The tattoo had read 'Aldo'. He'd be here in half an hour. I'd better hurry up and get ready.

Lots of things happened on 10 May 1980. It being a Saturday, various matches were won and lost. In London, Trevor Brooking led West Ham to a 1–0 defeat of Arsenal, and over in the States the Houston Astros beat the Atlanta Braves at baseball. Most notably, however, an irritable Mount St Helens was having a bit of a tantrum and limbering up for what, a week later, would end 130 long years of peace and quiet and become the worst volcanic disaster in the history of the United States.

None of these, however, would have been uppermost in my mind, even had I known they were happening. All I knew – all that mattered – was that today was Saturday, which meant no school, no hassle and a trip out on the back of Aldo's bike, a 750cc Honda. A group of us – Aldo and I, plus his friend John and my best friend Juli – were off to Porthcawl for the day.

I checked the time, spent some minutes carefully applying make-up, then scrutinised myself in the mirror. My hair was freshly washed and my face newly painted. I looked, I decided, not too bad. Not something I'd much been accustomed to thinking; unlikely as it might seem for a girl of my height (just under six feet), I was altogether more used to feeling bad about myself, the legacy of years of relentless bullying, and the accompanying stress of a change of school and thus friends. But a great deal had changed in a very short time. Much as Aldo had been key to my growing self-confidence, it had been a fashion show at school that had really inspired me. I was tall. I was slim. I had loved my moment in the spotlight. And though I wasn't so naïve as to think that the world was my catwalk, I had begun to feel at last that I had choices.

But that was for the future. Right now, I had nothing more pressing to think about than what to wear. I grabbed jeans, a stripy T-shirt and my suede stiletto boots. I yanked them on and skipped down the stairs.

Dad was in the living room, reading the paper. I joined Mum in the kitchen. She looked up. Then up and down. Then she sighed. 'I do wish you weren't going out on that bike today, Mel.'

'I'll be fine, Mum,' I answered, as I habitually did. She sniffed.

'Well, your dad and I don't like it.'

'I know,' I said again. 'But I'll be fine. Stop worrying.'

'Just be very careful, okay?'

I thought I could hear Aldo pulling up outside. Good, I thought, kissing her cheek. No more nagging. My parents were, and have always been, amazing people: deeply loving, supportive, the very best in the whole world. But like any other teenager, I was deaf to my mother's fears. Unaware of how often her words would chillingly revisit me, I grabbed my leather jacket from the newel post and helmet from by the door. Then I yelled a goodbye and went to greet Aldo.

Back in the early eighties, the seaside towns of Porthcawl and Port Talbot, where we lived, couldn't have been more different. Port Talbot was dull. It felt dull, at any rate, to me and my friends. Though it nestled prettily beneath the green and brown bulk of the Emroch and Dinas mountains, Port Talbot's equally dramatic southern skyline was a towering jungle of concrete and metal; a line of huge blast furnaces, steel gantries and grey buildings that filled the foreground of the view across Swansea Bay. The steelworks dominated the town. From the red dust that settled on every sort of surface, from windowsills to car roofs to optimistically hung washing, to the unspoken assumption that to my mind seemed universal, that being destined for the 'works' was the norm. I didn't want that. I wanted more. I wanted better.

Porthcawl *was* better. It was different. Exciting. Though it was only a few miles east down the coast, being at Porthcawl always seemed to feel a little like being on holiday. As a child, it had been one of my favourite destinations. It was a good-time place where the sun always shone and there was always ice-cream to eat. A place where I could play on the rocks and swim in the rock pools that were left, warm and magical, by the retreating tide. It had mystery, too, in the stories of shipwrecks, and the brave derring-do of the lifeboat crew. Porthcawl had a heart that was beating, whereas Port Talbot always seemed a little like my poor dad's chest – one big, sprawling, unhealthy wheeze.

Not that Port Talbot didn't have a seafront of its own, but ours, Aberavon, though briefly lively during warm summer weekends, could boast little in the way of excitement. Our own funfair, Miami Beach, had always felt just like what it was – a somewhat down-at-heel reminder of a time, now long gone, when people's expectations of holidays were much simpler. By the time I was in my teens it had been all but pulled down. In the winter months, the beach was a desolate sort of place, which skulked in the shadows of the steelworks.

Porthcawl just didn't feel like that. Indeed, by this time it was thriving. Its own funfair, Coney Beach, was a big draw for everyone and in the summer months it was filled with throngs of day trippers, and was held in particular regard by the biking fraternity. It suited me, too. At my height, I could almost always get served in the pubs. I felt the familiar stirrings of excited anticipation in my stomach. Volcanoes could do what they liked across the globe. All that was on my young mind that Saturday morning was what a great day I had ahead.

Funny how the brain works. It hadn't been a particularly memorable sort of day, but set against what was to follow, the rather ordinary details are still pin-sharp in my memory. We drove to the Knight's Arms, our favourite biker pub in Porthcawl, to find it quiet – it was still early in the season. We chatted, we had some lunch, and the boys went to sit outside, while Juli and I went into the back to play pool.

Juli had been my best friend ever since my change of school had reunited us the previous year. We'd clicked before, when we were younger, and now we clicked again. Even so, we made an odd sort of pair. Where I was a jeans-and-leather-jacketed patchouli-scented rocker, Juli had embraced everything punk. She was wild about Siouxsie & the Banshees and the Sex Pistols, had hair that often looked like a multi-coloured fright wig, and augmented her wardrobe with her granny's old frocks, which she accessorised with crazy bits of jewellery. In deference to the bike ride, I supposed, she was wearing something quite demure for her tastes – a black boiler suit – but, typically, finished off with pink shoes.

After our game of pool we went outside and sat on the guys' bikes, while they continued to chat in the sunshine. In such undramatic and, to my older self, seemingly empty ways are whole chunks of teenage life gladly swallowed up. We'd had fun, but decided to head home when it was gone four. If Juli wasn't home by five-thirty at the latest, she'd be for it. Her parents didn't even know she was out on a bike. Just with me – a bad influence anyway.

'You want to swap?' Juli asked me as we waited for the guys.

'Dunno,' I said, surprised. 'Why, do you?'

She shrugged. 'I just thought that now I've tried John's Suzuki it might be fun to take a ride on the Honda.' She smiled at me, and suddenly I realised that she might have another agenda. Perhaps this was more about me than her. More specifically, about me and John. Though he was way out of bounds – he had a very scary girlfriend – Juli knew how much I fancied him. She also knew that despite his going steady, in private he'd intimated that he was interested in me. Was this a manoeuvre to organise things so we could spend a bit of time alone together?

But I felt – and very strongly – that that wasn't what should happen. I shook my head. 'No,' I said. 'Let's leave things as they are.' The most significant 'no' of my life, as it turned out, and even now I'm not sure why I'd felt the way I did. Later I'd come to find solace in that. However much I might have wished that what happened hadn't happened, I was infinitely more grateful it hadn't happened to my friend.

Aldo always rode fast. He didn't seem to have an off switch. When we were out on our own he drove reasonably sensibly, but put him in the middle of a big group of bikers – on big bikes – and the testosterone kicked in. He went for it, always. There was never any point in telling him to slow down, let alone pointing out that with one ban for speeding already behind him they'd throw the book at him if he was caught. I tried it once, early on, and soon learned. He would simply growl at me and go faster.

But this wasn't – hadn't been – that sort of day. Just the four of us, two bikes, and an uneventful ride home in prospect. Why should it be otherwise? The route back was undemanding enough and the roads were, more often than not, quiet. I knew those roads well; the places where he'd let out the throttle and gun it, the corners and the straights, the scenic stretches through the burrows, the odd glimpse of sea, and the sweep of mountains that loomed to our right. Today's journey to Porthcawl had been largely uneventful, and I had no reason to suppose the ride home would be any different.

But fate, it seemed, had other plans. Aldo lived with his parents, two brothers and dog on Golden Avenue, a part of the Aberavon beachfront. We were driving towards it now, along Princess Margaret Way, when that absolute no-no, a *smaller* bike, passed us. Before I'd even thought, irritably, that he probably would do so, Aldo had already given chase. The road seemed to shimmer and dance beneath the wheels. I felt the force of rushing air trying to push me backwards and gripped hard; one hand clenched around the seat strap beneath me, the other, behind me, clutching tightly to the bar. I remember feeling a bolt of proper fear now, as the road curved away into a sharp right-hand bend that took it inland, away from the seafront. This wasn't just any old bend – it was Jeff's bend, named after a biker who had died trying to get round it some years before. I felt the bike dip beneath me and automatically leaned with it. How bloody ridiculous, I recall myself thinking. So close to home and he has to get involved in this. Not for the first time, I silently cursed his childish male pride.

But the curse must have died on my lips at that moment because suddenly I was no longer riding pillion behind Aldo but airborne, and moving at speed. And then nothing. Only absolute silence and blackness. No thought. No sensation. Just nothing.

I don't know how long I was out, but it soon became obvious that my blackout was only momentary, because the next thing I remember was a sound. Wherever I was – and I didn't have a clue – there was something approaching.

Something loud, something low. Pushing through the fog in my head with increasing insistence. A low rumbling sound. Getting louder.

Conscious again now, I opened my eyes, but the visor on my helmet was down so all I could see was smudged and dirty plastic. Like trying to see through a pair of grubby glasses, all I could focus on was the smudge. But the noise kept on coming. I turned my head towards it and the smudge became an outline, and then, almost as if propelled by some malevolent deity, I saw the bike, on its side, bare of driver and pillion, barrelling towards me headlight first. I heard a girl screaming. That's not me, I remember thinking, as it hit me. That's not me doing that. I passed out again.

In my head I went home then. At least, close to home. I was sitting beside Dad, in his ancient Morris Minor. He'd usually finished work by the end of my school day, so after the long walk to school, then home for lunch and then back, my treat was to have a lift home at the end of the day. I loved the Morris Minor. Loved sitting up front with Dad. Loved its feel, loved its warmth, loved its fusty pungent odour.

They say smell is the most strongly evocative of the senses, and, coming to again, I realised where the memory had come from. That same smell was pricking in my nostrils now.

Full consciousness returned in a rush of realisation. I touched the grass I was lying on. It was damp. There was no car. No Dad. Just the screaming. And the ground all around me soaked in – yes, *that* was it, that was what I could smell – it was *petrol*. And something else. There was a man. I squinted at him. He was waving his arms. He was wearing a brown coat and a cap and in his mouth – I gasped as I realised – was a lit cigarette. I tried to shout and felt a sudden warm wetness in my mouth. Oh God, no, I thought, watching him walking towards me. I'm going to burn – Oh, God, don't let me burn.

But I obviously wasn't the only one who'd seen it. The man – I didn't know him – was quickly intercepted, and suddenly it seemed there were people all around me. But they melted away as fast as they'd arrived, as the blackness came and swallowed me again.

This time I went nowhere, and all too soon I was back on the cold ground with strangers staring down at me. The only warmth was in my mouth, but then also in my heart, as Juli's face suddenly appeared. For a moment I felt calmer. She was here. She would help me. But she was crying and telling me to try not to move and saying sorry and holding onto my hand. I tried to tell her it wasn't her fault but when I spoke a red mist sprayed all over my visor. Now everybody seemed to be shouting at once. 'Internal bleeding!' 'What's happening?' 'Where's the ambulance got to?' But almost immediately I realised what had happened. I'd bitten the tip off my tongue, and the warmth in my mouth was my blood.

I was grateful when the blackness claimed me this time and so, evidently, was my body, because I must have been unconscious for some time. When I next came round it was to the sound of approaching sirens. That was all I could hear now. No other sound at all. I'd retreated into a safe house somewhere in my brain, shutting the door on the horror. I knew I wouldn't be able to keep it out for long, but I chose to remain there, hiding, and praying. Our Father, I chanted desperately in my head, who art in Heaven …

chapter 2

I was about to die, I decided. That was it. My body had been chopped in half in the accident and I was going to die at any moment. I don't recall quite what I did with those thoughts at the time, but one thing became suddenly clear. That if I didn't, I was going to get the mother of all rows off Mum and Dad. They'd been right. I'd been wrong. Whatever happened now – life or imminent death – I'd never felt more scared.

The man who had asked me to move my missing legs and feet reappeared. He was talking again. 'Be still,' he kept saying. 'Try to keep very still. And don't worry.'

I didn't answer because by now my tongue had become swollen. I could feel a flap of it hanging free. So much blood in my mouth. I didn't want to swallow my own blood. Someone then said something about how clever we'd been about the helmet. Juli and I had not let anyone take off my helmet. Someone – I didn't have a clue who – had tried, but we'd both of us, ironically, been insistent about it; we'd done neck injuries in biology class the previous week. Something useful to know, but not the sort of thing I'd ever dreamt would apply to me.

Another face loomed. Another man. Another smile. 'Hiya,' he said. 'We're taking you to Neath General Hospital.' He moved down and seemed to be feeling my legs – or at least, the place where my legs should have been. The terror flooded in again, and with it revulsion. I couldn't see. Was he picking up bits of severed limb? But if that was the case, why wasn't he looking disgusted? Why wasn't everyone around me throwing up?

I tried to keep focused on what I was seeing and hearing, but the velvety blackness kept rising to engulf me, cloaking all sensation, all thought. I seemed to be almost floating above my own body, riding turbulent air, surveying my situation and, strangely, finding clarity in distance; in one single precious moment almost all became clear. This was real. It had happened. I was badly, badly damaged. My life as I'd known it was over.

The kind voice intruded and I was back in my broken body and lying on the sodden turf. He had yet another question. A strange one, to my mind. 'Melanie,' he was saying. 'What's your date of birth, love? What's your age?'

'I'm fifteen,' I told him finally, my voice thick and strange. How did he know who I was?

Neath General Hospital was situated about a mile to the south of the town centre, on a steeply sloping hillside, facing west. The journey from Aberavon beachfront would, under normal circumstances, take about a quarter of an hour. What happens in the first 'golden' hour following an injury can have huge consequences on the outcome so it's an important chunk of time for an accident victim.

But nobody seemed in much of a hurry. I must have blacked out again at this point because I have no memory of being loaded into the ambulance. But somehow I was in one. And so was Juli. I hadn't a clue where Aldo and John might be – only that Juli had told me Aldo was OK.

I could hear someone talking on what must have been the radio. 'We're bringing in a teenager with a serious injury …' Juli became agitated. If that was the case, then why were we travelling so slowly? No speed, no sirens, no nothing.

'Because with a spinal injury,' they told her when she asked, 'smoothness is of the essence. We have to go slowly so we don't do more damage.' The atmosphere was tense, their words hanging heavily on the air. They seemed all too aware they had two terrified teenagers on board, and the fate of one young life in their hands.

By the time the ambulance had entered the outskirts of Neath, almost a whole hour had apparently passed. I'd spent much of it drifting in and out of sleep. I dreamed turbulent dreams. I dreamed about the princess in *Arabian Nights*, who'd defied her parents and fallen in love with a poor boy, with whom, despite their anger, she'd walk the beach at night. She'd been cursed by a sorcerer. He told her that if she continued to defy her parents, he'd turn the sand on the beach to knives beneath her feet. She didn't believe him but it happened even so. Her life had been ruined. Had my life as well? Had my stubborn refusal to stop seeing Aldo brought a sorcerer's curse upon *me*?

Consciousness returned as we neared the hospital. And with it, I began to feel increasingly agitated. I knew I was in big trouble. What would Mum and Dad say? Had somebody already told them what had happened? Would they be standing at the hospital entrance, waiting? Would they give me one hell of a row? For the first time in a long time I really felt my age; I was every inch a vulnerable child.

The ambulance had by now been reversed up to the entrance and the double doors opened to a hubbub of noise and activity. So many people. So much chattering and noise. So much sense of everyone knowing what they were doing. I felt almost as if I was some sort of celebrity. All this industry and attention focused solely on me. The feeling of relief was overwhelming. I heard a voice – 'On my lift' – and the next thing I knew I was lying on a hospital trolley.

I was here. I was safe. I thought I might leave them all to it and go to sleep now, but nobody around me seemed to want that. I was asked my name repeatedly, encouraged to stay conscious. The questions I'd been asked when lying on the petrol-soaked grass were all trotted out once again. Could I feel this? Could I feel that? Could I try to move my legs? But my own head was buzzing with entirely different questions. Could they please not tell my parents that the motorbike had crashed? And, most importantly, when could I go home?

When I asked, nobody seemed to have an answer for that one.

* * *

Eight miles away, in the small valley town of Pontardawe, an orthopaedic surgeon by the name of Mr R. M. Davies was finding excuses not to do the gardening. It was, he knew, a good day for gardening, and the garden, he conceded, needed doing.

Thirty-seven years old and at the peak of his career, he'd been appointed consultant surgeon at Neath General thirteen months earlier, and moved his wife and young family down from Cardiff; thirteen months during which the garden of their beautiful stone house had become more than a little overgrown.

They'd chosen their new home with care. After years of leading the nomadic lifestyle of a surgeon in training, this was finally a chance to settle down permanently. To re-establish old roots and also put down some new ones. Stability for the three children at last.

The house, which had been originally built in 1912 for himself by a local builder, was perfect for a growing family. Solid and spacious, it was set into the western slopes of the Swansea Valley, from which vantage point it enjoyed magnificent views across to the east, towards Neath, and looked down benignly on the road to the hospital; a place he'd already come to love.

But, fine though the afternoon had shaped up to be, somehow gardening didn't much appeal. Nor, particularly, did the thought of washing his car. But the driver in him invariably won out over the gardener and, short on excuses to get out of either chore, he was busy with his sponge when the call came.

Back at the hospital, it having been agreed that my life was not in immediate danger, the on-call registrar, Mr Sam

Kamal, had asked that I be taken down to X-ray for a series
of films. I was by now not so much under the knife as the
scissors; everything metal had to be removed, so they'd set
about – literally – chopping it all off, from the studs on my
precious jacket and my jeans and my T-shirt, right down to
the wires in my bra.

The results of the X-rays confirmed the doctor's fears.
There was crushing and deformity to three of the vertebrae
in the middle of the dorsal part of my spine. This was the
reason why it continued to feel as though everything below
mid-chest was missing.

This was the sort of serious accident that needed senior
input. Mr Kamal had already rung and alerted his consultant, so that by the time the seriousness of the situation had
been confirmed by the X-rays the man himself had dropped
everything, thrown on a jacket and, his post-car-washing
snooze and family supper now mere wishful thinking, was
already en route to the hospital.

Being called in on nights and weekends was as much a
part of life for a doctor as the nine-to-five routine, but as he
never knew exactly what sort of trauma would be awaiting
his attention when he got there Mr Davies did what he
always did: he mentally prepared for what he might find.
The situation was serious and the possibilities were many.
He knew the patient was fifteen – not a lot older than
Lizanne, his own daughter – but little more than that. How
was she coping? Did she have any idea just how bad things
were? Was there any chance that the situation might be
reversible? On the basis of what he already knew he thought
it unlikely, but could there be even the smallest hope? On a

practical level, were the family present? Stoical? Hysterical? Expecting the unrealistic? And, as Neath Hospital served a very close-knit community, did any of the staff know the family?

He parked in his space behind the ward block at the bottom of the hospital building and hurried up to find out what was in store, little knowing that he was in exactly the right place at the right time, in ways that would only become clear decades later.

I have no memory of the first meeting I had with the man who was to go on to figure so prominently in my life. Perhaps, by that time, the staff looking after me had all but given up in their ongoing quest to keep me lucid. But my consultant apparently introduced himself and explained that he'd been warned that I'd had a serious injury to my upper back after being involved in a motorcycle accident. He said he needed to examine me himself to confirm this, and also to check that the X-rays gave him all the informa- tion he needed. But he could have been speaking to me in Swahili. By now I'd been introduced to the mesmeric joys of morphine and found them a great deal more deserving of my attention.

My parents both worked full-time at the offices of the steelworks: Mum as a shorthand typist and Dad as a clerk. Weekends were a time for catching up with chores and relaxing; so, not unusually, at the time of the crash, Mum was cleaning the house while Dad was down at his old cricket club, Cwmavon. Later, they'd planned to head down town to watch a performance by a local male voice choir.

But then the call came that would turn their arrangements on their head – both for that Saturday night and for many years to come. Ironically, it was an old Cwmavon friend of Dad's who rang Mum. The friend lived, by what seemed another remarkable coincidence, on the corner where the crash had happened. She had witnessed the accident, and established my involvement. I'd had a bit of an accident, she informed Mum, and was about to be taken by ambulance to Neath General Hospital, 'just to make sure nothing's wrong'. My mother was obviously shocked and concerned, but reassured to some extent by what the woman said. She went upstairs to get ready to go to the hospital, reasoning that the cricket would just about be finished, so by the time she'd got changed Dad would be home and they could go together.

Neither was in any way prepared for the gravity of the situation that would greet them.

By the time Mr Davies had finished his examination, however, my parents – who had arrived not long after I had – had been advised of the reality by Mr Kamal, and were now waiting to speak to him, desperate for news. News it was his task, as my consultant, to give them, however sad or unpleasant that task was going to be.

He found them outside the resuscitation room, standing stiffly in the corridor, obviously anxious to hear something but at the same time fearful of what that something might be. They were frozen with fear but still clinging to hope, and my father found it in the sudden realisation that here stood a man he held in high regard. Mr Davies was his beloved rugby club's honorary surgeon, a young man who'd done great things with injured Aberavon players. Surely he could do the same for his daughter?

For Mike Davies, however, the feeling wasn't mutual. No doctor wants to find himself too close to a patient. Detachment and clear-headed thinking are too important for emotional involvement ever to be a good thing, particularly where serious injury is concerned. But standing before him was one of his fellow rugby club stalwarts. A man with a pretty fifteen-year-old only daughter who'd suffered the most appalling catastrophe, and whose future (*all* their futures) had, bar some improbable miracle, been utterly turned upside down.

It seemed a member of staff *did* know this particular family. He just wished it didn't have to be him.

Even so, the task at hand was to be honest and realistic with these two distressed people and, as delivering bad news was best not done standing, he invited my parents to go into the sister's office and sit down. He began with the best part – that my life wasn't in immediate danger – but said that the injury to my spine would probably take a few days to declare its intentions, as it were. His assessment of my prospects was not encouraging, sadly; they would need to prepare themselves for the real possibility that I would spend the rest of my life in a wheelchair. He would also need to operate to stabilise my back, to avoid a progressive deformity. If, as he expected, I would have to spend many months in hospital, a stable back would make rehabilitation easier. The only glimmer of light he could offer that day was that should the unexpected happen and there be an improvement in function, we would see it in the next forty-eight hours.

For my parents, this would be the hardest two days of their lives.

For me, however, things were almost too surreal to register. In the days that were to follow I would come to terms, in some ways, with what had happened, but mostly my youth and optimism would win out. It would be another three weeks before reality bit and the stuffing would be knocked out of me.

chapter 3

I was five when my parents told me I was adopted, and was then, as now, in a hospital bed. I was eating ice cream and jelly at the time, on account of my recent tonsillectomy. I was theirs but not theirs, I remember them saying. They were my mother and father, but not my *real* mother and father. This wasn't, however, important. All I needed to know, as is still the case now, was that I belonged to them both, that they loved me very much, and they would take care of me always.

My birth mother was an unmarried teenager from Plymouth, in the days when to be so was tantamount to a criminal offence. She had even named me Caroline – I was Caroline Sandford. Nothing was ever said, or known, about my father, and she had, we were told – and had no reason not to believe – been pressured to give me up for adoption. Luckily for me, over in Wales, a married couple who were unable to conceive and who were by now in their early thirties had decided to register with the Western National Adoption Society. Thus, at five and a half weeks of age, as a result of my suitable colouring and complexion, I became Melanie Bowen, whereupon I was taken to the

family home in Port Talbot, there to live with my new
parents, Dewi and Margaret, and also Margaret's mother,
my new gran.

I have no memory of how I responded to this news. In
actual fact, I don't think I did, very much. It registered. It
sank in. It meant little more. All that mattered, aged five,
was the jelly and ice cream. That, and how soon I'd be able
to go home.

It was early on Sunday. The morning after the accident.
And going home wasn't an option today. Or any time soon,
for that matter. Late the previous evening I'd been transferred to a two-bedded side room, attached to Ward Eight,
and separated from it by double swing doors. This, I
learned, was to facilitate my care without causing too much
disruption – I needed to be turned at least two-hourly to
prevent pressure sores developing on my inert lower body –
and also to afford a modicum of peace and privacy from the
other, mostly elderly patients, some of whom were frail and
demented.

Mum had been installed in a camp bed beside me, the
second proper bed in the side ward having to be kept free
for emergencies, and it was here that she would sleep for the
coming three weeks. Soon the room would be overwhelmed
by what would feel like my own body weight in flowers and
chocolates and cuddly toys, not to mention visitors, but for
now it was just the two of us – Dad had gone home to get
some sleep – while the very big thing that had happened to
our lives was taking its time sinking in.

Mum was stoical. And possibly thinking about family too. Had it occurred to her that the dependent baby they'd adopted fifteen years back had now, in many practical ways, become one again?

'You know what?' she said to me, perched on the chair beside my bed and looking as if she understood exactly what I was thinking. 'We're going to cope with this, Mel. Just think of your gran.' I often did. She had died of kidney failure when I was ten. It had been I who'd come home to find her collapsed in the bathroom. She'd passed away in hospital a few days later. Mum smiled. 'Well, *she* managed, didn't she?' I nodded. She then grinned. 'Went up and down stairs on her bottom for years.'

This much was true. Riddled with arthritis, my gran had spent the last few years of her life doing just that. I could see her doing it now. And the thought, bizarre to contemplate as it might be, was a comfort. The idea of not being able to go to bed in my own bedroom was one that had preoccupied and upset me very much.

Mum squeezed my hand and looked at me with clear, unblinking eyes. Then she said, her voice strong, 'And you will do the same.'

Stairs were, however, for the future. The here and now consisted of the bed that I lay on and my total dependence on everyone around me – a very alien state of affairs.

I was scheduled to see Mr Davies later that morning and, if my first encounter with my consultant was too hazy for recall, my second was anything but. From the moment

Sister announced his impending visit to see me – he was doing his Sunday ward round – my every waking thought was focused on what he might say. As the hours ticked by with no miraculous improvements forthcoming, I had a question no one so far seemed able to answer properly, namely, would I *ever* walk again? If anyone could tell me that, surely he could.

Everyone has a stereotypical image when they think the word 'doctor', and mine was, I imagine, no different from that of most teenagers. He certainly ticked all the important 'doctor' boxes. Tall and imposing, with a habitually stern expression and the sort of aura that only comes with that cocktail of great intelligence and lofty status, my consultant entered the room – I was alone at this time – and all at once I felt intimidated and slightly in awe. He sat down on the edge of my bed, looked me straight in the eye, and when he took my hand in his I knew, without question, that things were every bit as bad as I'd feared.

And I was right. He confirmed, via a clearly worded run-through of the facts, that he seriously doubted I ever would. I felt the wetness of a single tear tracking a course down my cheek, and the pressure on my hand as he tightened his grip. 'Will you be all right?' he asked me quietly, his face full of concern.

I bit my lip and blinked to try and indicate yes, all the while wrestling furiously with my face to hold back the flood I didn't want him to see. To this day I don't understand why it was so important he didn't see it, only that some force inside me felt this overwhelming need not to break down. To keep a grip on myself. To appear strong: the legacy, in hindsight, of a childhood full of school bullies, and a mechanism for survival that was almost instinctive. It was only once he'd left to continue his ward round and Sister O'Rourke had swept in – she must have been waiting outside because she did so immediately – did I lower my defences enough to let the tears flow. And flow they most certainly did.

I simply couldn't seem to banish the negative images from my brain. I had become a cripple. Not only would I never walk again, but I would be unable to stand up even for a second. I would live in a wheelchair, the focus of ridicule and scorn. I would be totally vulnerable. Would the bullies gain the upper hand again? Would I end up in an institution? Would people think I was brain-damaged? Would I *become* brain-damaged, have a breakdown because I couldn't cope with my new situation? Now I'd started crying I wondered why I hadn't cried before. Now I'd started, would I ever manage to stop?

This situation taught me a very important lesson: that crying as a paraplegic while flat on your back isn't some-thing it's safe to try at home. I imagine one of Elaine O'Rourke's sharpest memories of that time was of me nearly choking to death on my own snot.

The operation was scheduled for the major theatre list on Tuesday afternoon – a wait that for many might have seemed interminable, but because of the constant nursing attention, the two-hourly turning, the plethora of visitors and the regular morphine, it actually came very fast. Too fast, perversely, where Mum and Dad were concerned, because its coming so speedily effectively saw off the cherished forty-eight hours in which they'd allowed themselves the luxury of hope. As for me, I continued to feel cut in half, in my head every bit as much as my body. A spell of oblivion, however frightening the prospect of surgery, would probably be no bad thing.

Surgeons are, both by profession and by nature, inveterate fixers of things. Of bones and ligaments and tendons and unruly bits of body; the natural habitat of the surgeon is doing engineering work on interior structure, the desired state of affairs, always, success.

Mike Davies was every inch the surgeon. He had eleven letters after his name to testify to the fact that fixing things was what he was trained to do. Fortunately, for most of the time, this was what happened. His speciality, orthopaedics, involved dealing with the treatment of a large number of chronic conditions, sometimes non-surgically, with varying success, but surgically in a majority of instances, and for the most part with gratifying results. Only in a very few situations and patients would the outcome be distressing or critical.

He got upset, then, if faced with the unmendable. And that was exactly what I was. Which meant that what had seemed to me to be a rather marked detachment in his manner was both to preserve his professional distance and also the manifestation of his very real frustration that this was a patient he couldn't fix, even with the best will and expertise in the world.

Once I was on the operating table, he was struck by my almost-six-foot height; in bed, I'd seemed very obviously young and slim, but this – as is often the case when patients are in theatre – was something he'd not so far noticed. Similarly striking, and highlighting the sense of tragedy around me, was the total absence of external signs of damage. The only scar on my body would be that made by his knife: the nine-and-half-inch vertical incision that he was, this very moment, about to make.

I was to become fashionably bionic. Though it had by now been established that there was little hope of my ever regaining the use of my legs, there was something he *could* do: that was to ensure that, for both health and aesthetic reasons, my slender young back would remain straight and undeformed. The object of surgery, therefore, was to fit me with a pair of stainless steel rods, which would lie along the length of my spine, hooked in place under the arches of my top and bottom vertebrae.

Called Harrington rods, these two had been pilfered. Ordered in by neighbouring Morriston Hospital in Swansea, they had been earmarked for correcting spinal deformities in children. This was quite an expansion to their orthopaedic service, and they were rightly proud. However, as they'd not yet admitted their first suitable patient, they could put up little argument against Neath acquiring them now. Thus they were, and continue to this day to be, mine.

If surgery was to mark me physically, it was also to be a benchmark. Coming around after the operation, I soon became aware that what had previously been a generalised ache in a band around my chest – and for which I'd been knocking back all that morphine – had been replaced by something entirely different. My pain was now specific to the site of the surgery, though obviously – and curiously – in only half of the scar, the part that lay above the level of the spinal cord damage. I grew to be comforted a great deal by my pain. It seemed proof, at least, that my body was fighting back. And comfort was something I needed in quantity. There were no more 'what ifs' or 'perhapses' or 'maybes' up for grabs. This was the situation. These were the facts. The time for wishing and hoping was unequivocally gone. It was time to start addressing reality.

There is a reason why nurses are called angels. If it would be a bit bizarre to describe my circumstances as heaven there were, even so, definite parallels. I had exited one life and started another, and my guides, at least through this transition period, were the closest thing to angels I'd seen.

Sister Elaine O'Rourke affected me particularly. Up until then, though I'd had many moments of lucidity, she had been little more than a presence drifting in and out of my morphine mist. A beautiful presence in a navy blue uniform, who'd come to my bedside, wipe the mucus from my nose, rub my hands, speak to me and wash the tears from my cheeks.

Now, coming round and feeling someone massaging my arms and hands, the presence became a real, and familiar, human being. Striking green eyes. Chestnut brown hair. And lovely open smile. She was smiling at me. I smiled too, and said hello. Her smile widened further. 'Hello back,' she said, squeezing my hands.

And so began a relationship that was to guide me through the darkness. I remain devoted to Elaine to this day.

Not that I was going to let the darkness overwhelm me, in any case; I owed it to everyone around me to, at the very least, try my very best. I soon developed an unconscious strategy: a selective approach to the English language, both as spoken to me and as said myself. Given the words 'can' and 'will' and 'want' and 'able', I could function. Given 'can't' and 'won't' and anything prefixed 'will never', and my eyes, treacherous and untrustworthy organs, would let me down every single time.

As a system, this seemed to work well. Following the example set by both my parents, Elaine and her wonderful nurses, I concentrated, with every single fibre of my being, on all the positives of my new situation: the things I could do, the things I might soon do, the improvements and adjustments and successes, small and large, which meant that every day things would get better. In this I had not just mindsets but role models too. Mum and Dad never seemed to falter for the tiniest instant. Their optimistic demeanour was unremitting, and their attention to attending to the tools I'd need for progress gave me every bit as much backbone as the rods I had inside.

At night, however, my system faltered, and I floundered. With the rest of the patients, plus Mum, fast asleep, I had no one to beat off the clamouring demons. Alone and afraid, all the positives eluded me, crowded out and chased into corners by the negatives, which mushroomed in the darkness to mammoth proportions. I was terrified of dying but could see no life either. No future, no nothing. No point to my life. How could I ever be in control of my life again? I would be totally dependent on others for ever. And as for dependents of my own – what now? All the parts of me necessary to create life could still function. I couldn't feel them but they could still do the tasks they were designed to: accept manhood, then support and cherish a foetus to term. But I knew there was no way I could look after a child now; after all, my own birth mother, able-bodied as she was, had been acutely aware that raising me was beyond her – and I was a paraplegic of fifteen.

Thus I cried and I prayed to God that as I'd never, ever asked him for anything *surely* he'd listen and do something for me now? I cried till it hurt and then carried on crying. The only thing that would stop me was when the nurses came to turn me. It was almost as though if I let *them* see me crying, it would unleash a despair of such devastating power that I'd never be able to stop crying again.

But dawn came, every day, and chased the bad things away. They were borne on what seemed an unstoppable wave of people and happenings and endless activity. If life on Ward Eight could have been bottled and sold as a tonic, it would have flown off the supermarket shelves. Seeing all my classmates was a tonic in itself – particularly Juli, with whom I shared an unspoken pact that my injuries were not to be dwelt on. I was also aware that whingeing patients probably didn't get any visitors, so I made sure none of mine would ever leave my bedside having found it a miserable experience being with me.

And if the nurses – my beloved Elaine, and the night-watch of Pat, Audrey and Ruby – were chief among my rescuers from the dark well of self-pity on whose rim I often teetered, there was someone else with more prosaic matters in mind.

My Auntie Madeleine made it her mission to feed me – me and most of Neath General Hospital, it seemed. A busty blonde bombshell from Belgium, she had met Dad's brother Elwyn in Mons, just after the Battle of the Bulge, and he'd brought her home and married her after the end of the Second World War. And it seemed bulges, right now, were her *raison d'être*. Auntie Mad liked to bake, and in quantity, too, so there was hardly a day that went by when she didn't sweep onto the ward with a hat-box full of bounty: choux buns, éclairs, apple turnovers, rock cakes … All were fallen upon in great raptures of longing by both patients and ward staff alike. I always, quite properly, got first pick of the spoils, but it would be some days before I could eat one.

My desire to eat, it seemed, had gone AWOL. Between the accident and the operation I had no food whatsoever, my shocked body having little in the way of nutritional needs. I survived with nothing more substantial than a saline drip. Post-op, however, it was clearly important that I recommence dealing with proper food. This was some-thing about which I had grave reservations. I well remem-bered almost choking on my own blood after the accident and so had little confidence about eating while lying on my back. More importantly, though, I didn't feel hungry.

Denied the sensation of hunger in my stomach, I had absolutely no appetite at all. What would my body do with it once it was in there? How would it process it? Could it even do so?

Drinking was easier – and came a great deal more naturally. My mouth was dry from the op so I actively needed liquid, but even then, once aware, I became seriously agitated, having visions of lying there in a great pool of wee. Elaine O'Rourke, however, was quick to reassure me. She showed me my catheter, plus the drainage bag that hung at the side of my bed.

And I was reassured. Until another thought hit me. On the day of the accident I'd just started my period. Had anyone noticed? Had anything been done? Was I right this minute lying in a pool of blood instead of wee? I'd been plagued by the stress and monthly hassle of heavy periods since I'd started them, horribly early, aged ten.

If wee was an issue this was infinitely more so. Cringing with embarrassment, I asked Elaine.

'Don't worry,' she said. 'It's all stopped. It often tends to happen in cases like yours. The body goes into a state of spinal shock which can stop a period dead in its tracks.'

As positives went this was a seriously good one; the first bit of really encouraging news I'd heard. Was there any chance that this could be permanent, I wondered?

Er, no, Elaine explained. Only temporary, sadly. Something a month later I was to find out. And how.

At the moment, however, food was the issue, and if prizes could be awarded for cake-related effort, my Auntie Mad would have scooped the Gold.

And perhaps all that exposure to the *joie de vivre*-inducing properties of cream cakes paid off. Because, one evening, I finally felt hungry. I didn't know where the sensation had originated from, but it was definite, and it made me feel happy. It was Mum who fed me my first meal; not a cake, as it happened, but a supper of cheese and tomato quiche. She'd been told to take care; I was still flat on my back and had to take it very slowly, but once the floodgates opened I was a keen and speedy learner – once I'd started to eat, I didn't stop. Mealtimes were no longer a challenge but a highlight. It's a universal law that hospital food must always be unpalatable, dreadful and bland. Nobody had thought to tell anyone at Neath General, however, and as a result, quite in defiance of orders, they continued to serve meals that were delicious.

What goes in, however, has to come out. I don't recall consciously considering that aspect overmuch, perhaps because if the concept of plumbing was sensitive, my fifteen-year-old self simply couldn't countenance the thought of anything food-waste related. Way too gross.

But I was not to remain in ignorance for long. I was lying on my side one morning, at the beginning of my second week in hospital, engrossed in Peter Benchley's *Jaws*. I'd seen the film in the cinema several years earlier, and in my current situation a long meander into others' fictional misfortunes was turning out to be just the sort of diversion that appealed. My pressure care areas had been done and dusted – all around was the scent (still evocative today) of the Johnson's Baby Powder they always used. I became aware, though, that the staff nurse, Angela, was still nearby.

She was doing something behind me and humming a tune. Knowing I'd been 'done' now, I lowered *Jaws* and asked her what it was.

'Me, love?' she answered. 'Oh, just building a wall.'

'A wall?' I asked, stupefied. 'What do you mean?'

She paused in whatever it was she was up to. 'I've given you a suppository,' she explained. 'And now I'm, well, shall we say, dealing with the result.'

When you are fifteen almost everything has the potential for embarrassment of such magnitude that you want the ground to swallow you up. Just existing on the planet can be reason enough if it's a bad hair or double-zit sort of day. I was frozen with horror and excruciating mental images of what scene would greet me had I been able to see. Not only the sight, but also … ugh. *Ugh*. It was simply too terrible for words. As if it might help in any way, I lifted the book back to my face. Could this nightmare be happening? Yes, it could. It clearly was. Clearly had been before now, if my biology was sound. And no one had told me; no one had even mentioned it. I had never felt such acute mortification in my life. Yes, I knew people had to do things to keep my body working, but could I really cope with *this* thing for the rest of my life?

Angela, experienced nurse that she was, remained completely and utterly unfazed. I heard her chuckle. 'It's just a part of my job,' she said conversationally.

This didn't help. 'But you run a pub!'

She did, too, with her partner. The Railway, in Neath. She'd told me early on, when we'd chatted. In no way did that and the fact of what she was doing for me now make any sort of comforting sense in my brain. It wasn't that I expected her to regale her regulars with details of my bodily functions – I didn't think that for an instant – it was simply that she did *that* and also did *this*. It just seemed so unutterably mad. And we'd become friends, hadn't we? How could *she* bear it? Having to stick her fingers in my backside?

But she knew what I was thinking. 'And I'm also a nurse, dopey. And this is what nurses *do*. And anyway,' she said, her voice full of smiles and flecked with laughter, 'it's a very good wall. Want to see?'

No, I absolutely didn't want to see. I'd have nightmares. I retreated to the safer world of sharks.

Not all the manifestations of my new situation would be quite so challenging to confront. Less life-and-death important but equally memorable were the small things that really did matter.

If Elaine O'Rourke had claimed number one place in my affections from day one, when she popped in to see me one evening before a night out, she refuted all other claims to it. She was, quite simply, one of the most beautiful women I had ever seen. Teenage crushes take many forms, but few can be more intense than that between a young patient and her nurse. She looked beautiful in her uniform. Tonight, in a red dress, with her hair flowing down over her shoulders and her make-up all done, she looked beautiful beyond belief. So much so that I realised that was what *I* wanted – not to be looked at with pity but as the young woman I used to be.

I told her, the following day, on the ward.

'You know,' she said, 'there's no reason why you can't make up your face if you want to.'

I could? This thought had not yet occurred to me, because I stopped seeing myself as a pretty young woman the moment I learned I couldn't walk. Aldo, who'd broken his collarbone I now learned, had come and been sent packing by my auntie. Not because I blamed him – to climb aboard the bike had been my choice – but because whatever we'd had left between us was now gone. As for John, he'd been attracted to a functioning young woman; I absolutely did not want to see him like this, and I certainly didn't want him to see me. But Elaine knew a lot more about self-esteem than I did.

'Of course you can,' she said. 'And you should. You can use your arms, and we have mirrors we can fix to the bed so you can see. Why don't you have someone fetch your cosmetics for you? I know you use lots of mascara,' she said, grinning. 'Because it was me who had to wipe it all off when you came in!'

She leaned down beside me and picked up the small hand mirror that lay on the cabinet beside my bed. We looked into it together. She smiled. 'See?'

She had her hand on my head and was stroking my hair as she spoke. 'And this,' she decided, pulling on a strand of it, 'needs washing.'

Having a makeover when you are a newly post-surgery spinal patient who is required at all times to lie supine, or prostrate, or on one side, is no mean undertaking. Sister Elaine O'Rourke, however, wasn't one to let a technicality thwart her ambitions, so once she had dismantled the head of the bed, rustled up the requisite three nurses to shimmy me up it till my head hung over the edge and – crucially – hold me in place there, found several bowls, a plastic cup, three plastic aprons and (this the most testing) a quantity of shampoo, my transformation from the dragged-through-a-hedge look to glamour-puss could begin.

Much water was slopped over Ward Eight that afternoon. Much water and enough laughter to reverberate around our corner of the hospital in sufficient volume that our activities were brought to the attention of Nigel, the hospital hairdresser. Nigel, today, would barely attract comment, but back in 1980 he was out on his own. He took the concept of 'mincing' to rarely seen heights, had shocking pink hair that rivalled Juli's in lustre, and a ring almost anywhere a ring could comfortably go. He was also the hospital's best gossip. After assessing my locks ('Good God! What are these? Ugh! Streaks! And these *roots*!') he set about his styling, furnishing me with titbits as he went. 'So,' he said. 'What's this Mr Davies like, then? I've heard he's *really* big … in bones! Ha ha ha!'

But if his line in banter was of the kind that had nurses rolling helpless in the aisles, his hairdressing skills were seriously good. Standing up, or so I fondly imagined, the finished style would have had me looking every inch the pre-Raphaelite lovely. As it was, lying down, though the curls were still stunning, they massed around my head like a halo. If I were to venture a description of my look, it would have been 'Shirley Temple has fight with small tornado'.

And it didn't go unnoticed. Having applied sufficient make-up to distract the eye, I hoped, from my somewhat arresting coiffure, I must have looked as though I'd stumbled into Ward Eight en route to a travelling panto. I looked diverting enough, certainly, that when Mr Davies was finishing his afternoon ward round he stopped in his tracks by my bed and did a double take. He narrowed his eyes and looked sternly down over his glasses. 'Has …' he asked, 'something, er, *happened* to you?'

But if Mr Davies was sufficiently motivated to comment, that was nothing compared to the reaction of my dad. He came so close to collapse as to need to sit down – with his piles, not something he did lightly. It was my Aunt Irene, however, who best summed up just how important this development had been. Visiting the following week when my make-up was slightly less florid, she recalls a gratifying sense of things turning a corner. 'She's done her eyes,' she remembers thinking, 'so she'll be fine.'

At that point, in many respects, she'd been right. Despite the terrible thing that had happened to me, I felt cocooned in a bubble of love. I'd had endless visitors and presents and belly laughs and hugs and my care simply couldn't have been bettered. Small wonder it seemed I'd be fine.

But it wouldn't be long before the real truth would dawn – that the worst, in many ways, was still to come.

chapter 4

Monday 2 June 1980, and despite my every wish being wished as hard as could be, the trolley arrived that was to take me away. Today, just over three weeks after the accident, was the day when my time at Neath General was officially to end, it having been decided that now I was stable enough to travel. It was time to start rehabilitation.

I wasn't quite sure what rehabilitation meant, much less involved, only that the process, up to now little discussed, was one that could take an extremely long time. If not *all* time. No one ever told me otherwise. The idea that I might spend the rest of my life incarcerated in an institution was so appalling to contemplate that I actively tried not to. Never sought to voice it, let alone discuss it. Just as I had while lying on the grass soaked in petrol, I adopted the 'close your eyes and it'll disappear' approach.

Which seemed the only approach *to* take, because, for a fifteen-year-old child, it really *was* unthinkable. The only major trauma of my life up to now had been finding out that I had been adopted. And that hadn't felt like any sort of trauma at all. All I knew was Mum and Dad, all I loved was Mum and Dad. What I didn't know of the circumstances that had brought us together, I couldn't have cared less about. This was different. This wasn't about the past, but the future. The life I could no longer see for myself. A life that, so far, had been measured in small familiar increments. Birthdays and Christmases. School days. Weekend days. This term and that term. A week away on holiday. Even my three weeks at Neath – so singular an experience – had gradually attained their own comfortable rhythm: the treatments, the mealtimes, the visits, the ward rounds.

But all that was to change. I would not be coming back here. I might never go home. How could I ever go home? Home was a house on the side of a steep hill, with a multitude of steps and stairs and no accessible bedroom or toilet. But where else would I go? Mr Davies had already told me that my rehabilitation could take up to six months even in the very best – complication-free – circumstances. Even *with* a wheelchair-friendly home to go to. I pined uselessly for every single thing I'd now lost, from the comfort of my own bed to being able to make my body work right up to the O levels I wouldn't now be taking, exams that no longer had even the slightest significance. Or point. Who was going to employ a cripple?

But for the most part, I prayed. I was no stranger to praying, of course. I was like any other normal teenager – didn't much bother with God when things were good, but bothered Him ceaselessly whenever they weren't. Could He please fix my imperfections, make whoever I fancied like me, arrange it so my Maths test was easier than expected and generally ease my passage during turbulent times?

But the business of praying, when it's miracles you're after, is an altogether different thing to do, chiefly because you have to start off by apologising for all the selfish, insignificant things you've already pestered Him about over the years, before going on to try and make a convincing sort of case about just how truly madly deeply you need Him to be there for you now. And if He'd not seen fit to undo the damage I'd done to myself, could He at least find some way to give us hope for the future? Just the tiniest glimmer was all I asked.

Because I wasn't just praying for myself. Despite my growing terror about what the future had in store for me – Would I ever see home again? Would I be crippled and useless and incarcerated for ever? Would I ever see the outside of some grim institution? – none of this felt quite as bad and unrelenting as the ever-present guilt about my parents. They had done nothing to deserve this. They had adopted a healthy baby girl (my mother often used to comment how lucky we all were; there were so many disabled babies up for adoption, after all. How wonderful, they'd agreed, that I was perfect in every way) and now, just fifteen years later, they had a six-foot useless great lump for a daughter, one that would be totally dependent on them all over again. It wasn't just my own life I'd thrown away by my recklessness. I'd thrown all that love and care back in their faces as well.

*   *   *

The place where I'd been billeted for the next stage of my treatment was called Rookwood Hospital. It was a large Spinal Injuries Centre in Cardiff that took patients from South Wales and the South West of England, and about which I knew nothing whatsoever.

As was the case with my parents. Their only exposure to the business of spinal rehabilitation up to now had been the much fêted and publicised Stoke Mandeville Hospital, at that time inseparable from its then most famous patron, Jimmy Savile, whose tireless support and incredible energy had put the place firmly on the map. Working on the eminently sensible basis that somewhere so famous and so widely supported might be just the place for their daughter, they petitioned to have me sent there. After all, if I was going to have to spend God only knew how big a chunk of my life away from home, and in a totally alien environment, at least they could push for the best, and best-loved, one. The one, though they hardly dared voice their desperate hope, that might still offer some tiny chance that I would one day manage to walk again. But their reasoning fell on deaf NHS ears.

In rehabilitation terms, as Mr Davies was swift to point out, I would be equally well served in either place. And being sent all the way to Stoke Mandeville made little sense. Not if I wanted to see anything of my family. Stoke Mandeville was over 100 miles distant, Rookwood, in Cardiff, just 30. Besides, it was the centre intended for our region, and as with hospitals and schools one tended to go where one was told. So though Stoke Mandeville would come to figure later in my life, for now Rookwood, it was decided, it would be.

I was terrified. I'd been terrified from day one, of course, but as my final week at Neath General ticked by and 2 June got ever closer, my terror took on a new intensity.

By now I had settled into a routine at Neath General and trusted the staff looking after me – the very personal parts of me. I'd been eased through the metamorphosis from my old life to my new one by powerful tranquillising and painkilling drugs. Now I was about to be dragged off to an institution where I wouldn't have such support – not to mention my mother's constant presence through the nights. Did people ever come out of institutions? Weren't they places where you went to die? It didn't matter much to me that Rookwood was closer than Stoke Mandeville. It was still far away, and would be full of equally terrifying 'inmates'. Who would want to travel and visit me there?

My terror became a constant, unwelcome companion. It visited me every time I let my guard down for an instant and crept into bed with me at night. Up till this point I simply hadn't *time* for such terror. Too many routines. Too many distractions. The days full of people and things to be done, the nights eased by the comfort that was the presence of my mother, breathing softly beside me, just an arm's length away. All this was to stop. To be replaced by – what? It didn't help that none of my nurses knew anything about Rookwood either. The only person, in fact, who had ever been to Rookwood was my consultant, many years back when still a junior doctor, and presumably because he hadn't heard of any murders, mass lynchings or other criminal atrocities, he was completely satisfied that it was the best place for me to be.

As with any lack of solid information – a small testimony from a grateful former patient would have done – Rookwood soon acquired the status of a terrifying unknown, a situation not helped by my increasing conviction that the reason no one admitted to knowing anything about it was because it was going to be so grim and dreadful they dared not speak of it in my presence. Even the name conjured dark forbidding images of tar-black flocks of huge angry birds roosting and cawing in malevolent forests; a Dickensian nightmare made real.

The departure itself was protracted. Once aboard my trolley to retrace, for the first time, the route I'd taken in reverse just three weeks ago (apart from my trip to theatre for my op, I'd not seen outside the ward, much less sniffed fresh air) I was soon joined by a procession of staff. Almost everyone in the hospital turned out to say goodbye – even off-duty nurses, who'd come in specially to wish me well. There seemed not enough words to convey my gratitude to everyone, much less space in my throat for the lump that was lodged there; it really did feel as if I was being uprooted from a substitute home that I'd only just got used to and being taken away to a strange place full of strangers for an indeterminate period of time – and that was assuming I survived. I didn't know much but I wasn't stupid, either. A long life was no longer something I could take for granted. How could I when so much of me no longer worked? The human body was not designed to be like this.

Perhaps if I could just hang on in A & E long enough, they'd forget why they were gathered and we could all go back in and pretend it wasn't happening. But it wasn't to be. All too soon, the ambulance had backed up into the porch-way to admit me, and suddenly it was just me, Staff Nurse Liz, who had been given the responsibility of escorting me, and my small bundle of possessions, on our way to the big city and whatever we'd find there. I stared at the ambulance ceiling, my throat sore, my eyes puffy and my head full of regrets. The last time I'd visited Cardiff, I recalled, was to have the tattoo of Aldo's name removed; my grand gesture towards a bright shiny future as a model. Now some other girls' future. Not mine.

The ambulance shuddered into life. Liz settled herself into her seat beside my trolley and took my hand. 'I'm not sure if this is a privilege or a torment,' she confided. There had apparently been no shortage of volunteers to undertake this particular away-day from the hospital, about which I was touched, but all had also agreed that the prospect of delivering me into the hands of the people at Rookwood, depositing me there and then travelling back alone, was not one they viewed with any relish.

Nurses see patients come and go all the time, of course, but in hindsight what human could fail to be moved by the plight of a vulnerable teenage girl, so horribly disabled, who was about to be packed off into the unknown?

Once again, the ambulance was to proceed agonisingly slowly. Though it had been decided that my back was now strong enough to cope with the transfer, it was still on the condition that the journey be as smooth as possible. As the

M4 motorway had yet to snake its way this deep into the
South Wales countryside the route took in mostly trunk
roads and lesser ones. As a result we caused lengthy tail-
backs of traffic, most cars (either out of deference or caution)
seemingly unwilling to overtake. Perhaps the sight of the
ambulance moving so slowly made them think a little more
before hitting the gas. They must have wondered who
was in there and what terrible fate had befallen them. I
couldn't see myself, of course, but from what Liz kept relay-
ing, our procession must have looked a little like a funeral
cortège.

Somewhere, caught up in this tailback, were my mother
and father, ensconced in the family's aged Morris Minor,
which they'd had to bring along, rather than ride with me
in the ambulance, as the latter had to return to Neath almost
immediately, while they would stay at Rookwood for a
while to help settle me in. Having no idea where Rookwood
was, much less how to find their way there, they had elected
to follow us. My greatest fear on that journey, when not
engaged in being terrified for myself, was that at some point
we would lose them altogether. Without sat nav or mobiles
or a map (Mum couldn't read them), they were entirely
dependent on keeping us in sight. But with many junctions
and roundabouts and traffic lights involved, this was, even
on a journey this slow, a challenge. And given Mum's almost
legendary navigational history, I had a very real fear that
they might never get there and be doomed to patrolling the
streets of Cardiff for all time.

It wasn't hard to germinate such panics. During my time
at Neath, Liz and I had become great conversationalists.

Despite my physical difficulties (it's hard to laugh properly when lying on your back, plus the level of my paralysis meant my lung function was impaired, not helped by my having smoked for four years), Liz had always been adept at bringing out the teenage bravado that invariably saw me through difficult moments. But now, as the ambulance crawled for its interminable hours, neither of us could find anything to say. Seeing Liz, a year on, I was to find out that she'd cried without let-up for the whole journey back, but right then all I was aware of were my own racing thoughts. I was heart-in-the-mouth anxious. I didn't want to be here. What I most wanted to do was to leap up and run away. But running wasn't (and, I knew, deep down, would never again be) an option. So my woes circled round me like rooks themselves, while I remained in my dark place contemplating my dark future. A place no platitudes or chin-up type words could seem to broach.

Rookwood Hospital was – and still is – situated in Llandaff, on the western edge of Cardiff. It's set in an elderly house and an assortment of low, antiquated-looking buildings, within sprawling grounds dotted with fat cedars and impenetrable thickets. We would come to joke later that should a patient fall out of their wheelchair and end up in one, it would be weeks, perhaps months, before they'd be found.

Rookwood was half a mile or so from Cardiff's Llandaff Cathedral to the east and further away, to the west, tracing our route towards home, from the green spaces of the Welsh Folk Museum. To visit Rookwood now would be to find little changed. It still looks a little like a faded stately home that has been commandeered to provide a base for a bunch of troops.

But however evocative of better days the exterior surroundings, what the ambulance doors eventually opened onto was the back end of a single-storey ward block, far from the grand entrance, which was set among a collection of lock-ups and bins and looked every inch the sort of army barracks you'd see in a black-and-white war film. A set of double doors was presumably the entrance, but it was not them that grabbed my immediate attention. For beside them was a wheelchair, in which sat a woman of about thirty, a pathetic-looking soul in twisted tracksuit bottoms, who didn't even seem to be aware that we were there. She just sat slumped, looking blankly at the adjacent brick wall.

It was a vision that would stay with me always. Was this it for *me* now? Was this going to be my life? Would my days now be spent staring vacantly at nothing? If I'd been scared before I was doubly so now. I would not, I *could* not, become like that woman. But how, I thought, panicked, was I to stop that from happening? As I was unloaded from the ambulance, the blue of the sky – the first I'd seen for so long – seemed to taunt me. I was flat on my back. I was useless. A giant baby. I couldn't do anything for myself any more. My whole life, in all its most intimate aspects, was now in the hands of other people. Strangers. And where were Mum and Dad?

* * *

It came as no surprise that the first smell I encountered on passing through those double doors was urine. The smell I'd previously associated with telephone boxes, dank underpasses and the corners of multi-storey car parks seemed every bit as fitting in this bleak and cheerless environment. I wouldn't have been even remotely surprised to find matted-haired vagrants shuffling up to meet me, or beached up, semi-conscious, against the ward block walls.

A heavily pregnant nurse appeared to greet us and spoke in staccato terms to Liz. Her words, spoken low, were impossible to decipher, but one thing was clear. She seemed to have no intention of talking to me. All I knew was that I was now being wheeled I knew not where, and the sense of being out of control was acute. Liz held my hand and tried to keep me informed. Our destination – the female ward – was approached via the male ward, though in fact the distinction wasn't clear. The two wards were only separated by a set of partial screens. There were doors, apparently, but as I was to find later, there might as well not have been because they were never shut.

Our passage through this section was illuminating too, accompanied by mutters of 'Here's a new one' and also wolf whistles. Liz was very pretty, so male attention was unsurprising, but wolf whistles? Here? It felt horrible and wrong. She held my hand tightly and, with the help of the ambulance crew, lifted me carefully into bed. Then, our journey done, we were offered a cup of tea.

Not the biggest, most significant thing in the world, a cup of tea. Not most of the time, anyway. Cups of tea were a regular occurrence at Neath General; they punctuated the days just as surely as the ward rounds, the mealtimes, and Auntie Mad's cakes. At Neath I'd always been given my tea in a cup and saucer; they prided themselves on such details. Tea served in a cup and saucer felt normal – *tasted* normal – no matter that, being flat on my back or my front, I always had to drink mine through a straw. And not just any straw either. The nurses kept a supply of coloured bendy ones for me, which someone had taken the trouble to go out and buy; different nurses, different colours, and always a new one.

Here my tea arrived in a plastic feeder beaker. The sort babies have; a murky-looking, semi-transparent trainer cup. Liz automatically removed the trainer top and asked if a straw could be provided instead. This didn't seem too outlandish a request, and the ward nurse went straight off to fetch one. What came, however, gave us both the shudders – a length of plastic tubing, horribly similar to that used for bed-bags, which was unceremoniously dropped into my cup. By this time Mum and Dad had arrived on the ward and joined us, having, to my great relief, finally found their way there, via goodness only knew what diversion. Their faces said everything. They too were disgusted. The tea cooled in its beaker, undrunk.

And then, all too soon, it was time for Liz to leave us. The ambulance had been delayed for long enough. How I envied the patients she was going back to care for. How I dreaded that, as of now, our connection would be severed. How long would it be before I saw her – or any of my lovely nurses – again? She hugged me a final time and whispered in my ear. 'It won't be that bad,' she said. 'It won't be that bad.' And it wouldn't be forever. If I was to get through this, I *had* to keep telling myself that. Even so, we both cried, and as I watched her walk away, accompanied by another round of cat-calls and whistles, I thought I'd be happy to curl up and die right there. I clung to Mum and Dad while my sobs refused to quieten. She was wrong. It already *was* that bad.

chapter 5

There are events that happen in any life that become significant only once put in context with what follows them. My moment on the catwalk was one such.

Four days after my admission to Rookwood, Mum and Dad brought in a photograph for me. It was the one that had appeared in the *Western Mail* newspaper several weeks earlier, as part of their coverage of a not particularly important news event: the Glanafan Comprehensive School fashion show. I was fourth from the right of our line-up of models, all of us decked out in that season's new nightwear; there was sufficient nylon that had we rustled too much there would no doubt have been enough static electricity to launch a zeppelin.

'Thought we could put it on your locker,' Mum suggested. 'You know. Something to cheer you up.'

Mum had a point. Having spent much of the preceding few days in what I had come to decide was an extreme form of solitary confinement, to retreat inside my head was beginning to feel not just a means to escape the horror of my situation, but more a series of visits to a much nicer place – a dreamscape, almost, populated by a version of myself that was no longer imprisoned in this hateful bed.

Not that I'd wanted to be a model at the outset. (I certainly didn't want to be a model as a life choice – I just loved the feeling that if I'd wanted to, I could.) When it had first been put about that they were looking for models, my response was the same as pretty much everyone else's. A mass teenage lack of self-esteem, coupled with an equally natural fear of being made to look silly or uncool, meant our fall-back position was that anyone who dared put herself forward as a wannabe Twiggy would, without exception, be a tart and a poser, and utterly in love with themselves. Not the sort of girl, we all agreed firmly, that we'd want to have *anything* to do with. Dorothy Perkins, the store running the event, would, we decided, have to look elsewhere for their complement of catwalk crumpet.

But our group dynamic (not to mention our natural adolescent mistrust of things organised by adults) didn't prove much of a match for our girlish human nature. As the hour passed that stood between break-time and lunchtime, it seemed it wasn't only us that had had a major change of heart. By the time Juli and I turned up at the gym, we found ourselves in the midst of a heaving mass of girlhood, by turns giggling and strutting and giggling some more.

It seemed that despite our refusals to have anything to do with it, almost every girl in the fifth form had suddenly changed her mind. Someone even mentioned the Pirelli calendar.

This wasn't exactly New York fashion week, but there was a real sense of anxious anticipation as the three women from Dorothy Perkins, who up until now had been observing the preening teens with a stern and slightly jaundiced eye, gathered the mob into three separate groups. Under their critical gaze, we were directed to walk a single length of the gym floor.

When my own turn came it was with less surprise than I might have felt, given my earlier pronouncements, that I found myself 110 per cent committed to being a tart and a poser. Whatever it took, so be it. Besides, I was really enjoying myself. I strutted my stuff, head up, shoulders back (as I'd read somewhere), willing the woman to notice my height and my grace, and desperate to hear that magical 'yes'.

But my moment of glory was short-lived. Even before I'd fully had time to assimilate the long-term potential of my new status as catwalk beauty (being spotted, getting famous, lying on tropical beaches, sipping cocktails with umbrellas in, being swept away by Paul Michael Glaser and so on) I was the recipient of a sharp poke in the arm.

One of the shorter (and unchosen) girls glared up at me. 'You were always going to get in, Bowen,' she hissed. She nodded towards Juli, who'd also been picked. 'You and *her*. Any lanky bitch was bound to. And you know something else? You're going to look a right *prat*.'

Prat or not, I was delighted. No amount of bitching or barracking or bile could take the shine off the thrill of that day.

Next up, of course, we were to be 'styled and sized', both novel concepts in themselves. Not that I was a stranger to fashion and make-up. Though my wardrobe consisted mostly of T-shirts and jeans (I grudgingly owned two skirts only because they were a part of my school uniform), I loved make-up just as much as any other fifteen-year-old, and considered my unruly mop of curls to be a blank canvas on which to experiment with all the cheap hair-colouring products of the day. I'd been dark, I'd been fair, I'd been every shade of red, and was currently posing as a sultry chestnut brunette. Perhaps highlights? I knew I would have to consult Juli. She might have tired of her current strawberry blonde locks, and it was important that the two of us didn't clash.

Dorothy Perkins being one of the trendier names on the high street, we didn't harbour too many worries about what they'd be kitting us out in. Despite their constant edict that it was the clothes and not our excitable selves we'd be exhibiting, we knew better. It was us *in* the clothes that would make all the difference, so every one of us embraced the role of self-regarding *prima donna* with the sort of commitment almost never seen in class.

The night of the show itself was unforgettable; I would like to have added 'for all the obvious reasons', but it rapidly became clear that modelling, though not quite rocket science, did require a degree of poise and expertise. So it was that the most memorable aspects of the show involved strangulation by feather boa (it was said for months afterwards that the poor girl's eyes bulged so much that the whites of them could be seen from the back of the hall); near disaster by necklace (stray beads were still being found in corners of the school hall for months afterwards, and on the night the only solace was that she didn't take out the headmistress with a flying tackle); and finally, near choking by baby-doll nightdress, my own contribution to the evening.

This last was also an early lesson in the idiom that less can be more. In my element, clothed in a red satin baby-doll nightdress and skimpy knickers, I swept down the catwalk amid some gratifying whistling, and, avoiding the eyes of my parents (they were both purple), I paused for my twirl at the end of the runway as I'd been instructed during rehearsals. It was at exactly that moment when a man in the front row took a bite from a bar of chocolate and it seemed that the proximity of my thinly veiled derrière brought on a violent bout of choking. He eventually received assistance from a fellow audience member and the panic in the hall quietened down.

I don't know to this day if the two were connected, but at the time I was quite sure they were. 'Fancy that,' I remember thinking as I shimmied back up the catwalk. 'My bum nearly killed someone. Fame at last!'

But my fame was to be as short-lived as it was glorious. The intervening three months might as well have been a lifetime. Mum fixed the photo to my locker, as she'd suggested, and it wasn't long before it was spotted by one of the nurses. She pointed at the picture. 'Was that you?' she asked. It was all I could do not to contravene my own rule and break down at the import of her words. Not 'is' me, but '*was*' me. A person no longer here. Not the biggest distinction, but one that cruelly, however unintentionally spoken, addressed the stark reality of what I'd become. I *was* still me, wasn't I? *Wasn't* I?

* * *

The routine at Rookwood would soon become familiar, but for the first few anguished days I felt adrift and alone. From the moment my parents first arrived on the ward to join me, I was aware that all too soon they would have to leave me again, that they were no longer fifteen minutes but a whole hour away, and that I would have to get used to being without them every night, and instead, in the company of strangers.

And not just any strangers. The staff at Rookwood were different; to my ear, they 'talked funny'. With my lack of years and travel I'd never heard a Cardiff accent before.

After Liz left to go back to Neath, two auxiliary nurses arrived to carry out their usual routine. It might be doing them a disservice, given my traumatised state, but to this day I don't recall them introducing themselves to me, much less engaging me in conversation about what they had to do. I felt like an outsider – a new kid at school; only, generally, at school, all the new kids start together, so you have, at least, comrades with whom to share your disorientation. As for Mum and Dad, they were all at sea as well. They'd both lived through the horror of a world war, yet Rookwood still managed to terrify them.

Ward Six – my ward – held little in the way of hopeful allegiances. There was no one close to my age in the female section when I arrived, and none in the male section either. I imagined this must be a little like prison, though in prison at least the convicts got to move around a bit. I was imprisoned by my body and without control over any single aspect of my life. It felt less that I was spending further time in another hospital and more that I had actually started what was to be the rest of a life spent in captivity. I couldn't seem to get past the notion that even when I'd finally made it out of bed, I'd still be confined to this urine-stinking hell-hole; the only difference was that I'd now be in a wheelchair and could haunt the place much as that woman I'd seen staring, unseeing, at a brick wall when I'd arrived. I knew I would have to learn to cope with things minute my minute, but didn't have the first idea how.

The minutes passed, even so, and within the first twenty-four hours it became obvious that meals at Rookwood weren't going to be a highlight. There was choice, certainly, but that choice never seemed to vary. It was invariably Spam (or a Spam-lookalike) accompanied by limp salad, or one of two varieties of stew. The latter was either brown with unidentifiable lumps or white with unidentifiable lumps; not remotely haute-cuisine, not even meals-on-wheels; the inmates, appropriately, as I soon came to learn, labelled it 'muck on a truck'.

But the food did at least have one thing going for it. It was so vile, I found it hard to eat. This was a circumstance that was to bring me a small but definite crumb of comfort. A week or so into my relocation, I received a visit from John, the guy I'd secretly carried a torch for, the guy who'd made it clear he felt the same. I had mixed feelings about seeing him again. On the one hand seeing anyone was a welcome relief. I'd refused to see Aldo at Neath General, and I felt ambivalent about agreeing to see John now. All attempts made at physical normality at Neath (the hairdressing sessions, the carefully applied make-up) seemed almost nonsensical in this desolate place.

My body didn't feel like my own any more, in either a physical or emotional sense. Though it was so much more than simply a reaction to the unwittingly ill-judged comment of one nurse, the idea took hold and wouldn't go away. She'd been right; the 'me' to whom she'd referred no longer existed. The 'me' who lay inert on a bed in Ward Six was a different animal entirely. The young girl who had had to have her clothes cut off her body for surgery had now become someone who needed her clothes cut up to put *on* her, to make the dressing process easier. A small thing – an eminently practical thing, obviously – but one that seemed a metaphor for everything I'd lost.

And also gained. I didn't get many opportunities to see myself as I now was, but the business of dressing and undressing afforded depressing glimpses of how much things had changed. I'd always had as many self-esteem issues as the next girl – maybe more – but one thing about which I'd always been proud was my svelte stomach, which was concave. Less than a month after the accident and it was no more. Looking down, *lying* down, it had been replaced by a hillock. A hillock that made me look several months pregnant, the legacy of a body that no longer moved and muscles that were no longer toned. It was this aspect to which John (understandably stuck for small talk) alluded as soon as he arrived. As memorable comments go, his was a gem – one I knew even as he spoke that I'd never forget.

'Where,' he asked, 'has your flat stomach gone?'

It was an inauspicious start to an inauspicious visit. Our conversation limped on, increasingly pointless and depressing, and he never came to visit again.

* * *

If my few visitors (and they were indeed few; travelling by public transport from Port Talbot to Llandaff was complex and expensive) were a welcome respite from the relentless tedium that made up the days, the nights were anything but. I'd never been to one, but I felt sure that if Ward Six at night time were in need of description then the tag 'fish-market' would suit it very well. And that wasn't just because of the all-pervasive odour. The noise and activity simply never seemed to stop; it was cacophony central every night.

Much of this was only to be expected. Unable to move ourselves, we had to be turned and attended to regularly, but unlike Neath, where I was seen to quietly, calmly and with consideration for sleeping patients, it seemed that in here noise simply didn't matter. Although the nursing station was well away at the far end of the male section of the ward, I could still hear everything they did. And if, by some miracle, the noise generated by loud conversations, doors banging and what sounded like a banquet's-worth of clattering crockery failed to keep me awake, there was also the continual problem of *us*. As spinal patients, none of us – ridiculously – were able to reach our call buttons (day or night) because they were positioned out of reach on the wall behind our beds. We had no choice, therefore, but to shout for attention. And then, of course, at each other, for having been woken up.

Such sleep as I did get in the early days at Rookwood was visited by dreams, good and bad. Then, as is still the case now, I often dreamed I was walking. Better still, I sometimes dreamed I was flying: over green fields, blue rivers and lakes and mountains in bright sunshine, swooping up and down on the currents of air. I'd feel so free I would hate waking up. But then, also as now, most of my dreams were nightmares; the anxious awareness of footsteps behind me, a malevolent presence I could never identify, and the fear of being unable to run away. The worst nightmare of all, though, was waking every morning, seeing the ward and having to face my situation again.

But however the machinations of my unconscious mind might have helped or hindered the process of coming to terms, nothing was to have as much impact in those early days as what I was soon to start seeing around me.

Up until now, I'd been cocooned in my own little bubble of perfect, unique misery, but Rookwood was soon to remind me that I wasn't the only one to whom fate had been cruel, that there were people who were worse off than me. About six weeks after my own admission, another road traffic victim was admitted. She was nineteen and had also been knocked off a motorbike, sustaining head and neck injuries. Consequently, she couldn't speak, and though she could move her arms and legs, those movements were spastic and uncontrolled.

Like me, Bridget had a 'before' picture on her locker, one of a staggeringly beautiful young woman, with long black curls that fell almost to her waist. Much as the contrast in my own situation hurt me, it was as nothing to hers. Her face was now horribly contorted and dribbling, and the glossy curls had all been cropped. What was worse, to my mind, was that her mother had a mirror and seemed constantly to feel the need to show her the state of her appearance – to this day I have no idea why.

It wasn't just looks that mattered either. One of my most enduring memories of that time was the boy across the ward who had lost the use of both his arms and his legs, so didn't even have the luxury of two functioning limbs.

One day, he asked my mother if she would scratch his nose for him and this upset her so much that, once she'd done so, she had to leave the ward in a hurry so that he wouldn't see her tears. The memory today still brings a lump to her throat.

Slowly, then, I began to take stock and take heart. There was really so much that I could do for myself; my situation could be so much worse. In comparison with these people I was lucky. Me? Lucky? How could I possibly feel *that*? I didn't know, I didn't care, I was simply grateful that I did.

I just hoped the feeling wouldn't go away.

chapter 6

While it was clear that my walking days were definitely over, it was still important that my back had the best chance of healing straight and strong. This mattered not only for posture but also for balance; I had a whole body to lug through life with me but only half the usual amount of sensation. The first six weeks of my time in Rookwood, therefore, were spent lying flat in my bed while the bones in my back healed in the correct alignment, supported by the operative rods.

During this time, as had been the case since the day of the crash, I had a catheter. This was not, however, considered ideal. The plan was that during the last two weeks of this stage the catheter would be removed and 'bladder training' would be undertaken, in preparation for what would be the next stage of my rehabilitation: getting myself up into a wheelchair.

How this training was to be achieved was a mystery. How did you train something you couldn't feel? The theory, as explained to me, was simple. A proportion of spinally injured people, apparently, had 'reflex' bladders; it was hoped that once the catheter was removed, mine – whether

I could feel it or not – would somehow re-learn what to do. That, given time and training, it would hang on to its contents until I prompted it to do otherwise. The regime, based on this, was simple. I was to drink at least three litres of fluid a day, trust in the miracle of autonomic physiology, and then, on the hour, to 'express' it.

The idea made me feel like a heifer. I must drink, drink and drink – three litres is a LOT – and then, once a bed pan had been shoved underneath me, I must make contact with my bladder by means of rhythmically tapping my lower tummy below my belly button, on the hour, to kickstart the process of emptying.

This wasn't the load of mystical hogwash it seemed (no crazy chanting or joss sticks were required) but something that apparently had its roots in proper science. The theory was that the physical stimulation that the tapping produced would, more often than not, be successful. Tap it, it seemed, and you could turn on the tap, and your expressing would be a success.

There are lots of things that make the average adolescent want to curl up and die. But for most teenage girls, already beset by insecurities about looks, hairstyles, choice of clothes, numbers of friends and so forth, any angst that came under the umbrella 'bodily functions' was perhaps the richest seam of trauma a girl could ever mine. Bodily functions were personal. Private. Going to the toilet, particularly the non-wee variety, just wasn't, as I suspect was and is the case for most women, something one generally shared. Something no human would ever *want* to share. Indeed, much of my and my friends' time was spent in convincing each other, particularly boys, that we didn't have bodily functions at all. If – horror – we had to use a loo in a public place for 'number 2s' we would stuff half a roll of loo paper down first so no one could hear what we were doing. Not something most people bring up in conversation but something many of us did, and, I don't doubt, many women still do today.

For me – no different from anyone else in most regards – this represented a stress of monumental proportions from the moment the reality sank in back in Neath. And sunk in, it had. By now, though I doubted I'd ever actually get used to the idea, I had at least become to some extent inured to the humiliation that dealing with my waste products involved. Both my bladder and bowels needed evacuating, clearly, and I had learned to switch off that part of my brain that, if left to consider my plight for too long, would leave me both desolate and scared. It was almost too much to take in the fact that while I could put stuff *into* my body, someone else, for the whole of the rest of my life, would have to deal with what came out of the other end.

There seemed no way of sugaring that particular pill but at least, should this 'training' prove successful, I would be able to wrest a modicum of control from the wee situation, and with it, a measure of dignity.

Dignity, understandably, was in pretty short supply on Ward Six. If the muck-on-a-truck cart could lower our spirits, the 'crap cart' (again, imaginatively named by the inmates) was a thing of rare grossness. Didn't matter if there were visitors on the ward. It was always business as usual with the crap cart.

It was almost impossible to ignore. Its clanking and clattering soon became a familiar sound, which heralded two hours of purgatory.

Literal purgatory, every other day. Beginning at the far end of the male ward, curtains would begin to swish and suppositories would be administered. All this would happen to the accompaniment of the slap of rubber gloves, squirts of KY jelly, and a running commentary on who was going to be next. The plan was for the suppository to be left for about half an hour before the nurse in charge would return to check for a result.

If you had a visitor, this was always an extremely tense time. All you could pray was that things wouldn't get moving until the cart came back to you again. That nothing would happen while your visitors were at your bedside, not even your nearest and dearest, and certainly not your friends.

Not *my* friends, definitely. Didn't matter how much I loved them, or they me. They were fifteen-year-olds. Which meant, I didn't doubt, that they were not averse to recounting the gory details to all and sundry in the schoolyard at break-time. At times like this, I felt there was no way I could ever face anyone in Port Talbot again.

And then the evacuations started. To this day, I'm not sure which odour was worse: that of the results of the business of evacuation (which grew in sickening intensity with every

new patient 'done'), or the cloying scent of the air freshen-
ers so copiously sprayed to – ineffectually – try to mask the
first. Indeed, the two, in a fine example of Pavlovian condi-
tioning, have become so inextricably intermingled in my
brain that I still have major trouble finding air-freshening
sprays that don't take me, queasily, straight back to Ward
Six.

But at least we could do something about my bladder. In
theory, at any rate. Except it turned out that, however many
fine qualities my bladder possessed, being 'reflex' didn't
seem to be among them. Which meant that the two-week
training programme that commenced at the end of my
fourth week at Rookwood (in preparation for my being
transferred to a wheelchair in week six) turned into three
and then four and then five … In the end it was to mark the
start of a five-*month*-long period in which urine loomed
fearfully large in my life. And this after a period when it
hadn't loomed at all. Going to the loo had become an arte-
fact from my old life, something I simply didn't do any
more. My wee was excreted into a small plastic bag that
hung from a hook at the side of my bed, and I played no
active part in it getting there.

All that, however, was to change. Once training
commenced a whole new routine established itself. Sadly,
it wasn't the one planned. What should have been a drink-
tap-express situation was, in fact, something entirely different. I drank, I wet myself, my nightwear and sheets were
changed, I drank again, I wet myself again, the whole lot

was changed again. I now existed, it seemed, in a urine-scented miasma. Though I obviously couldn't *feel* that I was mostly lying in a puddle, I could smell it, and I well knew that visitors could too.

'Please,' I begged, 'can't I just have my catheter back?'

'No,' came the answer. It was out of the question. Catheters, I was told, were only for the sick. And unfortunate souls locked in comas. They, it was pointed out, obviously couldn't help it.

But *I* couldn't help it. The process wasn't working. And to make matters worse, it was positively harmful. Lying endlessly in wee does no one any good. Apart from the obvious stress and humiliation, I began to succumb to an endless round of infections – something that never stopped in all my time at Rookwood. Nothing trivial: acute vomiting, rigors, crashing headaches. The latter, I learned later, were a part of my condition – to give it its fancy name, Autonomic Dysreflexia, a situation in which the autonomic nervous system (that part of the body's electrics which controls functions of which we should be unaware, such as blood pressure, heart rate, gut function and so forth) over-reacts to a stimulus. In this case it was a response to the inflammation of my bladder; the inefficient emptying was causing the recurrent infections.

In short, it was my compromised body's way of letting me know that all wasn't as it should be in the areas I couldn't feel.

Nevertheless, we persevered. The 'we' in this case being nurses with a clearly unshakeable belief that it would work in the end, and an unhappy and vulnerable fifteen-year-old girl with insufficient authority to stop the urine-soaked nightmare from continuing.

My compliance with the issue of bladder training wasn't just about lacking sufficient assertiveness to question the regimen they'd decided upon, any more than it was about scientific fact. Doing as I was told, generally, seemed the best way forward, as events I witnessed early on showed.

In the next bed on my left, the final bed in the corner of the ward, was a woman called Lesley. She was thirty-one, had been admitted a month or so before me, and was already up in a wheelchair. Like me, she'd been the victim of a motorcycle accident, but the circumstances couldn't have been more different. Lesley's bike had been her own, and her accident had not been the result of any maniac driving; she'd been travelling, at no speed whatsoever, through some roadworks, and the bike had ended up in an unmarked hole in the road.

Fate had been especially cruel to Lesley. Given the circumstances, she could easily have expected to come through with little more than a few bumps and bruises. Instead, she'd had an especially unlucky landing, crushing her spinal cord at the upper mid-dorsal spine, resulting in the same level of paralysis as mine.

Like me, she'd lost the use of her legs, plus all of the muscles below the mid-chest level. Loss of these muscles had big implications for breathing, obviously, and also balance. I knew this because during the physiotherapist's first visit to me after admission, she helpfully brought charts of the body, in order to show me what was what. They looked a little like police outlines of murdered corpses, and showed the stark consequences of different levels of spinal injury. Mine, and Lesley's too, were shaded black below the mid-chest; this was the part of my body that wasn't going to play an active part in the rest of my life.

Lesley and I agreed that in one moment the course of the rest of our lives had changed irrevocably. It was good to be able to talk about it to someone who was going through it too, but it was also terrifying. I think it was then, talking to Lesley, that things *really* hit home. That we were both changed for ever, that there was never going to be a cure, that this – *all* of this – was never going to go away.

Apart from our injuries, Lesley and I had marked differences; I was six feet tall, and needed an extension on my bed, where she was four foot eleven. Months later, when standing between the parallel bars in physio, we looked a little like Mutt and Jeff. We had also had very different treatment for our injuries: post her accident, she had been managed traditionally, with bed rest, whereas I had had my fractures stabilised with metal rods. She was adamant that the conservative line followed in Bristol (and also, ironically, at my parents' choice, Stoke Mandeville) was the gold standard, while I found myself sticking up for Mr Davies's operative approach.

I was probably not qualified to judge either way – we were both of us up the same creek without a paddle – but my sense of loyalty to my brusque consultant was keen. I often found myself bringing his name up in conversation and wondered if *he* wondered how I was getting on. I was later to find out that he was perfectly at ease. He'd sent me to the acknowledged 'best place in South Wales'. Of the day-to-day horrors and humiliations of Rookwood, he obviously knew absolutely nothing.

Originally from Sheffield, Lesley was intelligent and funny, with long brown hair and a habitually determined expression. She'd had a good job in the Civil Service, based in Bristol, and also her own home, to which, it was sadly and increasingly clear, she would in all likelihood never return.

She'd also had a boyfriend but he soon became an ex because he simply couldn't cope with her injury. She had very few visitors and, as a result, liked very much to be included when mine came – as one or both of them did every evening. At times both Mum and Dad and I found this intrusive – after all, I had Lesley to talk to all day; when my parents came, time spent with them felt very precious. But I was also aware of how lonely she was; how covetous of my lovely family.

Lesley too had been using a catheter, and, like me, she'd now been moved onto a training regime. It wasn't working out for her either. But Lesley knew her mind and, unlike me, she wasn't going to take things lying down.

However much we might wish it otherwise, there is basic human nature involved in all our interactions, and I was learning about that pretty fast. The situation of being help-less is not natural. It puts you immediately in a position of dependency, which is one in which no sane person wishes to exist. I no more wanted strangers to deal with my faeces than I wanted to have to deal with theirs. And I particularly didn't want pity. Which was unfortunate because pity, in all its forms, was such a part of the experience of being as I was that you could practically sniff it in the air.

The position of my bed – indeed that of the last four beds at the end of the female section of Ward Six – felt like the end of the world. Geographically, from a hospital layout perspective, that was precisely where it was. A dead end. The end of a long ward at the end of a long corridor which was one of several spokes that fanned out from the entrance. There was, therefore, no passing traffic. Unlike Neath, with its endless bustle and activity and comings and goings, no one had cause to be at the end of Ward Six unless they had come to look after one of the four patients there. And apart from the nurses and various medics and domestics, the only people who had reason to be on Ward Six were the families and friends of people like me. People who for all the world wished it wasn't so, that they didn't have to find themselves regulars here. And who would? This was not your usual hospital ward, with its round of admissions and recoveries and discharges. The patients – and their visitors – were here for the long haul. Jolly farewells were few and far between.

You could see it in everyone's expressions. The way, as they approached, to see whoever they were seeing, they reconfigured themselves to suit the gravity of the occasion. How they'd glance in your direction and then crave the chance to look away. You could sense they realised they were entering a desperate place.

I couldn't blame them. I wished so much that, like them, I had the choice to leave, but, as time wore on and the extent of my disability dawned on me, the thought of the outside world was becoming just as frightening as my continuing confinement in the ward. I was so grateful for the love and support of my parents; being able to confide in them was the single greatest thing that kept me from the black hole that could spiral me down into overwhelming despair. With them beside me, I knew I could just about cope.

Lesley didn't have that. All Lesley had was Lesley. And her way of avoiding the black hole of despair was to take herself off to the pub. Within 'pushing distance' of the hospital there were two of them: the Maltster's Arms and the Black Lion. Both welcomed Rookwood patients. After one particular evening's escape with some rare visitors, Lesley returned a little the worse for wear and arrived back rather noisily on the ward.

Noise itself wasn't an issue – it was almost always noisy – but her stentorian rendition of 'She was on the bridge at midnight …', though completely hilarious to us patients, didn't go down terribly well with the nurses.

By the time she'd reached the female end of the ward, she'd decided to stop serenading her fellow patients and was now keen to try and engage us in polite conversation about how we'd spent our own evenings.

Two nurses appeared behind her and told her it was time to pipe down. It seemed that, for Lesley, it was a final straw moment. Something had been steadily building inside her – something big. She suddenly erupted.

Whirling around, and in doing so almost falling out of her wheelchair, she told both the nurses to f**k off. Needless to say, this did not go down well either. In an instant, she was manhandled into bed, both cot sides were raised and her wheelchair was removed. Not just removed, either, but – or so it seemed to me – confiscated. Maybe it could be seen to have been a health and safety issue, but I didn't doubt for an instant there was a power play involved. Indeed, the nurses seemed keen to make that fact very clear. In the fracas, I heard her tell the nurses she was wet, but they, by now, didn't seem to care. As they left, having noticed me staring wide-eyed and horrified, one of them stepped across to my bed. Perhaps she had read my expression as one not of shock but of defiance. There can be no other explanation for what she said. Which was that I could expect more of the same treatment should I decide to step out of line myself.

I lay in bed, my heart thumping, long into that night, listening to the sound of Lesley's sobbing. Her bed remained unchanged till the following afternoon.

If finding out all about power and control was proving taxing, there were other, less dramatic but equally important lessons to learn. Towards the end of my six-week period of total bed rest, one of the nurses, during a turning session, noticed some blood on my sheets. This development was not unexpected. Sister O'Rourke had already told me, back at Neath, that my periods would soon be returning, and, in some ways, their doing so was proof that my body was returning to 'normal' after its long weeks in spinal shock.

It was also, to my great ambivalence, a reminder that I was still a reproductively functioning young woman. A sexual being. But what was the point of having periods? I'd never been keen to have children anyway, but now it was academic because what man would want me? After all, Lesley's boyfriend hadn't wanted her any more, had he? How was I now – as a cripple in a wheelchair – going to be desired by any boy or man? Before my accident, with a mixture of embarrassment and pride, I had grown used to being wolf-whistled on a daily basis – whether in my school uniform or in my casual clothes. I had been proud of my body and filled with normal girlish glee that it could provoke this reaction from grown men. I had not yet been in love but, just like any other girl, I had hoped in due time to be swept off my feet and transported to a romantic ever-after.

My English classes had taught me the great love stories – *Romeo and Juliet, Robin Hood and Maid Marian* – and, like almost all girls back then, I'd watched the film *Love Story* and been enthralled by the love affair between Ryan O'Neal and Ali McGraw. That it culminated in the heroine's untimely death from leukaemia now took on an almost unbearable poignancy. She'd been lucky; she'd been loved *before* it had happened. Was I likely to find someone to accept me as the cripple I'd already become? It felt impossible. *I* couldn't accept me. I even envied Ali McGraw's character's tragically early but theatrically glamorous death; I could see no prospect of heaven on earth for myself, however short, before my own likely premature demise.

As with the business of my bladder, however, the resumption of my periods was not about sex. It was just one more embarrassment among many.

The nurse was brisk and businesslike about it. What sort of protection was my preferred choice? I told her I'd always used tampons up till now, and another nurse was dispatched to go and get one.

She returned soon after and it was duly inserted, while I lay there and considered the long-term implications my monthly period would bring with it. Exposure to the crap cart meant that while I remained at Rookwood there was little that could further mortify me. But after that? Would Mum do it? Would I find some way to manage? What did other women in my position do about it? All questions that burned but remained unasked and so unanswered. I was naturally shy about such intimate matters. It was bad enough living it, without having to discuss it.

Two hours passed and it was time to be turned once again. Another nurse this time, who also saw blood. 'Looks like your period has started,' she said.

'I know it has,' I answered. 'Another nurse has already put in a tampon.'

I wondered at this point if I might have had a leak. My periods, after all, were sometimes horrendously heavy. Not so. The nurse made a closer inspection and, inexplicably to me, started laughing. And this wasn't just laughing, this was *serious* laughing. The sort of laughing that left her fighting for breath and helpless with her unexplained mirth. It was some time before she got herself sufficiently together that she was able to share the cause of the hilarity with me and all the other patients within earshot, who I didn't doubt were listening intently by now.

'It's been put,' she explained, her eyes still wet with tears, 'in – how shall I put it? – the wrong orifice!'

I imagine she probably thought I too would find this funny. Indeed, in the telling – and it's been something I've told, often – it generally makes people smile. But at the time I could no more have laughed about what happened than I could insert the wretched tampon myself from a position lying flat on the bed. My natural sense of humour about such things deserted me. I was wholly, toe-curlingly horrified. I simply couldn't believe that there was a nurse on the ward (a nurse who looked about *sixty*) who either didn't know where a tampon should go or, worse, cared so little for putting it where it belonged that she just shoved it anywhere it *would* go. Where, I thought wretchedly, would she put my next suppository? I felt violated. I'd been lying bleeding for two hours, with a tampon in my rectum, entirely unaware that anything was wrong.

I didn't know the reason – could she really not have *known*? – but one thing became blindingly obvious. That the trust I'd put, of necessity, in all the carers around me was misplaced. Was mistaken.

Was gone.

chapter 7

Sport. The final frontier. Well, not exactly the final frontier. More the first, last and everything-in-between frontier. Sport, for people like me, or so it seemed, was the *only* frontier. At the very least, the only way forward.

Two weeks into my time at Rookwood Hospital, a way forward was something I very much needed to find. Confined to bed, however, the prospect looked tricky. I couldn't move any part of my body beneath my nipples so there seemed little chance of my making any sort of bid for escape.

I had obviously had a number of shocks during the five or so weeks of my new life as a paraplegic. I had become somewhat battered, both physically and emotionally, and, or so I thought, somewhat inured to the relentless round of bad news my life seemed to have become. But there was more.

The doctor in charge of Rookwood was a Mr Chawla. Before taking up this post, he had been a surgeon, but his career in that specialty had apparently been cut short after a sustained period of ill health.

I didn't know then – and still don't – whether it was considered good practice to let me settle in before dropping the bombshell (today I suspect there might have been a retinue of dedicated stress counsellors and concerned professionals in attendance) but whatever the protocol of such matters it was during a regular ward round on an ordinary day that Mr Chawla imparted the news that I had, in all likelihood, just fifteen years to live. Indeed, that fifteen years was an optimistic guess. In truth, I'd be lucky to see thirty.

He took pains to explain in some detail why this should be. The pronouncement that I'd be lucky to see my fourth decade was apparently all to do with the health of my kidneys. Kidneys, like all body parts, have a finite life-expectancy, and mine, as a result of the paralysis, would be coming under much greater pressure than was normal. This was because I would be recumbent for much of my time, and the reduction of physical activity would reduce kidney filtration of the blood. There would also be pooling of urine in the kidney pelvis, leading to an increased chance of infection. In addition, the lack of gravitational assistance an able-bodied person would naturally get from standing and walking would mean bladder drainage was also slowed down. This meant a constant risk of overfilling, which would lead to the formation of stones. Stones meant more infection, more infection meant more risk of it rising up the body, it rising up the body meant the risk of kidney infections, the recurrence of which meant progressive damage to the kidneys, and damage to the kidneys, in the end, meant I'd die.

And if my kidneys didn't kill me outright, there was a whole jolly plethora of other things that might. Chest infections (I couldn't cough properly), skin sepsis (from pressure sores), neurological complications of the injury, diabetes, heart disease, liver disease, osteoporosis. It seemed not so much a catalogue of possible disasters as a shopping list the grim reaper could peruse and choose from at will.

I wasn't much surprised, therefore, when I later found out that the biggest contributors to potentially fatal ill health among the disabled are the symptoms related to failure to cope and depression – namely excessive smoking, drinking, drug use and general self-neglect.

It was no wonder that once Mr Chawla had left my bedside, I immediately lit up a cigarette. (Strange as it seems today, smoking was still permitted in certain hospital wards in 1980. In Rookwood, smoking in bed was as much a part of ward life as the clanking of the crap cart.)

But it wasn't all bad news. The message that came after the litany of despair was as simple and positive as it was unexpected: participate in sport and you won't die quite so soon.

I don't recall anyone actually saying those words to me, but they didn't have to. I wasn't stupid, after all. I knew that almost everything that was likely to finish me off before I'd had a chance to experience the twenty-first century would do so for one reason only. Because I was inert. Because I was inactive. Because slumping in a wheelchair feeling sad all the time would gather the moss of disease and destruction as surely as night followed day.

But if the idea of staving off death wasn't sufficient inducement to embrace this sporting life, Rookwood, in all its ways and routines and ethos, took pains to point out that there were a whole host of other benefits to enjoy. For starters it meant I could wear velour tracksuits. This was thought to be a more compelling inducement than those unfamiliar with the times might recall; as well as being much kinder on the skin than conventional clothing, what with all those buttons and seams and rivets and so on, the velour tracksuit (shoulder pads obviously optional) was *the* fashionable look of the eighties. And where velour left off (should velour be to one's liking – it certainly wasn't to mine), camaraderie kicked in. I could, it was pointed out, look forward to living in an environment in which my fellow sportsmen and women were all just like me. An enriching environment in which no one would much care should I wet or soil myself mid-competition. Best of all, though, was that I'd be spending time doing something that would take my mind off my predicament.

I had massive problems with every bit of this. I had spent all my school years loathing any sort of sport. I loathed the stupid skirts, the silly shorts, the freezing cold, the freezing communal showers, the sand in your knickers in the long jump, being made to play goal defence in netball on account of being tall and, most of all, being forced to fraternise with all the insufferable types who found sporting pursuits easy: the lithe and the talented, the robust and the speedy, the skilful of hand and keen of eye.

Because I wasn't one of them. I had always been a dyed-in-the-wool fag-round-the-back merchant and, frightened though Mr Chawla's prediction about my lifespan made me, I really couldn't see why or how this would now change. Yes, I could do sport, but I still couldn't *do* sport. I'd lost the use of a substantial part of my already unsporting body. How was that going to make me an athlete?

To be fair to my parents, they had tried. My father was, and still is, a keen follower of cricket, and like many a sports fan he was a keen player as well. During my childhood, it was a rare day when a trip to the beach or the park did not include his bringing along a cricket ball, which he would throw high into the air and encourage me to catch. But I was canny at seven; one look at his gnarled fingers, damaged by years of catching a speeding ball, made it patently obvious this course of action would be unwise.

Later on – presumably once he'd given up his aspirations that I should become a second-generation cricketing-ace Bowen – he and Mum would take me to his own cricket club, where, should I be able to make out his tiny form behind the stumps, he was a fine wicket-keeper. I could watch him and the rest of the team in action, while Mum and the other wives made salmon and cucumber sandwiches.

There being little of note ever happening on the pitch, I would help them. It was either that or sit at the boundary line and watch the grass grow. It seemed to me that playing cricket mostly involved standing doing nothing and, once they'd become bored with that, rousing themselves into action by walking across the field of play and coming in for tea.

If my early years had kindled nothing in the way of a sporting passion in my breast, my teens had seen off any hope entirely. I didn't want to spend the rest of my – apparently short – life in a tracksuit. Be it velour or finest silk, I wasn't a tracksuity sort of person. I liked figure-hugging clothes. Plus it didn't take terribly long for it to dawn on me that there was a reason why disabled people dressed in shapeless shrouds; when you are institutionalised and dependent on being dressed by others, it takes a great deal of will to insist on wearing clothing that is markedly more difficult for them to dress you in.

Most important, however, was my reluctance to accept the idea that to be constantly surrounded by people like me would in any sense be a good way to live. Whilst I did, and still do, appreciate that there is much comfort and camaraderie to be found in spending time with people who understand your particular set of challenges, that wasn't how I wanted to spend all my time, any more than I wanted to let incontinence dictate the way I lived my life. I didn't wish to hide behind the sympathy of the similarly afflicted; I wanted to find the empathy of the whole population I had every intention of getting back to live amongst.

Which was not to say I had any sort of downer on those with disabilities who did find fulfilment through sport. I had, and always will have, nothing but admiration for those whose pathway back to life outside a rehabilitation unit has led them to achieve heroic feats of sporting prowess, win medals and inspire hope. But sport, right then, didn't feel a workable option, and I concentrated on doing what teenagers do best – being resistant and hostile and negative about it for the entire five months of my stay. After all, sport had always made me feel like a useless great lump. Now I was one, I didn't need it confirming.

* * *

In retrospect, my resistance to the very thing I was being pushed to embrace in the interests of staving off early mortality was pretty perverse. I *was* very frightened about the future, no doubt about that. I'd been good at biology in school, and as each damning medical fact presented itself, I understood all too well how real this all was. The universal panacea 'it won't happen to me' had already been blown out of the water five weeks back, so I certainly couldn't practise denial as a strategy. Instead I took heart from Mum's response when I told her what Mr Chawla had said: that thirty was a very, very long way away, and that I really mustn't worry about that now. I also recalled what Mr Davies had told me, early on after the accident had happened. 'Be grateful,' he'd said, 'for what you *have* got.' He meant my arms. 'Regard everything else as a bonus.'

That's what I'd do, then, I made myself decide. I'd do as I was told. I would do the hateful sport. I'd be positive. I'd wait for my bonus.

The first bonus, I realised, once I'd got to know Lesley, would be to carve myself out some independence. From the moment it became clear what the future had in store, I'd become mentally resistant to the very idea that, from now on, I'd be labelled 'disabled'. I was determined to be all done with labels. However clichéd the notion, those early weeks of adjustment had done serious things to my psyche; I had begun the process, for perhaps the first time in my life, of really discovering who 'I' was. Gone was the adopted 'bastard' child, the victim of the school bullies, the wolf-whistled-at teenager. I defined myself now by incremental achievements: how I coped, minute by minute, hour by hour, day by day, with the endless round of seemingly intractable challenges I was facing. How I felt as each one was achieved. The tag 'disabled', therefore, did not sit comfortably with me. Somewhere, deep inside, I knew the reverse to be true. I was actually becoming *enabled*.

But a wheelchair meant freedom, and I needed some of that. First, however, I had to be fit to use one. It wasn't anywhere near as straightforward as it looked. Before it happened to me, I'd have assumed you were simply plonked down in it and off you'd go. This was not the case. The level of my paralysis meant I lacked sufficient working muscles to hold my upper body upright. Were I to be propped up I would simply keel over again. Without a working musculature in my torso to support me, my hips became a hinge with a life of their own; unbalanced, my head and chest would just crash down and land on my knees. There were other problems to overcome too. Changing the orientation of my body meant changes in blood flow – typically a big rush to the limbs. It took a great deal of acclimatisation and practice for me to sit up without passing out or feeling sick.

But we got there, and soon it was time to start getting me used to having my legs put over the side of the bed. Once again, the rush of blood to them made me dizzy, but little by little I got used to the sensation, and could reliably achieve my prescribed fifteen-minute goal.

After so many weeks barely registering their existence – I couldn't much see them, after all – having my legs hanging there in front of me was a strange and emotionally uncomfortable sensation. I simply couldn't fathom how these heavy-looking limbs had no feeling. I recognised them, certainly. They were my legs, all right. Everything about them was familiar to me: their size, their shape, the texture and colour of the skin, even the little scars on my knees where I'd fallen playing hopscotch in my 'previous' life. Yet they didn't *feel* heavy as they hung there over the bed, didn't feel mine. Didn't feel anything at all. I would sit there and stare at my feet and my ankles, and will them – really will them – to move. But they wouldn't do it for me. They wouldn't obey. They felt as if they were somebody else's.

Nevertheless, I kept at it, and the day eventually arrived that saw me take possession of my very own wheelchair. In keeping with all NHS-issue wheelchairs of the time, it was a *tour de force* of heavyweight tubular steel engineering. I didn't know what it weighed but I imagined it to have been fashioned as a sideline by a factory that made Centurion tanks. As I was soon to find out, pushing it was hard work, pushing it uphill frightening and barely possible at all, and the prospect of anyone folding it up and lifting it into, say, a car was about as daunting as any normally built human could imagine. But it was also my passport to the first taste of freedom I'd had in a very long time.

Not that freedom came without a price, and mine was one of vanity. To help support my trunk, I had to wear a skin-pink custom-made thermoplastic body-brace. If it had been fashioned in black leather, it would have been a designer basque. As it was, it made me look a little like a shop-window mannequin. It also had a bizarre-looking sternal extension, which poked up uncomfortably between my boobs. I soon established the need to put on a T-shirt first, in order to spare them from being sliced clean off.

Once kitted out, it was time to get aboard and suffer the second indignity of the wheelchair experience – that I was soon to look even more ridiculous. NHS wheelchairs were not designed with self-esteem in mind. The armrests were so high that my arms, draped over them, looked like those of a gorilla, and the position of the footplates was even more bizarre: my long legs were hitched up unnaturally high, my knees pressed together almost at chest height, while my feet – miles apart – looked as if they'd had a bust-up and broken off diplomatic relations. I looked like a rag doll who'd been dumped in a corner. This would not do. I tried a different tack. But pushing my knees outwards meant they flopped out so far that I looked as if I was about to give birth. I realised I had only two options on how I faced the world: I could either look like Pippi Longstocking or a porn star.

Still, whatever I looked like, the chair meant one thing. The chance to move around. To get out of the ward. To join my fellow patients and finally feel empowered after so long spent immobile and staring at ceilings. One early jaunt around the corridors of Rookwood, however, made it clear just how superficial this sense of independence really was.

One of my fellow patients was a military gymnast. Arthur was a couple of years older than I was, and had broken his neck during a display. He was all but completely quadriplegic, with weak and often spastic arms and hands. His wheelchair wasn't operated by push-power but was electrically controlled by a hand-held joystick. On this particular occasion he was at the rear of our convoy, on the way from the ward to the gym. Lesley and I were in the middle of the group – there were about five of us in all – so the first I knew of his hand being in spasm was the menacing roar of a motor gone mad, a loud yell, and a violent jolt from behind. The jolt was Lesley's wheelchair cannoning into mine and causing mine to do likewise to the lead one. Everyone seemed powerless to stop the progress of Arthur's chair, and soon we had all been unseated. One by one we were thrown from our chairs to the floor in the chaos, and the corridor became an instant scrapyard: littered with flailing bodies, buckled metal and heartfelt cries of 'Sorry!' from Arthur while his wheelchair – with him, mercifully, still strapped in – finally whirred itself to a standstill.

We all laughed at the time, but the incident made me think. It was one thing to be helpless in a hospital corridor, but the world outside was beginning to feel extremely scary.

chapter 8

After two months at Rookwood I had definitely become
fitter. Once I was up in my wheelchair, the pace and
rhythm of my life in rehabilitation had become much more
intense, with huge benefits to my mental equilibrium.
Despite still falling prey to regular bouts of despair and
anxiety, I found the days to be regularly punctuated by positives. Just being upright became a source of much pleasure,
and though, at the same time, it often felt scary, a real sense
of purpose took hold.

The first stage of my new sedentary existence was to sit
up in the wheelchair unaided, in my fetching pink brace,
safely parked beside my bed. One day, early on, I was sitting
thus, one hand clutching the mattress for reassurance,
watching Lesley. Further into her new life and now
comfortable in her wheelchair, she was sitting enjoying a
cigarette at the dining table in the middle of the ward. She
looked as if she could have been sitting at any table, in any
place; in short, she looked natural. *Normal*. So why on earth
was I sitting by my bed, and not with her?

'D'you have an ashtray there, Les?' I called, even though
I had one on my locker. She turned around and smiled. She

was a mere three feet away. I resolved that I must cast off and join her at the table, in order that we might enjoy a cigarette together – do that most normal and everyday of things.

Three nervous pushes and I had crossed to the table. I reached out a grateful hand for the safety of its surface, while Lesley stubbed out her cigarette. Then, with what I hoped was an impressive show of confidence, I put my own cigarettes and lighter on the table. Moments passed while I steadied myself for the next bit, which was to open the packet and offer her another. Like me, she smoked constantly and didn't much care. When your life expectancy was deemed to be a scant couple of further decades, you tended not to worry about the perils of smoking. The idea, back then, felt ridiculous.

Lesley accepted the cigarette, I took one myself, and there followed my greatest achievement in two months – I was actually able to do something for someone else. By now, of course, Lesley was reaching for her lighter, but I'd already struck mine and proffered her the flame. She took it and inhaled deeply as I lit up too – just two girls together, enjoying a simple moment. In my mind and my heart, though, I was flying.

Along with many of my fellow patients I now had a Monday to Friday routine. Each day started with breakfast, then an hour in physiotherapy, which was situated just along the corridor from the ward. Here we would go through a daily set of passive movements with our physiotherapists (not without good reason did we dub them physioterrorists; they were an army in white tunics and navy blue trousers) in order to maintain the range of movements in our paralysed joints. Without this they would soon become deformed, through joint contracture – not a terribly appealing prospect. The physio department remains unchanged to this day: a huge expanse of room, tiled floor, vast windows, crammed with various instruments of torture.

Chief among these were the parallel bars. As part of our recovery, it was considered essential that we 'stand' for half an hour daily. This was not standing as the able-bodied know it, more the self-supported propping of a big floppy body, only achievable by means of ankle-to-thigh splints and a great deal of effort from the arms. It was also necessary, if you weren't to collapse like a puppet, to stand with your chest thrust out as far as you could manage but with your bottom, bizarrely, tucked in. This essentially meant more of the porn-star aesthetic – thirty minutes of continuous pelvic thrust.

Physio, of necessity, was followed by a comfort break back on the ward. This, too, was all about learning. In this case, how to get on and off toilets efficiently, a life skill of major importance. The idea was that you'd get yourself positioned, tap on your belly and pray, and then – hey presto! – you'd wee. In reality, it never worked like that for me. My bladder would empty when it suited itself, invariably long after I'd left the toilet. So I quickly learned another approach to the situation. If you didn't drink anything you didn't need to go, so I decided – erroneously, as my fragile health would soon prove – that it would be in my best interests if I simply didn't drink anything all day. I could then practise the ergonomics without having to deal with the plumbing, which made the whole thing a great deal less stressful.

Our next port of call would be a trip to the gym, an altogether more rigorous undertaking. Getting to the gym at Rookwood represented my first proper taste of the outside world since I'd lain on that petrol-soaked grass at Aberavon beachfront. It was based some distance from the main building, adjacent to a large expanse of green we'd never run around on, and close to a brick tower which, to my fifteen-year-old eyes, bore an uncanny resemblance to an antiquated version of Margam Crematorium, which was just down the road from where we lived. I was never quite convinced that recalcitrant patients wouldn't, if the staff were particularly pressed, end up being incarcerated – if not actually incinerated – there. It did look unsettlingly like Auschwitz.

Getting to the gym, in the early days particularly, was a Herculean feat of mind over matter (and one of hope over experience, to boot). Somewhat curiously, given the role the hospital played, there were no special facilities laid on to separate us novice wheelchair users from the endless stream of traffic that came and went. No separate wheelchair routes or, in many areas, even pavements. It didn't help, either, that the gym building was sited very close to one of the main car parks.

Once we were out of the main building, it was simply a case of join the roadway and pray. There were visitors, obviously, plus ambulances, delivery vans, staff cars and so on, and all of them seemed united in the belief that the speed limit (a somewhat optimistic five miles per hour) applied to everyone else except them. That's how it generally seemed to me, anyway, and as the road was the only way to get to the gym, I had no choice but to take a breath and rise to the challenge, using every ounce of concentration and courage that I had.

As well as the traffic, there were potholes to consider; if you weren't mown down by a passing white van, you could easily be ambushed by some frightening crevasse. Though as nothing to the car or the pedestrian traveller, a pothole, for a paraplegic, was a very real danger. It didn't take much to tip a fast-moving wheelchair. Still, unlike the cars, at least the holes generally stayed put. It wasn't long before I had each one logged in my brain, and had learned the best way to slalom round them.

Not that knowing the course made you infallible. Another untaught lesson (there were lots of those) was learned early. A small stone on a rough part of the drive jammed a castor, bringing my chair to a juddering halt and flinging my head down onto my knees. It was only the foot-plates hitting the asphalt that stopped me from being thrown face-first onto the ground and anointing my cheek-bones with gravel. For some moments I hung there, cling-ing desperately to the armrests, entirely at a loss what to do. Mercifully, Lesley wasn't too far behind, and with a strength I'm not sure even *she* knew she possessed, she managed to get sufficient leverage on the seat back to haul my chair upright again. By now I had slipped dangerously far forward so she had to manhandle me back into position so I wouldn't simply slither straight out again.

Not a life-changing skill, but a prudent one to learn: to scrutinise, scrutinise, scrutinise. If it had happened in one of the furthermost reaches of Rookwood, I might have been marooned there all day.

The gym itself felt exhausted, a little like many of its patients. My only experience of such places was the gym back at school, and the two couldn't have been more different. The school gym was alive with squeals of childish exuberance – not everyone felt about gymnastics as I did. PE, for some girls, was considered fun. Even the run-down and sweaty boxing and wrestling rings I'd seen in films had a cachet, a definite heartbeat. They were places where endeavour was rewarded. But healthy sweat was not a feature of Rookwood gym, and the equipment was shabby and dilapidated. You could never forget it was part of a hospital, not only because of all the patients' pillows strewn around, but also because, in keeping with just about every ancillary building, it still felt like a hospital. It still *smelt* like a hospital. I couldn't help wonder – did we?

Even so, I realised I could work there in ways that I couldn't in the hospital. Paradoxically, given the place and the situation, my resolve was encouraged in this tumble-down gym. This was mostly to do with the fact that, unlike school, there was no sense of unrelenting pressure. No bouncy adolescent gymnasts, overkeen to impress instructors. No unpleasant competitive edge.

Though it was not without its quotient of glamour. One of the remedial gymnasts in charge of us was, I soon learned, a former Mr Wales. But, like his colleagues, Chris Barr didn't bully or nag us, much less try and tease out any hidden Olympic potential. He just told us the sort of exercises we should be attempting each day, then left us to our own devices.

It was a tactic that worked. My periods in the gym were soon to become one of the highlights of my day. This was largely because here I could concentrate on strengthening the parts of my body that I *could* control. This was an immense psychological step because my time in bed had largely been spent concentrating on the bits that didn't work any more.

Our visits to the gym were mostly about weight training – building up the muscles in our arms. Vital work for limbs that in many practical senses would have to become substitute legs, which would power our means of getting around.

Not only did heavy wheelchairs take one hell of a lot of pushing, they also needed getting into and out of, which meant transferring and then balancing your entire body weight in often difficult and/or public situations. Beds and toilets and cars all posed their own unique set of problems. Strength and co-ordination were key. Our range of exercises included lateral pull-downs, shoulder presses, bench presses and curls, together with work on our pectoral and trapezius muscles. In short, we had to exercise every single working muscle, from the neck and shoulder girdle to the fingers. This all needed to be achieved without the benefit of core stability, or abdominal strength, which is something I took entirely for granted until it was gone, like so many good things in life.

It was no surprise that we were invariably exhausted at the end of a session. So much so that the (mostly uphill) journey back to the ward for our lunch was an extra bout of weight training in itself. And as soon as we had eaten and been to the toilet (in my case, generally just for the practice) we went back down the hill and did the whole thing again.

Slowly, and strangely, I began to notice a change. I was growing stronger, clearly, but something else, too. I realised that the gym-loathing, sport-phobic, PE-sceptic, able-bodied girl I'd once been had now discovered that perhaps there *was* something in this. That the physical exercise was a brilliant antidepressant and that exhaustion was better than any sleeping pill. So, while no one would convince me I had any sporting potential, I could see that movement and action and making demands on my body were, if I was to come through this and actually get a life, going to play a vital part.

Macramé, however, was not. The timetable at Rookwood had our days structured thus: physio, then gym, then lunch, then more gym, then a spell in occupational therapy. OT was again situated not in the main building but in a single-story block to the left of the main drive, which we could head off to straight after gym. It was staffed, like the physio department, by a small, committed army, though in this case the trousers were a more militaristic bottle-green, and the white tops accessorised by green cardigans.

I knew – and still know – very little about the science and thinking behind occupational therapy, but then, as now, I doubted that handicraft projects were the acme of best ways to proceed. They had their place, obviously, but as I couldn't imagine that any part of my future life would be enhanced by the deft completion of a cross-stitched cushion cover or tissue holder, my teenage enthusiasm for OT was in rather short supply.

But we had to do *something* to while away the hour not already allocated to honing our gladiatorial skills, and 'with our hands' seemed to be the obvious choice. In my case, it soon became my 'have a fag and swear' break, plus, if I was alone, the chance to shed the odd tear. Of course, if I gave in to crying, there were consequences; having given in, I got cross with myself and swore more, which naturally necessitated another fag to calm me down, which, on top of the last one, made me hack uncontrollably, which nine times out of ten made me wet myself, obviously, which upset me and made me cry all over again.

School work had been proffered as a further option. Mr Chawla had suggested it soon after I arrived, but my routine now meant I had precious little time. Once I'd finished my rehabilitation activities for the day, Mum or Dad would be arriving. I also had to visit the loo every hour. I simply had no space, either emotionally or physically, to take on any further commitments. And, in truth, I was resistant to it even if I had. Though almost all of my teachers came to visit at some point – my old maths tutor and his wife had even named their new baby Melanie, which touched me – they never mentioned bringing any course work. Perhaps they knew my mind even better than I did. School now seemed a part of the life I'd been removed from. It didn't seem applicable.

Handicrafts apparently were. Thus, on my first visit to occupational therapy I was offered the chance to try my hand at either macramé or basket weaving. On other days,

I don't doubt, there would be embroidery, perhaps tapestry, the possibility of knitting – all of which, I'm quite sure, might have enriched my life in some way, if only I could raise the enthusiasm.

By rights, I should have been a natural. Mum knitted and sewed to an impeccable standard, and showed every sign of enjoying it. I don't doubt that, had she sufficient time and raw materials, she'd have constructed our house out of sewing and knitting, with a crocheted chimney on top. She also made all my clothes for me. At least, till I was ten, when we had a huge showdown on the occasion of my discovering jeans. Jeans were sacrosanct, untouchable. You couldn't knit jeans. Though, had she had denim-coloured wool, she might have tried.

Unlike Mum, I was hopeless at both. Even threading a needle was beyond my meagre capabilities. Should I finally see any success in the OT department, it was odds on that by then I'd have stabbed myself so much that I risked expiring in a pool of my own blood. This wasn't all down to ineptitude either. I knew I'd been inoculated against any love of needlework on the day, aged about eight, when I sat on the points of Mum's sewing scissors, which had slid down between the cushions on the sofa. Both my bottom and my psyche still bear the scars.

My uselessness at sewing did not go unnoticed, and my school needlework teacher, Mrs Hughes, took pity, giving me a simple snake draught excluder to fashion while the cleverer girls got to make cleverer things. Even in this my humiliation was public; in an effort, perhaps, to address my low self-esteem, she proceeded to display it to a less than impressed class. My stitches, however, were so clumsy and enormous that the stuffing – chunks of foam – fell out like so many bricks around her, even as she held it aloft and lauded my pathetic skills.

Not being good at needlework, however, did have a certain cachet, and like-minded, needle-phobic girls soon found one another. One day, when Mrs Hughes had left the classroom for a meeting, we domestically disaffected got together. Fired by a common goal to revolt against girly duties, we barricaded the door and connected all the reels of thread on all the sewing machines. We weren't entirely sure what would happen when we'd done this, but, to our delight, once we switched them all on, we manufactured vast lengths of multicoloured rope. It was only once this utterly purposeless activity was threatened that the situation took a turn for the worse. One girl (Sandra, if I remember correctly; well-behaved, good at sewing) started muttering about going to get a teacher. We did what one does in such inflamed situations: we bundled her into the cupboard in the corner, which, among other things, happened to house the school's entire stock of sanitary towels. This must have unsettled her because she started protesting at what soon became a worrying volume. For some reason, we decided this was best dealt with by locking the door and telling her we'd throw away the key. This was meant, as these things are, as an entirely idle threat; we simply intended to launch it from the window till she stopped threatening to dob us all in. Unfortunately, however, under the window we chose was a small but perfectly positioned drain.

The key fell into it. The bell rang. We made a bolt for it and stampeded to our next lesson, leaving one of Sandra's friends to explain what had happened. Another key was found and she was eventually released. And bar a severe warning, we never got called to account for our high jinks.

Now, at Rookwood, I wondered at that unspoken code. That sense of camaraderie. That wealth of forgiveness. That community of girls – and that included Sandra – to which I knew I could no longer belong.

Instead, I could now make a stab at that skill which eluded and bored me so much. I should have been impressed. Many older inmates – hemiplegics, amputees, head-injury patients – had created tapestries and hanging baskets and all sorts of impressive things. But one look at the results of their often heroic efforts made me resolve one thing – that the *whole* thing, for some reason, upset me so greatly that I never wanted to look at them again.

My wilful truancy from OT sessions was, therefore, a rather self-righteous and belligerent form of rebellion. It just felt like such a massive waste of precious outside time that I was determined to find more gratifying pursuits. I didn't need to think very far before realising that, given the lush herbaceous borders and general foliage at the hospital, I could mitch off OT with the minimum risk of exposure, find a suitably sheltered spot and while away the hour. It wasn't always for the purposes of weeping and swearing, either. Once again, the disaffected found a way to be together. Sometimes, gratifyingly, we'd mitch off *en masse*.

Hanging out with like-minded patients was precious, because activity at Rookwood was relentless. Though not always in nice ways. Even the simple pleasure of being still and reading a book was hard to accomplish. If the constant turning and toileting wasn't distraction enough, there was the irritating constant of my increasingly unruly body. One of the features of paraplegia, as I was soon to find out, is the problem of exaggerated, unregulated reflexes. Normally the brain controls and manages this but in paralysed bodies the mechanism doesn't work, so my legs, a law unto themselves at such times, would bounce repeatedly and endlessly to such an extent that sometimes a member of staff would have to restrain them, as if they were a pair of excitable puppies. And when my legs weren't on the move my abdominals would be in spasm, catapulting me backwards and forwards.

When my body behaved itself I sometimes watched TV. Most of us had our own, as there was no ward television. With patients needing to be turned all the time, it would have to have been constantly on the move.

But there was little time and space for such things. Though I was much too far from home to see friends on a week-night, my parents kept up their nightly visits, together with many of my relatives. Sometimes they'd start up a round of charades on the ward: popular and funny, but also a some-what odd choice because with most of us physically chal-lenged in major ways, it made the business of miming somewhat tricky.

What I most wanted to do was the one thing I wasn't allowed to – go with Lesley and the others to the pub. Early

on, Mr Chawla had casually pointed out that while maintaining my fluid intake was of the utmost importance it
didn't necessarily have to be water. There can't have been
many parents who are charged, when visiting their hospi-
talised fifteen-year-old offspring, to come armed with a
four-pack of lager. But however much anyone might sniff
at the idea, the fact was that, in moderation, it helped a very
great deal. There would be years ahead when I'd learn alcohol and wheelchairs didn't always mix, but right then it
represented temporary salvation.

I would so much have liked to be able to go to the pub;
there, perhaps, I could have a short drink instead of beer,
and also, precious freedom from the hospital. Once my
catheter went, however, it was largely off the agenda. I was
too sick and tired of wetting myself. Though I'd obviously
spent time in pubs before my accident, the Rookwood staff,
knowing my age, would never have allowed it. My troublesome bladder tied me to the hospital, in any case. I knew
there'd be little fun in sitting in a pub – in *public* – and
everyone seeing I'd wet myself. Again.

On 30 July 1980 I turned sixteen. I'd never been much of a
one for parties and fuss, but this day also marked an important first for it was decided that I would be allowed out for
a few hours in order to celebrate my birthday. I'd been in
Rookwood for just over two months by this point, and was
deemed fit enough and competent enough that I could be
allowed to join the real world, if only for a short spell at
home.

Mum and Dad started making plans. Clearly the aged family car would have to go. They would now need one roomy enough to ease my passage in and out, and also to accommodate my tank of a wheelchair. The Morris Minor was duly dispatched and replaced by a two-year-old brown Marina estate.

It was with a great sense of occasion that Dad arrived on the ward to collect me on the morning of my birthday, and once again I was struck by how fortunate I was that I had parents who took such good care of me.

I was excited, and also apprehensive. On the one hand, I couldn't wait to see my home again, but I was also scared at the prospect of how I would cope. I felt largely confident about it, bullish even, but much as I did, I kept returning to the fact that this would be a huge leap into a whole new unknown.

I wasn't looking my best for this, the landmark moment of my post-accident life. I was wearing the standard 'uniform' of T-shirt and the hated velour jogging bottoms, and by now my hair was a dishevelled mess. My highlights had grown out, I had three inches of dark roots, and whatever style I'd once had was long gone. There was no time for make-up, which was becoming difficult to put on. Perversely, it was harder to manage now I was up and about in my chair. Whereas mascara had once been quite easy to apply, it was now a virtual impossibility for me when sitting. It needed both hands to be up at my face – one for the brush and the other for a mirror – and I'd not yet worked out how to stay upright and safe without at least one hand holding tightly to my chair.

But really, my appearance was the last thing on my mind – and certainly Dad's. He was much more concerned with the practicalities of the trip: how to get me from one place to the other without mishap. I had as yet no experience of getting in and out of a car, so I needed all the help I could get. Plus, from now on, there would be my wheelchair to consider too. Like it or not, and my feelings were still mixed here, it went where I went and I went where it went – we were now an inseparable team.

Happily, Dad had already considered this and had brought Ken, his great friend and cricketing team-mate, to the hospital with him to help with all the lifting and carrying. Neither of my parents could have carried me – of that I was sure – either individually or together. But Ken was undaunted. He was as big and strong as my wheelchair was heavy, and it soon succumbed to his superiority.

The journey home took an hour and a half and I panicked through every heart-stopping moment of it, praying that my body would behave itself and hoping that the hours I'd spent dehydrating myself (only a drop of water to take my medication since the previous night) would prevent any accidents in transit. This was my first excursion since being moved to Cardiff, and this time I was making it sitting up. I could see out of the windows and everything we passed seemed entirely unchanged. It was only me that was so, so different.

Once we arrived at our family home in Uplands, a sense of grim reality began to kick in. It was set halfway up the side of Mynydd Emroch, with a seriously steep driveway followed by four steps up to the front door. And this in a location where the valley road itself already towered over Cwmavon and Port Talbot. I had barely registered the gradient before, but now the fact of our location consumed me. It might as well have been the north face of Everest, as far as I – the *new* me – was concerned. Without Ken, who that day carried me from the car up to the house – and even in this I felt publicly humiliated: What would the neighbours think? Would they be sniggering? – I would no more be able to access the family home than fly to Mars, or, once I was in there, even more upsettingly, would I be able to get out of it again.

In the weeks to come, this worrisome thought became reality. Whilst coming home would be a positive in some ways, it would also see me stuck there, a virtual prisoner.

Right now, however, everything was just new and changed and disturbing. It was strange to see how Mum and Dad had converted the back living room into a bedroom for me (my bed had been placed slap bang in the middle of it, to facilitate access on all sides), and odd to think I'd never see the upstairs again. There was also the spectre of the hourly bladder machinations. We had no downstairs toilet, so a commode had been obtained for me. This, of course, meant I needed help; this was not like the toilets at Rookwood, all designed with disability in mind. Every hour, therefore, Mum and Aunt Irene and I had to leave my visitors (who were stationed in the front room), troop off to the commode, do what we needed to do and then troop back, whereupon everyone pretended we hadn't.

Despite all the hassles and toilet humiliation, my birthday went quickly. I had plenty of visitors – Juli, lots of relatives, a steady stream of neighbours – who ensured that I had little time to stop and let it all sink in. Mum had made me a sponge cake (I didn't like dried fruit) and inscribed it with 'Happy 16 Birthday'. I also had presents. Lots and lots of presents. Almost all of them, ironically, were perfume and make-up, as if bought – though unwittingly – to flag up the truth. What else did you get someone like me?

It seemed a scant few hours before it was time to start thinking about making the long journey back, and as soon as we set off – Dad driving, Ken again, plus Mum this time, too – I succumbed to what I realised were long-pent-up tears. I realised now that the house I'd been brought up in and so loved was going to present serious practical difficulties, not only as it had today, but always. Every positive thing seemed to have its own negative. Home was lovely, but also horrendously impractical. Rookwood was awful, and yet so horrendously suitable. If I wasn't to be marooned there, or somewhere like it, for all time, Mum and Dad would have to confront the necessity of moving from the house I knew they loved. Thinking this, I was overcome with grief and also guilt. Why couldn't I just die and let them have their lives back?

With Mum to soothe me, I gradually got a grip on myself, only to find myself in floods once again as we turned into the entrance at Rookwood. The sun was just setting and the outlines of the trees made stark shapes against the darkening sky. I purposely didn't look at the tower by the gym.

Above all else, my trip home had left me feeling different from what I'd expected. I thought I'd come so far, yet now – out in the real world – it didn't seem very far at all. Glad though I'd been to be with family and friends in my own home, there was a part of me that really did want to die at that moment, simply to escape my wretched future. I was happy but I was sad, I was alive but I was dead; the turmoil was overwhelming and, worst of all, I was convinced it was a feeling that would never go away.

When Lesley said, 'Aren't you lucky you've been home?' I really didn't know what to say.

chapter 9

Clearly, you can't choose your parents. And even if you could, would you want to? After all, by the time any such notion might surface – if, say, you were refused some insane teenage whim – your lives would be so bound up, so much the fabric of each others', that the question would simply not figure.

But my parents weren't like most other parents. They did make a choice. They chose *me*. It wasn't fate and biology that led them to their baby. It was a considered and lengthy process, a whole series of decisions – not all of them their own. Would they now be ruing that day?

I spent a lot of time thinking about Mum and Dad that night. I imagined their journey home. The things they might be thinking. The fears for the future that must have been percolating inside them as I lay and quietly wept in my bed.

They would have said little, I knew. Ken was with them, of course, and though they'd discuss things with him up to a point I could imagine them maintaining the same dogged composure, the same relentless optimism that they unfailingly did when with me. I imagined them thanking him, dropping him home, driving home themselves, Dad parking the car, his face set in that dear and familiar expression of concentration as they made their way up to and inside the front door.

What would they say to each other then? Who'd begin it? What twists and turns would their conversation take? I had (and I was now more convinced of it than ever) utterly disrupted and ruined their lives. And all through my own selfish, thrill-seeking actions. My refusal to heed their advice. Surely at some point they would reach that conclusion, however much they might protest otherwise.

It was with some surprise then that the following Monday afternoon I found myself the target of a smiling young woman, who breezed onto Ward Six with such an air of gaiety that she looked entirely at odds with her surroundings. Her hair was flame-red and her grin looked genuine. She was, she announced, my social worker.

Never having been allocated a social worker before, this left me somewhat bemused. I'd just finished avoiding lunch, and was in the last throes of getting ready to go back to the gym, and the last thing I'd expected was a visitor – much less one on official-seeming business. But she was soon to enlighten me.

It seemed my birthday trip home had been deemed a success. She had, she explained, spoken to my parents at length and, following the information she had elicited from them – all positive – had organised a case-conference, the net result of which was that I would be able to go on visits home each weekend, to commence with immediate effect.

It struck me, as she spoke, that perhaps I'd misheard: her interpretation of my visit back home seemed so diametrically opposed to my own. It hadn't left me elated, however much I might have wished it, but the opposite – more frightened and useless than I had felt at any time since arriving at Rookwood. However much I craved home and family and some semblance of normality, the obstacles now seemed impossibly huge. Yet here she was, all bounce and smiles and arrangements, telling me something entirely different.

This was a conclusion she simply couldn't have reached without Mum and Dad's wholehearted confidence that they'd cope.

I imagined this conversation and it filled me with hope. 'We'll get over this again,' was what my Mum always said. Had said throughout my childhood, whatever the crisis. Had repeated to me, over and over again, from the moment I woke up in Neath General Hospital. 'We'll get over this, love. We will.' It would be a long time before I would truly believe it, but for now it simply seemed that my parents meant business. That Mum's words held absolute conviction. That come what may, they – and I – *would* be able to cope. Slowly and surely, they were staging my rescue from the suffocating clutches of Rookwood.

Mum and Dad arrived that evening and confirmed that they had put everything necessary in place. So, come Friday at 4.00, they'd be allowed to collect me, and return me on Sundays at 10 p.m.

Whatever my private fears about how on earth we would manage, the prospect of spending my weekends at home brought a whole new perspective to my weeks. Now I had a goal, a thing to which I could look forward, something to hold on to when the monotonous routine threatened to play games with my head. I also had a motive to do the very best I could. If Mum and Dad felt they were up to the task, then so, I resolved, would I be.

Mostly, I needed to be strong. This became apparent straight away. They could obviously not expect passing rugby players to simply sweep me up and carry me anywhere I needed to be – not for the rest of my natural life, at any rate, however appealing I might find the prospect – so we needed to learn how to manage my body during all the transitions that I'd need to make daily. From chair to car. From car to chair. Up steps and down them. To the toilet and shower. In and out of bed. The list seemed endless.

It was important, therefore, given their diminutive frames, that I was able to contribute as much as possible. My sessions in the gym that week took on an even greater sense of purpose. Being fit, being powerful, was all.

By the time the first Friday came around, we'd already worked out a system for getting me into the car. If we could get my feet and legs positioned in the footwell, it was simply a question of me grabbing the grab handle above the car door and pulling as much of my weight as I could manage, while Dad gave a firm inward push.

Achieving this small thing felt good. This was a significant (even if metaphorical) step. And having achieved it, it could almost be imagined that as a family we looked, despite everything, quite normal. Had you glanced into our car as we trundled out of Cardiff on that still summer evening, you'd have seen nothing you wouldn't have expected to see. Dad and I up front, Mum in the back, travelling like any other normal family would to a home that was as normal as any other home, except that things would be done very slightly differently. I'm not sure if she said it, or if I simply sat and thought it. 'We'll get over this again.' Well, now we had.

An even greater triumph was getting me out of the car and back into my chair once we'd arrived back in Port Talbot. For starters it was slightly more precipitous. Though I had become a little more confident on such gradients as there were at Rookwood, my nightmares about steep hills and runaway wheelchairs were based not on fancy but fact. And if ever there was a place suited to propagating night-mares about runaway wheelchairs, No. 1 The Uplands would be pretty hard to beat.

The *cul de sac* itself was not that steep. Our house was the last of a row of about a dozen that ran perpendicular to the mountainside and had far-reaching views across the steel-works and Swansea Bay. Approached via a metalled track, it was the highest road of houses in a stack of some half dozen tiers. My journey to school – twice down and twice up again, Monday to Friday – consisted of traversing several long flights of railed concrete steps, leapfrogging gardens and descending, road by road, till I was down at 'ground' level, where the River Afan rushed southwards to the sea.

Wheelchair friendly, as they say these days, it wasn't.

But these were the big issues of the future, not the present. Right now, I was much more focused on the problem of reversing what we'd done relatively effortlessly at Rookwood, in a place where there was not a square inch of flat ground to be found.

I needn't have worried. Dad had thought everything through and had decided that getting me back into my chair while still parked on the road would be the most sensible option. After that, all we had to do was push me up the driveway, turn a right angle and pull me up the four steps to the front door.

I say 'all we had to do' but this was, in truth, a very big deal. I was six feet of heavy human – now weighing close on twelve stone – and the NHS wheelchairs of the time were very much *of* their time, adding perhaps another three stones on top, if not more. They were certainly at least double the weight of their modern aluminium and titanium counterparts. Still, motivation is an often-underrated assistant, and it was clear that unless we had the strength to do the job I might have to spend the night in the front garden. Again, we devised a system. I would sit, facing up the slope, bent almost double, and turn the wheels as best I could; Dad would bear the strain and do the pushing from behind, and Mum would add some pulling at the front.

The steps themselves were a little more tricky – as they would be – but Mum and Dad, however slight of limb (and, in Dad's case, short of breath), were not, for a moment, faint of heart. This time it was Dad who did the pulling, from behind and above, while Mum – I could contribute little at this juncture – had the luxury of pushing from the front.

Now that the gradient was reversed and I was facing *down* the slope it was vital that we all kept in mind that at no point must I be allowed to fall forward. With no sensation from the chest down it would be the work of seconds, as I knew, to have me pitched onto the concrete, and so face the possibility of disaster. Face the possibility of disaster quite literally, in this case; perhaps a night in the front garden, face down.

Picturing this made me smile. We'd only that week had a similar disaster – not with a wheelchair and a body, thank goodness, but with a freshly baked summer fruit flan. It had been a glorious day and my parents had brought my Aunt Irene and Uncle Don along to visit, picking up the flan en route to Rookwood. With it being so balmy, they'd thought it would be nice if we could enjoy it in the gardens in the early evening sunshine, once my regimen of exercise was done for the day. They'd even thought to bring napkins and paper plates.

The grassed area outside the gym was a spot favoured by all, and we were pleased to be able to take possession of one of the slatted wooden benches, upon which Mum soon set things up. She was just about to get the flan out of its box when we heard, in the distance, a grunt of extreme effort, closely followed by a curious fluffing, whistling sound, and the sight of something – none of us knew what, at that moment – skimming at some speed through the air and headed, alarmingly, straight for us. It thudded down to earth mere yards from where we sat, closely followed by an anxious cry of 'Are you all right?', to which someone – me, perhaps – barked 'Only just!'

We all peered through the trees to see the source of the intrusion and could make out a young and muscular-looking guy, who was, it transpired, taking advantage of the weather to cram in a little discus practice.

Thank goodness, we all agreed, that the discus hadn't landed – ho, ho, ho – in the middle of our flan. Our relief, though, was to be cruelly short lived. Mum, possibly worried that a further discus might be headed in our direction, quickly returned to the business at hand, easing our treat from its box to a plate. The flan, though, had other ideas.

Why do disasters always happen in slow motion? Is it simply to intensify the dismay? In any event, it was with no sense of urgency that the flan decided to slide in between two of the slats on the bench. Curious, given its sluggish progress, that it managed to resist all attempts to arrest it, and to avoid the desperate hands now stationed underneath. Before anyone could so much as grasp at a sliver, let alone taste it, it had sunk gracefully and entire to the grass beneath the bench, where it was fallen upon gratefully by an army of ants.

We were philosophic, in the end, on both counts. The ants were thrilled, we were sure, by this unexpected bounty, and as for the rogue discus thrower of Rookwood, he turned out to be a rather special person. Back then just a fellow inmate by the name of John Harris, he was to go on to become the paralympic world record holder. We felt proud to know both him *and* his discus.

* * *

Dad was in fits of laughter, watching Mum bending in front of me as we prepared, as a unit, to make our final ascent to the house. Listening to him, I realised I didn't need to see myself as a 'disabled' person, any more than they did. No, I couldn't walk, but I was *still* just a person. A person who, though dependent on a wheelchair, was still a person. Someone Mum and Dad were assisting to get somewhere else, and despite everything, it was rather funny. After all, it didn't *have* to be tragic, did it? Well, possibly it would be, if they dropped me mid-climb and I ended up sharing the same fate as the flan. But if I worried about that, I'd never do *anything*. I'd be stuck for all time feeling sorry for myself at the bottom of a set of metaphorical steps.

Everything went without mishap and suddenly I was back in the house. It didn't escape my notice, however, that getting inside had taken the best part of twenty minutes. Had the accident not happened on that May afternoon, I wouldn't have given a moment's thought to such things as the driveway and steps up to our house. Wouldn't have thought once about them, let alone twice. My mind would have been in a very different place. I'd have been back around midnight, having climbed off the pillion (perhaps I'd now be in my one little black dress and vertiginous stilettos), removed my helmet and kissed Aldo goodbye. Though my head, somewhat guiltily, would have been full of John. Had I made an impression? Did we have any future? Would he, right now, be thinking about me? All the while I'd be dodging the questions of my waiting-up mum, which invariably concluded with 'As long as you're all right'. I'd be thinking about Sunday and what I'd do then. And now all of that, *all* of it, had gone.

But I didn't dwell for long. There was too much to take in. Looking around I could see that my parents had turned the whole house upside down. I couldn't access the garden – it was just way too steep – but thankfully my wheelchair could fit through the doorways so I could move about freely downstairs. And they'd given over much of that to me, it seemed. The temporary bedroom they'd put in place in the back room for my birthday had, in the short time since I'd last been home, been augmented and made to look much more like a bedroom. *My* bedroom. They'd moved all my furniture – every last bit of it, right down to the beloved painting of a white horse that I'd chosen myself when I was eight. It now hung in exactly the same place above my bed as it had when it had been upstairs.

They'd worked wonders. Moving me downstairs meant moving the contents of the downstairs back room upstairs, and that was precisely (and logically) what they'd done. They'd turned what had been my bedroom into an upstairs sitting room for themselves – which would give me the space and the privacy downstairs to entertain guests independently. I felt a surge of gratitude. Both their gesture and industry moved me beyond words, and was to mark the start of a period of sustained happiness and hope. Seeing me happy of course made them happy. And so, in turn, made me happier still. For the first time I began to respond to their always frequent 'love you's, not with my usual self-conscious and non-committal mumble, but by telling them both how much I loved them too.

*   *   *

As the leaves began to turn and summer became autumn there were regular discussions about a date for my discharge. By now I'd been home every weekend since my birthday and these visits had been deemed a success.

Which was not to say they were easy. They had become a lifeline, certainly; home was the one place I could rest and unwind without the clamour and clatter and routines of the ward. But I was far from well – my continuing bladder problems caused almost unrelenting infections – and more often than not exhausted.

It wasn't surprising, then, that I didn't get out much. But it wasn't just fatigue that was the problem. It was life, and the business of living it. The shenanigans involved in the car-to-house manoeuvre were stressful, of course, but it wasn't so much that as getting organised to attempt the challenge in the first place. Where once I had done all the usual things – jumping out of bed, showering, throwing on clothes, grabbing breakfast, running for the bus to town – entirely unthinkingly, now it would take me the best part of the day just to get in any sort of state to have friends and family round, let alone attempt anything more ambitious. This would change over time, but at the moment it seemed to take forever. But perhaps my narrow focus – just to get through each day – was nature's way of stopping my attention from wandering to all the things I would or might never do again. All the normal teenage things my friends were still doing around me: going to pubs, the movies, the hairdresser's, the shops, playing pool, wearing platforms, swimming in the sea, sunbathing in skimpy little bikinis, flirting and posing, dancing at discos with absolute abandon, and, yes, even riding on the back of motorbikes.

And horses. If there was one thing that really broke my heart, it was that I'd never sit astride one again. I'd never had one of my own, sad to say – too much work, too expensive, and, ironically, deemed too hazardous – but since the age of about nine I'd been a regular at the local pony trekking centre. As with any new skill, I knew I'd never forget the first time I got up on a pony. The struggle to get a foot up into a stirrup, the shove on the bottom from the stable-hand to help me into the saddle, the thrill of being up there, of getting better, and stronger, the sense of satisfaction when I could make it up there on my own. The riding off – just the two of us – on whichever dewy-eyed beast I'd been lucky enough to be allocated that day.

I pushed away the memory and stored it safely inside. If my weekends at home were to prepare me for anything, it was to adopt a state of mind that, once I was home properly, would give me the strength of character to wrest back some control of my life.

Freedom, in the form of my escape from Stalag Rookwood, came on Saturday 18 October 1980, five months and one week since that early summer Saturday which altered my life so dramatically. I was still a child, but I now looked and acted like an adult. I'd been in an adult environment for months, and had, I was beginning to realise, psychologically outgrown my contemporaries. Unsurprisingly, I'd matured more in five months than, had my circumstances been different – been *normal* – I would have in two or three years.

It felt like the strangest form of irony. It was through my body having returned to a state of quasi-babyhood that my mind had become so clear and strong; that I felt confident in making informed decisions about how I'd manage my new situation.

One of those decisions was to go back to school, which presented me with another irony. In going back, if I wanted to retake my O levels, I'd be placed with more junior pupils. In other words, to go forward I'd have to go back.

But if that was the case, so be it. I was champing at the bit to be gone. Mum and Dad were on the ward bright and early and there was a palpable feeling of triumph in the air. We'd survived the accident, survived Rookwood and now we were on our way home. My parents had even let slip a secret – that they'd planned a holiday for us all in Blackpool. I couldn't have been more excited if I'd tried. I'd been there once before on holiday, when I was ten, and to return had been a dream ever since. Equine pursuits were once again a feature. I'd ridden a donkey called Flicka on the beach every morning, and my favourite fairground ride had been the carousel with horses. I was way too afraid to ride the likes of the big dipper, but, if I could have, I'd have ridden on those horses all day.

As it turned out, the trip was to prove deeply depressing: steps everywhere; booth-style seating; no fairground rides for cripples; no disabled toilets – from best childhood memory to nightmare in one step. But, in anticipation of it at least, I couldn't have been more excited.

My bedside locker was emptied with due ceremony. After that there was a long round of goodbyes to be made. All of this, to my hard teenage heart, was quite painless – only daft people cried when they were happy, or at weddings – until it came to saying farewell to Lesley. She wasn't on the ward and I didn't know where she'd gone, and I became very anxious that I might not get to see her before I left. Even so, it was a parting I was dreading. She'd been at Rookwood when I'd arrived there, and now I'd be leaving her there. And to what sort of future? Unlike me she had no one. And also nothing to return to. She'd lost both her high-powered Civil Service job and her home, and though she'd applied to Bristol Social Services for somewhere, there had as yet been no indication of what this might be, let alone some clue as to when it might happen.

Lesley's situation was a powerful reminder not only that life could be cruel and unpredictable, but also that my own prospects could have been so much worse. I had parents to take care of me, talk through decisions, help fight my battles, keep my chin up and steer me on a route to equip me for wherever my new circumstances might lead. Lesley had none of that. No one to support her. She was entirely at the mercy of whoever it was – and I didn't know who that might be – that was in charge of sorting out the lives of people like us, who were one day fit and healthy and then suddenly were not. There was absolutely nothing I could do to help her, except empathise. Be there. And now I'd be gone.

She returned to the ward at the very last minute and immediately lit a cigarette. 'You still here, then?' she asked in her usual brusque fashion. I wondered if maybe she'd hoped she might miss my departure. Sentimental displays were not her style at all. I nodded, all at once too tearful to speak. 'We'll keep in touch,' we both promised, through our tears.

Mum and Dad had gathered up my belongings by now, and came across to bid Lesley farewell themselves, and then, moments later, we were gone. Back through the male section – no wolf-whistles this time – then out into the main corridor and through the horrible, flapping plastic doors I'd so loathed. We emerged outside into a stiff autumn breeze and made our way to the car park for the last time.

Loading up, nothing seemed very much different from the weekend routine we'd been doing for so long now. But as Dad drove down the driveway to the main entrance gate, my heart felt suddenly full with the prospect of not having to come back here again on Sunday evening. Not next week, not next month, not next year.

We swung out into the road and then Rookwood was behind us. It was real. It was final. I wasn't coming back. If I had anything to do with it, not ever.

part two

chapter 10

After leaving Rookwood, my life was a different life from the one I'd envisaged. Things were still pretty challenging, but at the same time coping with the difficulties was rewarding, and it felt really good to be home. And surprisingly manageable. The months of daily visiting and helping with my care while I'd been there had paid huge dividends for Mum and Dad. There was almost nothing, day to day, that had been done for me in hospital that they couldn't do – and do tirelessly – at home. The skin care, the washing, the medication and so on – even the two-hourly turning through the night. Dad was excused the latter as he had to go to work, but with just Mum and me managing the manoeuvring between us, I gained strength and fitness in a fraction of the time that I probably would have done otherwise. How Mum coped with the chronic interruption to her sleep, I never really understood, but, as ever, her attitude was relentlessly can-do. As we settled into our new routine, it occurred to me just what incredible people my outwardly ordinary parents must be.

And not just in terms of their resilience. They were also old hands at dealing with authority, having climbed through several hoops sixteen years earlier in order to adopt me in the first place, and somehow, in the weeks prior to my discharge from Rookwood, they'd managed to convince Social Services that our entirely unsuitable home-on-a-hill, with all its steps, steep drives, two storeys, lack of down-stairs toilet – let alone bathroom – was a suitable place for a paraplegic to live. Which wasn't just one heck of a thing to pull off, but also, I realised, my passport back to life. Had they not done so, and had our home at the Uplands been deemed inappropriate, I'd not even have been *allowed* to come home.

We would, of course, have to move somewhere more suitable; they both knew that. But moving home took time – months or even years, in all probability – and they simply couldn't countenance the idea of my being imprisoned in Rookwood any longer.

This small thing, though successful, was still a reminder of just how much our new lives would be affected by deci-sions made *for* us; that my new lack of mobility would impact far further than just in the matter of physical constraints.

There was more to come. Mum and Dad had been busy in other departments too. We were all agreed that continu-ing my education was paramount, from both an academic and a personal standpoint. I needed, we all knew, to be among my peers, not locked away in a box marked 'disabled'.

My headmaster at Glanafan Comprehensive – another Mr Davies – unfortunately had other ideas.

'Not possible,' was his considered opinion when Dad went along to visit and discuss the possibility of my return, to take the O levels I'd missed sitting last year. It just wasn't practical. It would apparently involve too much reorganisation of classes, as all my lessons, and therefore my classmates' lessons, would have to take place on the ground floor. But much of the school *was* on the ground floor, my dad countered. And besides, what about the whole ethos of comprehensive schooling? Didn't the word 'comprehensive' mean accessible to all?

Mr Davies, however, was not to be budged. It would simply involve too much reorganisation and inconvenience. And besides, he added, delivering the ace he'd so far failed to reveal, my being there might upset the other pupils. And they couldn't have that happen, could they?

Disgusted, my father decided to call it a day. If Glanafan would find me such an unwelcome influence, then so be it. It was their loss, not mine.

It would be easy to single out Glanafan as particularly cruel and insensitive, but in truth, back in the early eighties there was little disabled provision in *any* sort of institution, and those with disabilities tended to be herded together and educated in special schools. Special indeed, as they seemed to work on the 'one size fits all' principle: whatever the nature or extent of your disability, that was the place you were sent to.

I knew nothing of the rejection from Glanafan at this point because Dad had wisely decided I didn't need to. Home schooling – the other option open to us – was one that didn't appeal to me at all. I wanted to return to the real world, normality. At least the closest to normality I could get. So it was arranged, once I was settled, that the council's special needs education placement officer would come to visit and decide what best to do with me next.

So it was that one day in late October the doorbell rang. Mum went out to answer it while I remained in the front room, waiting, in anxious anticipation, for the official in whose hands rested my educational future. He was duly ushered in and I proffered a hand in greeting.

Curiously, to my mind, he ignored it. 'HEL-LO!' he boomed in what I would soon come to learn was an impressive 'Does she take sugar?' sort of voice. Right then, not yet versed in the odd, sometimes comic and occasionally astounding ways that certain people tend to address the disabled, I just opened my mouth in disbelief.

He beamed at me. 'I'M MIS-TER FISH,' he continued, still with the same exaggerated enunciation and the volume racked up to max. I noted his name with childish delight and wondered if perhaps the poor man was deaf. But not for long. I soon recognised that he probably wasn't. Dad was pretty deaf, after all, and he never spoke in this way. I nodded an acknowledgement and he rattled straight on. 'AND I UNDER-STAND YOU WANT TO GO TO SCHOO-ELL?'

'Yes,' I replied, through disbelievingly clenched teeth. 'I'd like to go back and do my O levels.'

'OOOHHH,' said Mr Fish, and it wasn't really clear if he was trying to clarify which levels, or was simply in a state of mild shock. It seemed the former. 'RIGHT,' he continued. 'In that case I will see to it that you can go to a lo-cal spe-cial u-nit. Be nice for *you*,' – as in me – 'to get out a bit, and for *you*' – as in Mum and Dad – 'to have a break. I'll be in touch as soon as I can.'

So it was that arrangements were put in place, and I was to restart my education the following week. Dad took a day off work for the occasion and drove me to the appointed school – Sandfields Primary – to which the special unit was attached. I did wonder why it was at a primary school but assumed that was just where they had space for the unit.

Promising he'd be back to collect me at lunchtime, Dad left me in the care of Mr Fish, who then passed me over to the special needs teacher, a plump, grey-haired lady, who took me over to the single-storey, red-brick building where I had apparently been billeted. As soon as I entered the room it became clear that my classmates, seemingly without exception, were severely educationally challenged children with a wide variety of disabilities. Some were able to play with toys and building blocks and a few seemed to be coping with looking at books, but there was not a shred of evidence that anything approaching an O level syllabus was, or would ever be, taught here. Taking all this in, it became instantly clear that I didn't fit in with my surroundings. And when I was handed a *Janet and John* book, along with the exhortation to 'See how you get along with that,' my first impressions were confirmed. It didn't need a huge leap of intellect to realise that my ambition to sit my O levels had obviously not filtered through.

So it was that my very first day at the unit also turned out to be my last. And it wasn't even a whole day. Dad came to collect me at lunchtime, as arranged, and I didn't need to explain to him that there was no way I was coming back to the place. Not this afternoon. Not tomorrow. Not ever. He knew. He already felt much the same. We couldn't leave quickly enough.

Which left me at something of an educational impasse. Happily, though, fate had another surprise up her sleeve, and this time it turned out to be a good one.

Mum had given up work at the steelworks soon after my accident, after a period of compassionate leave. She continued, however, with her other great commitment: her work on the Magistrates' Bench. She'd been a Justice of the Peace for four years now and it was work she took very seriously. Having accepted the honour of being asked, she was ever mindful of her considerable responsibility, both to the community, in bringing offenders to book, and also to the individual accused themselves, many of whom passed through her hands. She'd obviously been given lots of training to equip her: courses on manifold aspects of the law, on police protocol, the psychology of offenders, the myriad effects of drug and alcohol abuse and the principles underlying sentencing. It would have felt wrong, after such training, not to continue to put those skills to good use.

And it was brilliant for me that she had. Also on the bench was Dr Edwin Jones PhD, who happened to be headmaster of another Port Talbot school, St Joseph's Roman Catholic Comprehensive.

Edwin Jones was a bit of a local hero. Having done well in school and earned a place at Swansea's University College, followed by three years studying Historiography at Cambridge, he was destined for an academic future as a lecturer on the other side of the world, in New Zealand. But something held him back. Happily for me, he followed his heart and not his head, and instead opted to train as a teacher. A good decision: he went on to become, at twenty-nine, the UK's youngest head of a Catholic comprehensive.

But it wasn't just as a teacher that Dr Jones was able to help change my life. On a family holiday a year previously, he'd seen for himself how difficult it was for the disabled to access education. While away, his family had befriended another family, whose son, like me, was wheelchair-bound. Hearing them recount how he'd been denied access to every mainstream school they'd tried – including, to his dismay, Catholic ones – he vowed that if placed in similar circum-stances as a head teacher he'd never willingly deny access to anyone at his school. His mantra was to teach the whole person.

Given both his history of trailblazing and personal experience of disability, it was probably no surprise that a chance mention of my situation regarding Glanafan – still entirely unknown to me – attracted his attention. He would, he told Mum, be more than happy to look into the possibility of accommodating me there instead. She outlined the problems they'd mentioned at Glanafan; after all, St Joseph's was on two storeys as well, and would have just the same difficulties to overcome. Not to mention pupils who might also be upset. But Dr Jones was not one to let details put him off, or give heed to the notion that my being in his school might traumatise his delicate charges. On the contrary, he couldn't see how being in the presence of disability could be anything other than a good thing.

So it was that this Roman Catholic school got their first non-Catholic-agnostic-sort-of pupil. And also their very first disabled one. Which was to turn out to be an enabling experience for us all.

This is not to say I was embarking on the experience with any degree of religious fervour. My attitude to the notion of God since my accident had been one of puzzlement and ambiguity. Was there anybody up there? Was there really a higher power? Or was I all alone in this thing? No one was pressuring me to find answers to my questions; Dr Jones made it clear to me at the outset that I wouldn't be forced to participate in any religious aspects of school life that I didn't want to.

But such was the school's total, unquestioning acceptance of me, so powerful was the sense that here was a place where I could rebuild my life, my faith in human nature and my fractured sense of self, that immersing myself fully in all aspects of school life felt entirely the right thing to do. For the first time since I'd been given it, I felt my wheelchair – that thing that threatened to define me – disappeared.

In January 1981 I was invited to join a school trip to Lourdes, and I was both moved and thrilled. For many teenagers back in the early eighties, going abroad on holiday was a seriously big thing. In a world not yet served by the 99 pence flight or the ubiquitous gap year, travelling abroad for the first time was an exciting rite of passage, often (though obviously not necessarily always) involving a first taste of air travel, foreign food, foreign music, sea that was brilliant turquoise instead of murky pewter, and, if you were lucky, the heady thrill of a holiday romance, conducted against a backdrop of gently wafting palm trees with scents of jasmine and the sweet taste of sangria. Me? I was off on a pilgrimage to Lourdes, with a group of priests, poorly pensioners and nuns.

But I couldn't have been more excited. It was another example of the school's willingness to share an essential part of their life and faith with me. I was clearly not on my own.

That was, if I was going to be able to go. The trip had been planned for May, but towards the end of January I started developing new and worrying symptoms. A painful swelling appeared around the top of one of the Harrington rods in my spine. My GP referred me back to my surgeon, Mr Davies, who looked about as pleased to see me as he had the first time he'd clapped eyes on me nine months before.

Though he certainly must have noticed the change in me. For starters, the frightened teenager who'd lain supine in a hospital gown and upon whose broken body he'd operated had now been replaced by a confident sixth-former. If anything would prove that he'd done a good job, the sight of me, all smiles and hairdo and freshly applied make-up (I was keen both to show off *and* to keep in his good books – I had a trip to be passed fit for) would surely do it.

I smiled. He didn't. And not for the first time, it crossed my mind that in his line of work, once he'd *done* all his work, he mostly hoped that the work would stay done.

Because he seemed just as grumpy as ever. But, as I was only to learn later, it was for a very good reason.

Two reasons, actually. One, seeing me had brought back to him the absolute horror of the sight that had greeted him when he'd opened up my back nine months previously; the carnage that, even as he'd operated on me, he wasn't sure he could do anything to put right. And two, the resentment he felt at the suspicion that my symptoms were caused by a rod having dislodged. He was a fixer. He'd fixed it. It should have *stayed* fixed. That it might not have irritated him greatly.

But whether dislodged or otherwise, it was, he assured me, nothing serious. Whatever he found, he could now safely remove them because they had already done the job they'd been put there to do. And as all that would need to heal would be the skin and the surrounding muscles, there was no reason why I shouldn't be fit and fully recovered in plenty of time for the trip.

But why Lourdes? He peered at me over his glasses and looked stern. I wasn't hoping for a miracle, was I? He didn't actually say so, but his face said it for him; if I was, then I was clutching at straws.

Unbeknown to me, my injury still haunted him, and he already had his own thoughts on this. Mine was the worst spinal injury he'd ever dealt with in his career as a surgeon, and having to review the original injuries again reminded him of his feelings at the time. Principally, on seeing the damage – the total carnage – his utter disbelief that I'd escaped even more horrendous injury, permanent brain damage, quadriplegia or death. Had that been an act of God in itself?

But he opted not to share this – perhaps he felt I'd already had my share of miracles? – and instead confined himself to simply raising one eyebrow and commenting that he hoped I wasn't travelling there with any unrealistic expectations.

Absolutely not, I told him truthfully, wondering as I did so if he was so good at looking fierce and disapproving because he practised every morning in the mirror. He certainly looked as if he might do. But then he softened, presumably as a result of seeing my enthusiasm, though it could equally have been because he was a very busy man and this particular excitable teenager had taken up enough of his time. He conceded that, however sceptical he might be about miracles, I might – probably would – find the trip beneficial; might gain, if nothing else, some inner strength.

I was re-admitted to Ward Eight on a Tuesday soon after, which felt curiously like a home from home. I was prepped for the op the following morning, and I realised, just before I felt myself sink under, that I was going off to find inner strength in southern France straight after having my own scaffolding removed.

Which seemed a rather neat kind of irony.

chapter 11

The crossing from Dover to Dunkirk was scheduled to take a little over two hours and I had a plan for it in place. I'd not had the best of nights; I was definitely going to be out of my comfort zone doing this, and the seven-thirty train from Swansea had meant a very early start. I was by now existing mainly on adrenaline. What I needed, I reasoned, was a chance to chill out with the other sixth-formers who were coming on the trip to Lourdes as helpers.

But my wheelchair had plans of its own. Well, just the one, to be honest. To thwart me. I'd never travelled by ship before but I'd never been car sick, so I had no reason to think this voyage would be any different from the rather glamorous and exciting experience of my imaginings. Alas, it was manifestly different, the combination of the rolling of the ship in tandem with the independent motion of my wheelchair making for an intense nausea. Ironically, Mum had expressed great anxiety that she would feel ill, having once been violently sick on a Tenby to Lundy ferry, but, as it turned out, while she admired the view and munched on turkey sandwiches I was compelled to abandon my intended exploration of all parts of the ship – in particular the promised bar – and forced to spend the entire journey looking like an impromptu prow maiden, clinging grimly to the foredeck rails, wind-lashed and grimacing, and remaining motionless for the duration.

Landfall at Dunkirk was, therefore, a great blessing. We disembarked onto the quayside in darkness – it was now late evening – but I doubt I'd have taken in much even if it had been daytime. I was more concerned about the logistics of the transfer from the ferry to the train, which would take us down through France overnight. It was a train of a kind I'd not seen before, with a narrow central corridor and couchettes on either side. I was carried aboard without incident, however, and we were soon underway. Now the tables were turned, unexpectedly, on Mum. She couldn't lie down without feeling really grim, and so was forced to sit up and remain awake throughout the night, while I, similarly sleepless, though feeling human at last, could lie and watch as the stations flashed by.

Not that there was much sleep to be had even had either of us craved it. Despite the severe infirmity of most of my fellow pilgrims – several were terminally ill, some at cruelly young ages – they seemed no less excitable than I was. The night was punctuated by a constant babble of chat and laughter, and when we arrived in Lourdes just after dawn, we were both feeling distinctly bleary-eyed.

But not for long. Canon Mullins, the priest in charge of our particular band of pilgrims – a body of people that had been gathered from various parts of South Wales – addressed us all with his loud hailer and the throng were swiftly unloaded from the train and onto buses, which would take them to the hospital that would be their base for the duration. Lourdes was nothing if not geared to its principal attraction, and the movement of large groups of gravely ill patients was managed with impressive precision.

Mum and I had been given an alternative base. As I wasn't ill, I didn't need to be in hospital. This was something about which I was more than a little pleased, because I'd seen more than enough of those lately. Instead a small hotel had been found for us nearby. Unfortunately, it was situated at the top of an extremely steep hill and we were stumped as to how we'd make it up there. Two of the school helpers came to our rescue, finding us a taxi and helping load our luggage, before seeing us off up to our eyrie. How we'd manage subsequently was not as yet clear, but we were too tired to worry.

The hotel itself was only the second I'd ever stayed in, the first being the one on our trip to Blackpool. In terms of décor, they looked little different. A riot of bang-on-trend seventies décor, a symphony in mustard and brown. There was one significant difference, however, in that, understandably, the porter spoke no English. Even more understandably, given that my modern language option at school had been Welsh, I spoke no French. As Mum didn't either, communication was patchy, and all we managed to establish once he'd shown us to our room was that it wouldn't be any good. The bathroom, though undeniably well-appointed, had a doorway too narrow to allow me and my wheelchair to get in. But the manager, who by now had been summoned, was undaunted. In no time at all he had another one sorted, the only trouble being that it was already occupied by a pleasant though undeniably stupefied young German guy, who politely vacated our superior accommodation as a lamb might head off to slaughter.

The only downside to this unexpected upgrade was that Mum and I had to share the spoils, in the form of the vast, king-size double bed. It was a novel experience for us both. It was up against the wall of the room on one side, and as it made sense for Mum to have the outside in case she needed to use the loo in the night, I felt somewhat marooned in the corner. It took a Herculean effort and no small amount of time to bounce or roll my way across the vast plain of mattress to get from bed to chair and vice versa.

Having only the vaguest notions about the town of Lourdes (I knew it existed, was some sort of religious place, attracted pilgrims) I had little idea what to expect. I had little idea what to expect of France in general, come to that, my only knowledge of the place having come from school maps, and my only impressions being restricted to the stereotypes of berets, strings of onions and garlic. Thus my senses were constantly assaulted by novelty: the all-pervasive aroma of coffee and baking croissants; the constant white noise of animated conversation; the cafés with outside tables – something not seen in Port Talbot, ever; the breathtaking views of the looming Pyrenees; the way everyone seemed to have time to stop and chat, *always*. Even more exciting, from a personal point of view, was that I'd got here, I was coping, all the obstacles seemed manageable, and the fears I'd had about any sort of foreign trip being out of the question for me were being happily quashed, hour upon hour. Indeed, this trip would pave the way for a lifelong love of travel and see me embarking on all sorts of adventures, but right now I just felt a great sense of relief.

After the marathon journey to get here, we'd ended up going to bed, exhausted, at 7 p.m., so by the following morning I was itching to get out and see the place properly in daylight. An early breakfast of whichever cereal we could recognise from the pictures on the boxes (augmented by the standard fare of croissants and fresh fruit and coffee) was taken in the hotel dining room – an assault on the senses itself. Once again, I was struck by all the noise and chatter, made more striking by the fact that the babble all around us was entirely incomprehensible: a totally new experience for us both.

Next up was mass – a central and regular part of the trip, obviously – which took place in the town's basilica. This was, more correctly, the conglomeration of basilicas and other holy buildings that were collectively known as the Sanctuaries: the Basilica of the Immaculate Conception, the Basilica of the Rosary and the Grotto of Massabielle. They were set one behind the other and together formed the principal focus of pilgrimages to Lourdes.

Unsurprisingly, given that this was an area capable of accommodating 80,000 worshippers at once, the sheer numbers of people were daunting. There were literally thousands gathering, including an unexpected and sizeable military presence. Mum and I soon learned why. This wasn't an exercise in overzealous crowd control. This was simply another form of organised pilgrimage, with the

Forces from many different countries all visiting Lourdes at the same time.

As we made our way towards the main precinct of the Sanctuaries, I got my first glimpse of the clearly large-scale commercial tourist operation that was in action here to capitalise on the presence of such a vast, and also constant, stream of pilgrims. It was less than edifying. Where I'd been moved by being in the presence of obviously sick people who prayed not for themselves but for others, now I saw a different aspect of what went on here. Dabbling in large-scale religious fervour obviously paid. As the gathering congregation – our own party was just a tiny part of the whole – were channelled towards the three holy sites, we passed a vast number of tacky souvenir stalls, selling everything from plastic crosses to cheap and nasty religious statuettes.

But they were soon behind us and, in any case, my eyes were not on them but the awe-inspiring spectacle of thousands of people all singing and chanting under the directions of the bishops, who were there to keep some semblance of cohesion and order – no mean feat with such an enthusiastic crowd.

Little by little, the huge throng made its way down into the precinct of the basilica. The buildings themselves were set on the slope of a hill, and so towered above us, majestic and imposing. The service, for most of us, took place right there, with the sun intermittently beating down overhead, or drifting behind welcome wisps of high cloud.

This was my first experience of a full Roman Catholic mass – at school I only attended assembly – and the impact was intense and unexpectedly exhilarating, especially the chanting of the verses and the soaring beauty of massed voices singing. The sense of kinship, camaraderie, support and love overwhelmed me. It felt like the biggest expression of care and altruism that I had ever, in my young life, encountered. Here I could see for myself *why* people worshipped, and I found myself forgetting all about the cynical commerce that preceded it, and crying at the sheer power of it all. This was not to form the start of a growing sense of faith, but more, a sense of the power and goodness of humanity. My lukewarm commitment to religion had been engulfed by the feeling that here was a greater spiritual presence than I'd ever known in my life.

But I could only feel pious and awestruck for so long and the trip had lots of other new experiences in store, not all of them entirely expected. As our first full day drew to a close, Mum and I had the exciting prospect of sampling the hotel's evening dining facilities. The set menu (which was written in French, so a journey of discovery in itself) comprised a bowl of lettuce each – curious; didn't salads normally contain things like spring onions and beetroot? – followed by some sort of meat dish. Neither of us could work out quite what the meat was, and I grew anxious, having heard rumours about it, that the meat might be – horror of horrors – horse.

There was a group of Sicilian soldiers dining in the hotel with us and one of them, no more than about twenty, I decided, had been winking at Mum for some time. Sensing our confusion (it wasn't a huge dining room), he promptly came over to set our minds at rest, explaining that it wasn't horse but rabbit. As the idea of Thumper being dispatched was only marginally less awful to contemplate than the idea of Black Beauty, we lost all further interest in what remained on our plates. And, in any case, the soldier had plans. Quite without warning – bar the winking bit, obviously – he asked Mum, with an expression that seemed entirely serious, if she'd be interested in accompanying him to 'go to orgy'. Therein followed five minutes of that most cringe-making of situations: Outrageous Mother Embarrasses Teenage Daughter. This was entirely new territory. My *mother*? Engaged in *flirting*? Because that, without a doubt, was what she was doing.

'Does the word "orgy",' she enquired, with a twinkle in her eyes, 'mean the same in Italian as it does in English?'

The soldier, whose English was clearly quite advanced in certain areas, nodded enthusiastically. 'Oh, yes, it does.'

Mum nodded unashamedly. 'Well, in that case ...' she purred. 'Yes. That sounds great fun. Why not?'

But the soldier's delight was to be dashed in an instant. 'Mum!' I blurted out, blushing crimson and mortified. 'You can't!' And to make certain, I followed up with a threat. 'You *can't*!' I repeated. 'I'll tell Dad!'

And, indeed, we did mention the incident once home and he seemed not in the tiniest bit bothered. His only response was to roll his eyes and laugh and say, 'Fancy, love. You could have been a Mafia moll!'

* * *

Despite moments of glorious sunshine, rain was a fairly constant companion during our time in Lourdes. This wasn't unsurprising for a town that nestled in the foothills of the northern Pyrenees, obviously, and rain, of course, felt appropriate. The people who came here were pilgrims, not sun-seekers, after all. If they were rained on, it was supposed to be borne without complaint. Whatever God willed, I supposed.

I don't know if it was just a natural release of tension after so much serious and contemplative activity, but one afternoon, towards the end of the holiday, both Mum and I found ourselves in mischievous mood.

It was, this particular day, raining torrentially. The sort of rain that came out of the sky in drops the size of snooker balls – the rain that was responsible for making the area so verdant. As was the norm, we ignored it. It would fall, we'd get wet, and no harm would be done. A neighbouring gentleman seemed to feel otherwise, however, and kindly shared the cover of his enormous umbrella with us both.

Grateful, we felt better able to concentrate on the proceedings, which, today, involved a sermon from one of the presiding Irish cardinals, who was using a microphone but still struggling to make himself heard. Indeed, we could make out very little of what he said; the combined volume of the rain thumping down on the umbrella above our heads together with the rush of the swollen river meant it was becoming increasingly difficult to concentrate on what were doubtless some wise and important words. I was actually more transfixed by the thought that given the electrics snaked all about him he might suddenly go up in a puff of blue smoke.

Perhaps sensing the damp crowd were growing restless, he turned the volume and the passion up a notch further, and now he did get our attention. 'T'ousands and t'ousands of people,' he bellowed, 'come to Lourdes every year! Dey come in search of peace! Dey come in search of health! Dey come here in search of salvation!' His up-tempo delivery had everyone engaged now. He took a breath. 'And *t'ree* of our pilgrims have DIED!'

There followed a bemused silence, as we all digested his words. 'D'you think that came out right?' I whispered to Mum finally. 'Because it sounds to me as if he thinks that's a *good* thing!' He didn't, clearly. He couldn't have. He'd meant, we felt sure, that given the desperate state of many pilgrims' health, it was a miracle that *only* three had succumbed. But given what he *had* said, and his hilarious Frank Carson-like delivery, we couldn't stop ourselves from spluttering with irreverent laughter.

The man with the umbrella was not at all impressed by our levity. He briskly whisked away his umbrella from above us, affording our equally disapproving neighbours a clear view of the heathens in their midst. Worse still was that he now positioned it in such a way that the rain (which had grown markedly heavier) collected and ran in an unbroken stream straight down the back of my neck. I blinked at the heavens and wondered about God. Had divine intervention wiped the smile from my face? I kept it that way for the duration.

* * *

God. The Almighty. Some form of higher power. I didn't
know quite what to call it, how to picture it, how to analyse
it, but my week at Lourdes, however fanciful the concept
might seem, was full of a sense of there being something
greater than the earth on which we lived out our lives.

I felt it in the kindness of strangers – the Flemish man
who carried me selflessly on and off a coach, despite having
an appallingly bad chest. I felt it in the inexplicable – our
experience of the ritual of immersion in the holy waters, and
how, as they assured us would be the case, you came out feeling warm and dry. I felt it in the beauty of the unity of
purpose in the candle-lit procession. But whoever or whatever was orchestrating things that particular week, they
definitely saved their best till last.

Principal among the must-dos on any trip to Lourdes was
apparently to light a candle at the Grotto of Our Lady,
which was situated on the bank of Lourdes' beautiful river,
the Gave de Pau. As a result, the crowds were routinely vast.
Mum had ventured down with a group of ladies she'd
befriended, but with queuing in the rain not being high on
my list of priorities (not to mention my reluctance to impose
on helpers at a time when they were looking forward to
relaxing after spending all day helping the needy) I hadn't
yet managed to include a visit. But on this, our last night,
there turned out to be an opportunity. Mum had gone to bed
early and I'd spent the evening with a group of helpers in a
large and lively bar in the centre of town. It was already well
after midnight but none of us were tired. When it became
clear in conversation that I'd not as yet seen the grotto, it was
suggested that now might be the time to visit. Decision

reached, we made our way from the bustling nightlife all around us towards the purity and stillness of one of Lourdes' holy places, a stroll of about a half hour's duration.

The rain had stopped and the night was warm and still, the backdrop of mountains huddled black and featureless beneath a dramatic night sky. Without light pollution, the heavens looked amazing: full of scudding pewter clouds, a bright but mostly hidden moon and an impossibly thick and deep sprinkling of stars.

Energised by our collective impulse we made our way down the steep and winding path that snaked its way to the riverbank and grotto, chatting about who we might light our candles for. As we descended, however, it grew so tranquil and quiet that it soon reduced our chatter to a low and respectful whisper.

Long racks of unlit candles greeted us at the entrance. It felt almost illicit to be here so late, unshepherded, and yet strangely as if that was the way it should be. The still night. The sense of peace. The absence of jostling hordes. We all selected several candles and set about lighting them with the lighters that many of us had brought with us. I lit four. One for Mum, tucked up safely in bed. One for Dad, who I wished could have come too, but who was back at home with only the cat for company. One for the school that had welcomed me so warmly and had generously brought me to this beautiful place. And finally one for my steadfast surgeon Mr Davies, whose skills had once again allowed me not just to be here, but also to continue on my journey through life as fit and well as it was possible for me to be.

We then left behind the flickering light of the candles and made our way further inside the grotto. The only sound I could hear was the rushing of the river. Our own excited voices, as one, were stilled, as we looked upon the statue of the Virgin. Suddenly the clouds parted and, emerging from behind them, the moon bathed the statue in what seemed to my eyes to be an impossibly bright light. I was transfixed, quite unable to take my gaze from it, and conscious of a feeling of peace and serenity that seemed to be flowing, like blood, through my veins. I knew in that instant, with an unshakeable conviction, that everything would be okay. That I could look forward to the future. That I would be able to cope with anything life threw at me. I felt warm. I felt calm. I felt exhilarated and also tearful. More at peace with myself than I'd been in my entire life.

The moon slipped back behind its cloud, the light dimmed, the grotto darkened. The moment – whatever it had been – began to fade. The chatter recommenced. We all discussed what had happened. Coincidence? Maybe. But what about that *feeling*? We couldn't have imagined that, could we?

As we made our way back, the feeling persisted. I wasn't fanciful and I didn't think fanciful thoughts. But *something* had happened. I felt different.

chapter 12

As a surgeon, I imagined Mr Davies had, over the years, got used to his patients doing as they were told. After all, for the most part, they were unconscious on his operating table so not in a position to argue. Plus he was a doctor so (as everyone knew) he was not very far removed from God.

It was a Thursday in January 1982 and I'd come to Neath General Hospital to try and coax him round to my way of thinking. Not because I was feeling particularly reckless or mischievous, but simply because I needed him on side.

I'd been at St Joseph's for fourteen months now, and my new life was taking on a shape and sense of purpose that prior to my accident I would not have thought possible. Far from feeling disabled, I felt I'd been reborn and was learning how to live again; and with that came the opportunity to go in directions I'd never been before. I was in school once again, yet I wasn't being bullied, and despite the wheelchair I actually felt a sense of new-found freedom.

I'd completed my O levels the previous summer and was now just beginning the second term of A levels – I'd chosen to do English and History. The latter of these, unfortunately, now felt like a mistake. With every fibre of my being, I wanted to go forwards rather than wallow in the details of the past. With hindsight, perhaps Psychology would have been a better choice, because I didn't doubt I was going to have to employ some. My hunch was that Mr Davies wouldn't feel much enthused about the plan I intended to run by him. And I certainly did have a plan.

One of the key figures in my time so far at St Joseph's had been my biology teacher, Mr Richards. Peter Richards (who was also, in no particular order: gorgeous, an ex-Birchgrove RFC Swansea rugby player and a part-time coach) had spent a great deal of time assisting me physically, and would stay behind after school on a regular basis to help me build up my stamina and strength. Much of the school gym equipment wasn't accessible to me as a wheelchair user, obviously, but a regular programme of upper body exercise (lateral pull-downs, triceps and biceps curls, bench and shoulder presses and so on) meant I was achieving as much as was possible. What Peter couldn't help me with, however, were the sort of standing exercises that could only be attempted with specialist equipment – parallel bars and leg splints.

Having had his own sporting career curtailed by injury, Pete Richards knew enough about physiology to know how beneficial this could be. After all, our legs and hips are designed to be upright, and a regular daily session of standing-based exercise would reap huge benefits both in terms of blood and lymph circulation and bone strength.

Some time previously, Peter had heard about a civilian with a disability who had gained admission to the armed forces rehabilitation unit at RAF Chessington, and who'd benefited greatly from their intensive regime. He suggested that, should I feel I might like to do the same, he'd make enquiries on my behalf. I should make clear here that had Pete suggested he take me to Alaska that instant to catch a fish, I'd be in my parka before he was – but his deliciousness aside, the idea really appealed.

Based near Leatherhead in Surrey, the rehabilitation unit at RAF Chessington admitted a small number of injured civilians only when space allowed. It was convenient for me, therefore, that in early 1982, when the possibility of my going was first mooted, there was a real chance of admittance. Though they were busy with casualties of the troubles in Northern Ireland, the British Forces were not then involved in any other major conflicts so there were a few spaces available.

Not that anyone could simply pitch up there. The rehabilitation courses they offered were rigorous and demanding and definitely not suitable for all. Acceptance on them followed a strict selection procedure, including recommendation from a suitable person (in my case, Pete Richards), the written agreement of the doctor responsible for the management of each individual case, and finally, that having been granted, a formal interview with the medical officer in charge.

The first was no problem, the last we doubted would be, but the bit in the middle, based on previous encounters, might, I thought, prove more tricky.

Yet without the agreement of Mr Davies for what constituted quite a radical upheaval I was going to be going nowhere, so I took pains to prepare my case well. I arrived in his clinic to be greeted by his usual stern and taciturn expression. Nevertheless I ploughed on. I told him I'd heard all about the benefits of Chessington, how my biology teacher had recommended me for it, how I'd built up my body strength to be the best it possibly could be and how I'd been advised by pretty much everyone I'd encountered that, as a paraplegic, I'd benefit from an hour's standing each day. To do this, I explained, I'd need callipers to stabilise my hips and legs, and, somewhat crucially, his approval.

As I anticipated, he wasn't about to give it.

Had I been inside my surgeon's head that day, I imagine I might have understood his scepticism better. He had, of course, seen patients with over-optimistic expectations many times. It wasn't so much the specific details of where I wanted to go – he hadn't, at that point, even heard of RAF Chessington – but the motivation that he suspected lay behind it, which, in his admittedly vast experience, was generally centred on false hopes. Whatever else his role from here on in my life, he felt it his duty to provide reason and truth. To quash any fanciful notions in the bud before a cycle of hope and disappointment became established and my mental equilibrium was shot.

All this, of course, I pooh-poohed. I had looked inside myself and I did not have false hope. I knew all the facts. I harboured no hidden hopes that I'd ever walk again. I had simply thought through the reality of my future and decided that being completely independent was non-negotiable. I already had independence in many things. By now I managed all my day-to-day care entirely without any help from Mum. I dealt with my bladder with my catheter and leg bag, and my bowels with daily suppositories that I administered myself, all of which restored my dignity. But that wasn't sufficient. Much as I didn't want to think about it, I had to consider the worst-case scenario of something happening to Mum or Dad. I knew it was vital to be able to drive and thus make myself fully independent. And it wasn't just worst-case scenarios I pondered. I wanted the simple pleasure of going somewhere – anywhere – on my own. I'd been managing to get myself in and out of a car for months now but to do likewise with my wheelchair would require upper body strength I simply didn't have.

But Mr Davies clearly thought there was more to it. He continued to stare hard at me, and began to frown. He was, he told me, deeply sceptical about what good it would do me, even were my protestations genuine. Where I saw only potential benefit, he saw only potential cost. However much I told him otherwise he insisted on believing that what I saw as a chance to get really fit and strong was in fact an ill-advised attempt towards gaining mobility on crutches and callipers – something he felt was not only misguided, but also held a very real potential for further trouble. He'd listened, unimpressed, to my version of what would happen, and the alternative scenario he painted for me was undeniably bleak. I'd in all likelihood get pressure sores from using the callipers, have dangerous falls and very serious injuries. And even were I lucky enough to escape all of those, I'd suffer crushing disappointment and possible depression, however much I told him I wouldn't. And for what?

He was at a complete loss to understand why I wanted to go to such a place. Why on earth, having loathed and

detested Rookwood so much, would I want to leave everything and everyone I knew and go back to spend months in
another institution? Why would I want to leave my home,
the lovely school where I was settled, and the A level courses
I'd started only four months before? He was, it was fair to
say, astounded.

From my own point of view, it made perfect sense.
However much I wanted to get my A levels, there was, at
that time, virtually no university that could accommodate
someone like me, which dented my motivation somewhat.
Attention to my physical progress, on the other hand, could
only reap massive benefits. Looked at objectively, however,
my enthusiasm for Chessington only made sense for two
reasons: one, that I had a bizarre fetish for being banged up
with strangers; or two, that, despite everything I claimed, I
really did believe it might give me back the use of my legs.

Which made convincing him otherwise a fairly uphill
struggle. But I already knew – literally – all about those, and
was not to be deflected from my quest. Annoyingly for me,
however, neither was he. Again and again he insisted on
pointing out that no matter where I went, be it Lourdes or
Chessington (or, indeed, Timbuktu), nothing tangibly
different would happen to me. I would still *be* me – to put
it bluntly, a paraplegic, with serious and life-threatening
problems to surmount. I was tempted at this point to
applaud the vote of confidence, but, with a wisdom fuelled
mainly by stubborn conviction, I kept my counsel and let
him lecture on. The idea was, he pointed out, as much by
expression as language, not only irresponsible but also
unreasonable and unrealistic to boot.

But he was my surgeon and not my keeper, so by the end of the consultation (having perhaps brought to mind the quotation about what happens when irresistible forces meet immovable objects, or else just exhausted and keen to move the day along) he offered what we agreed was a sensible compromise. He would not in any way endorse my intended plan of action, but neither, seeing as I was so dead set on it, would he actively stand in my way.

All of which suited me fine, because it meant I could finally get my hands on the equipment I needed for my next big adventure, without which I couldn't take the plan any further. Such high-tech kit didn't come cheaply. I beamed happily as I sat and watched him fill out the form that would see me granted what I'd come to secure, both an 'OK', and a set of hip guidance orthoses – my passport into Chessington. Much as I was tempted, I drew the line at giving him a grateful hug.

That hurdle vaulted, things moved quickly. I was measured up for my callipers the following week and while I waited for them to arrive I was invited to Chessington to meet Colonel Robinson, the officer in charge of the rehabilitation facility. It was in his hands that my fate now rested, as it was his final assessment of both my physical and psychological fitness that would decide if I was admitted or not. After my battle with Mr Davies, however, this turned out to be a mere formality, and as I left he commented that he looked forward to welcoming me there. I wasn't sure if this was down to my newly minted inner steel or whatever Mr Davies had put in his letter, but either way, the job was done. I was in.

My callipers arrived soon after, and were a masterpiece of engineering, in heavy block leather and steel. There was an encircling band that spanned my lower chest, an elasticated sling that fitted around my bottom to keep my pelvis forward while I was standing, pairs of locking hinges situated at hip and knee level, and an attached pair of brown leather ankle boots. Equipped with these, I presented myself at the camp on the morning of Monday 22 March 1982.

Chessington was a good deal further from home than Rookwood, and we'd been up at 2 a.m. for a 4 a.m. start. The journey had taken four hours in total, and my parents, having made it, would soon have to do it all over again. It was mooted that perhaps they should both get chauffeurs' caps.

After an impressively militaristic arrival procedure, we were shown to the quarters where I would be billeted in the Station Medical Centre. Based at the top of a hill, the SMC was a single-storey red-brick building with a sergeant's office on one side and a corridor that led onto a room that could accommodate four female patients. The male quarters were situated elsewhere but I didn't know where and no one was about to tell me; they were strictly off limits.

After my time at Rookwood the accommodation felt spacious, yet was also surprisingly feminine and cosy – I'd been expecting something altogether more barracks-like. Two of the other three beds were already occupied, both by female civilians who'd been in road accidents and who'd sustained severe head and neck injuries.

Kim, who was in the bed next to mine, was just a year or so older than I was. Her injuries had left the right side of her body spastic, and she was also unable to talk. Because of the weakness in one side of her face, she constantly dribbled into a hankie. Despite this, she could still manage to communicate, by means of a hand-held device that printed onto a paper ribbon. At the time I arrived, she was using a wheelchair like me, which she operated by dragging her foot along the floor, though in time she graduated to a walking frame.

Perhaps understandably, her inability to speak sometimes led the nurses to treat her as if it was comprehension and not communication that was the problem. It must have been hard work to deal with such a major disability and I wondered how on earth she kept her spirits up. I didn't wonder for long – she had a great sense of humour. After she was addressed brusquely by one of the nurses early on, she typed, 'Don't worry about her – she's an arsehole.'

The other occupant of our room was a girl called Sherry, who had suffered a similar injury – both her speech and one side of her body were affected. She was about Kim's age but appeared a lot younger. She was physically tiny and incredibly sweet-natured, and seemed to us terribly vulnerable. We naturally took it upon ourselves to act as her guardians during her stay, and we fast became comfortable as flatmates. Though our very different regimes meant we had little contact during the day (and also evening – people with head injuries are advised against drinking alcohol, so neither of them was much interested in the station's social life), we all became very close; parting to go home for the weekend on a Friday afternoon always felt sad, and being reunited on a Monday morning was always joyous.

There was a dining room in the SMC, which was used not just by us three but also by the male occupants of the unit – at this time mostly patients with head injuries, which they'd sustained when off duty or on leave. There was also one quadriplegic civilian and one serviceman suffering from a brain tumour. All this was to change dramatically within the month, but right now we were a small band of brothers.

Mum and Dad, by now used to the drill, helped me unpack and then left me to it. It was ten-thirty and I'd already had my orders: to report to Flight Sergeant Rayner in Gym 3. This was inconveniently situated (as were Gyms 1 and 2) right back down at the bottom of the hill. For a moment, memories of Rookwood made me pause and take stock, but I pushed off regardless. This was doing me good.

And in ways I'd only so far imagined it might. By the time I reached the bottom (going down involves its perils too) I was sweating and flushed, but that would be as noth-ing to the effect on my physiology that the sight that was about to greet me would have. I'd just put my hand up to push the gym door when it swung open without me, reveal-ing an image that I knew would stay with me forever. It was a young man, over six feet in height and rippling with muscles, with sandy blond hair and bright, bright blue eyes. And he was aiming his wide smile right at me. He was kitted out in tight white T-shirt and airforce-blue tracksuit bottoms – no trace of the Rookwood velour baggies here. I was rendered uncharacteristically speechless.

'Hi,' he said brightly, as my mouth dangled open. 'You must be Melanie. I'm Tadge Rayner. Flight Sergeant Rayner to the rabble, of course, but as you're a civilian … Good to meet you!'

Gawd, I thought, trying frantically to gather my senses. Even his name sounded as if it had been taken straight off a Hollywood billboard. Could things get any better than this? I regrouped. Perhaps yes, in the short term at least, for I then saw what he had clasped in his hand – my callipers. 'Right,' he said. 'Let's get started.'

He didn't waste time. In what seemed like moments, the callipers were assembled and affixed over my jeans and T-shirt, and he placed me in a sitting position with my legs dangling over a gym plinth near the wall bars. I was to stay here for half an hour while my body got used to the weight, and also to minimise the possibility of my legs and abdomen going into immediate spasm once he stood me up.

This was what came next. Tadge pulled me forward to the edge of the plinth, with my heels gently resting on the floor. He straightened my knees fully and locked the calliper joints. Then, with my hands resting on his shoulders – this was definitely the best bit – he grabbed the hip joints of the callipers and pulled them (and me) with them, while I pulled upwards against him. The hip locks were dealt with as soon as I was upright, and hey presto! I was at last standing. Looking a little like the bride of Frankenstein, admittedly – but as Frankenstein had scarpered and left Tadge in his place, I absolutely couldn't have cared less.

Sadly, this bit was all too brief because once assembled, as it were, I had to be turned and affixed to the wall bars. This was so I could 'acclimatise' for fifteen minutes, while he turned his attention to the increasingly unruly male service personnel who'd now joined us, all of them injured in Northern Ireland, and currently in the later stages of their rehabilitation. There were about twenty of them, jostling loudly as they entered, and passing comment, understandably, on the sight that greeted them – a teenage girl, strapped to the bars, facing the wall, looking like the victim of some sort of medieval torture and feeling like a dunce.

Things then changed. The softly spoken man who'd gently manoeuvred me into position on the wall bars suddenly became the NCO disciplinarian, and order and calm (at least among the soldiers, if not me) was instantly restored. He quickly set them to an exercise routine, which I could hear but, frustratingly, not see.

But before long – the promised fifteen minutes, I imagined – Tadge was back and asking solicitously how I was getting on. Confidently expecting to be unpicked from the bars and released from my very boring view of the brick wall, I beamed at him and confirmed all was well.

'Jolly good,' he said. 'Just another fifteen minutes to go.' Then he strode off and went back to his men.

If the prospect of regular assignations with Tadge was rather thrilling it was even more so when combined with the prospect of spending my days ogling twenty strapping (presumably – I couldn't see) and fit young men. But it was not to be. By the time I'd been freed from both wall bars and callipers, the gym had been cleared of all 'the talent' that I'd been promised, on tape, by Kim, before I'd left. ('Look at the arse on that', 'What I could do with him if I could keep still' and 'We may have had accidents but look around – men from army, navy and RAF bending over in shorts'.) Harumph, I thought. You can *so* go off people.

Things didn't improve. My next fifteen minutes were equally thrilling, consisting of sitting quietly in a chair on my own, in the corner, to check that the standing had had no ill-effects. Only then was I allowed to go back up to the SMC for lunch.

This, too, was going to prove a challenge. With 100 yards of parade grounds to cover before the 60-yard push up the hill, the twenty minutes I had before lunch was due to be served were nowhere near enough for the task in hand. It took forty-five, in fact, to make the SMC, with Tadge following behind at a distance that ensured that, should I come to grief or succumb to asking for assistance, he'd be available to help or admonish as required – a clear reminder that this was no holiday. But missing lunch didn't bother me unduly. Kim's other message strip before I'd left the room earlier had been, 'The food's so bad here it stops me dribbling.'

Hey ho, I thought wryly. Welcome home.

chapter 13

In the early days at Chessington, conquering the hill became a small obsession with me. Because the Station Medical Centre was at the top of it and pretty much everything else at the bottom, being able to get up it unaided was vital – not just in terms of missing regular meals but also in terms of missing any sort of social life, because the other great draw at the bottom of the slope was the NAAFI, where everyone hung out. Pretty much every social activity took place there. The building housed a large dining area cum function room, where films were regularly screened, and a separate bar with a pool table and jukebox. If I wanted to be a part of things I needed to be stronger, so I attacked the programme of exercise Tadge had devised for me with plenty of verve and motivation. The hill itself contributed hugely. It's difficult to appreciate unless you've actually done it, but to haul your own body weight up a steep slope (plus hefty wheelchair, of course) using only the muscles of your shoulders and arms takes the sort of strength and stamina that most people, particularly women, never have the need to develop.

I was also helped enormously by the encouragement of the lads, whose psychology Tadge understood well. Sharing the gym with (and now, pleasingly, with an uninterrupted view of) the Forces lads, I was given a set of strength exercises to attempt, while they – with varying degrees of enthusiasm – went about doing their own prescribed tasks. Tadge left instructions that, should I need help with the equipment, they could leave off their own exercises and provide assistance as necessary. It soon became clear how sound Tadge's thinking was, because they all felt the need to demonstrate their own expertise and fitness by doing some serious showing-off.

Once my own fitness was deemed to have improved sufficiently, Tadge removed me from my daily stint facing the wall bars and set me up with a pair of elbow crutches. Standing with these required confidence and balance beyond anything I'd previously demonstrated and also beyond anything I'd thought I could reasonably expect. Unable to feel my feet and legs, I still had to stand in my callipers, obviously, and incline forwards just enough to avoid falling helplessly – and catastrophically – on my back. But it was also a case of fine-tuning. If I leaned too far forward I'd put too much stress on my arms and be unable to complete my allotted fifteen minutes. From the side I looked a bit like a tall leather triangle, with my crutches about eighteen inches in front of my feet and placed about two feet apart.

For my first session, Tadge obligingly stood behind me to ensure I didn't fall backwards and to help me appreciate my new centre of balance. It's impossible to describe quite how weird and scary it is standing up when you can't feel your legs and feet. But it was a sensation I not only had to get used to, but also, were I to do it, to 'read'. On the second day of standing, Tadge positioned himself in front of me, gently nudging me from side to side, in order to encourage me to learn the small corrective adjustments to my stance that would keep me from keeling straight over.

On the third day, he had a *tour de force* surprise. Having got me into my usual standing position, he opened the gym door to admit two five-a-side football teams (his rehab group) who proceeded to practise their ball skills around me. Alarmed, I yelled, 'What am I supposed to do now?'

'Never mind them,' Tadge replied, grinning. 'You just concentrate on staying upright.'

As the ball kept approaching, two things became clear. One was that I was seriously frightened, and two (perhaps as a result of the first) was that I was probably better off dealing with the ball rather than running the risk of a player – or most probably two of them – bundling into me in pursuit of the thing. I therefore devised a ploy of knocking it away with one crutch while simultaneously transferring my balance to the other. This, of course, though he'd not said a word, was exactly what Tadge had had in mind.

I settled into Chessington life well and swiftly, and central to that were the people I met. As well as those who had had accidents of a 'civilian' nature (road accidents, neck injuries from diving or, on occasion, falling down drunk) there were many horrific stories of service-related injuries, particularly from the horrors of Ulster.

Tiny, for instance – so named because he was a Goliath of a man at six feet eight tall – had been the driver of a Land Rover which had been dispatched to a local school, where there'd been a report of a bomb. There wasn't any bomb; it had simply been a trap, and when he opened the rear door to let out the troops, a car pulled up and several masked gunmen opened fire. Tiny instinctively spread his body across the rear opening and took the majority of the bullets. By the time I met him in Chessington he'd made a good physical recovery but mentally still had a long way to go. He couldn't and didn't ever talk about the incident, and that part of his rehab would clearly be difficult and slow. Others had lost limbs or the sight of an eye, invariably through isolated sniper action. What they all – so cruelly damaged – had in common was their youth. Not one of them was over twenty-five.

I soon fell into a comfortable routine at Chessington: the weekly timetable of exercise and socialising, followed by weekends of rest and tranquillity back at home. It was almost like living a parallel life, quite away from the rigours of the real world. But the real world was about to intrude. On 2 April 1982, Argentine forces invaded the Falklands.

It was a Friday, so Mum and Dad came up to collect me as usual and we spent the weekend anxiously following the action on the other side of the world. In light of what had happened, I'd been asked to report back at the earlier time of 8.30 a.m. the following Monday. By now it was clear that a task force was being deployed and the atmosphere at Chessington changed markedly. On arrival that morning we could see straight away that security had been massively racked up. For the first time, I was issued with a security

pass and they took Mum and Dad's car registration. A flurry
of signatures followed.

Though my own programme of activity wasn't affected,
there was a clear increase of obviously military activity at the
base. Where I'd been mildly disappointed on first arriving
to find the much anticipated 'young men in uniform'
conspicuous by their absence (like Tadge, almost everyone
wore PE kit), I was now seeing uniformed men drilling on
the parade grounds. A double-edged pleasure; these men
were preparing for action. There was a palpable tension in
camp. The lads who previously tended to watch TV for
anything other than the news were now suddenly glued to
the unfolding drama.

Not that anyone was expecting an immediate increase in
servicemen wounded in action. The initial part of the task
force set sail on 5 April, and it would take some time before
they engaged with the invasion force. Even so, plans were
clearly being set. In all likelihood, any casualties would first
be taken to Aldershot Military Hospital and only transferred to Chessington once the initial acute treatment had
been completed.

For a while it seemed the casualty count would be low, but
then, on 4 May, *HMS Sheffield* was hit by an Exocet missile.
Twenty were killed and many others wounded, and suddenly
the reality of the horror was driven home. And as if I personally needed a reminder of the significance of the date, on
Monday 10 May – the second anniversary of my accident –
Argentina declared the entire South Atlantic a war zone.

Eighteen days later, there was fierce action led by Colonel
H. Jones (posthumously awarded a Victoria Cross) that

Wearing my St. David's Day costume in my parents' garden, aged 5. Silly hat (trad.), itchy shawl (trad.) and wellies (inspirational?).

Playing mini-golf in Stanley Park on holiday in Blackpool, aged 10. Ah, the memorable hole in one.

Modelling at the Glanafan School Fashion Show, spring 1980. I'm the one in the middle and Juli is standing behind me.

In St. Mark's Square, Venice, with Mum and Dad – such wonderful people.

The model student outside the front door of number one The Uplands, revising for my 'O' levels and getting a tan.

Outside RAF Chessington with Corporal Lynne McLevie, 1982.

Relaxing and rehydrating with Bernard Williams in the bar at the Washington Convention of the American Syringomyelia Alliance Project, 1992. Lectures work up a tremendous thirst.

My Mortitia Adams look for hit-woman Polythene Pam in the film *Kiss Kiss (Bang Bang)*, 2000.

Our Wedding Day, St. Theodore's Church, Port Talbot, Saturday 2 October 2004. Church, flowers, white wedding-dress, husband – the best day of my life.

A dream come true.

Flanked by two gorgeous men, hubby and the lovely Gwyn Jones, when filming for the TREAT Trust Wales DVD at Neath Rugby Club, 2006.

Mike's turn to be the lucky one with me and the beautiful Dame Tanni Grey-Thompson when filming for the TREAT Trust Wales DVD at the National Indoor Athletics Centre, UWIC, Cardiff, 2006.

'Hullo, good evening and welcome.' With the delectable Michael Sheen (taking a break from appearing as David Frost in *Frost/Nixon* at the Donmar Warehouse Theatre, London) filming for the TREAT Trust Wales DVD at the Aspire Centre, Stanmore, Middlesex, 2006.

Life is good! Mike and I whooping it up in our back garden, summer 2007.

successfully retook Goose Green. Sixteen other British para-troopers died, and among the casualties was one who subsequently joined us at Chessington. He told us the terrifying tale of having taken a bullet in the arm and lying wounded with his fallen comrades surrounding him. And then he heard the chilling sound of the Argentine troops all around. They were inspecting the fallen to check who was dead and then shooting any survivors. He had to lie there and play dead for fourteen hours.

By the end of that month the war had escalated greatly, with, ironically for me, many Welsh Guards involved. Over a scant three-day period at the beginning of June, scores of British troops had been killed or injured, and many of the latter were bound for Chessington. Having watched events unfold on TV day by day, we were all braced for horribly burned casualties. And they certainly came. Most of the burns victims were Welsh Guards from the *Sir Galahad* and the *Sir Tristram*. They wore identifying badges and were treated with enormous respect by everyone at Chessington. The burns themselves were a gruesomely arresting sight: faces with features destroyed, one or both hands with fingers deformed and contracted into fists, flayed legs and feet with destroyed stumps of toes. All were on show for the world at large to see: in order to protect them while still monitoring progress, these horrific injuries were encased in clear plastic bags.

The function room in the NAAFI had by now been fully converted into a dining room to accommodate the greatly swelled numbers. It was here that I first met Steve. I'd gone in to buy a sandwich rather than making the haul

up to the SMC for my lunch and he was in the queue
three places ahead. He was gorgeous – so much so that I
couldn't take my eyes off him; he was one of the best-look-
ing guys I'd seen at Chessington yet. Despite his being
with a group of burned guardsmen, I could see nothing
obviously wrong with him apart from a burned hand in
the usual plastic bag. Hearing him speaking to his mates
I could tell he was Welsh (and, incredibly, as it turned out
when we talked, from a place only twelve miles from my
home). But even having seen what I'd seen I wasn't
remotely prepared for the sight that greeted me as he
turned around. The whole left side of his face looked like
a lump of molten plastic, barely recognisable as human.
His ear had been wholly burned off, he had no eyebrow,
and his livid scalp was dotted with just the odd tuft of
hair. My face must have told him what my mouth could
not utter, because he smiled at me and said, with heart-
breaking politeness, 'I'm sorry if I've put you off your
sandwich.'

'Not at all,' I answered quickly, feeling awed. 'In fact, do
you mind if I join you?'

What a contrast, I thought, as he and his mates and I
chatted. I'd gone looking for pleasure on the back of a
motorbike. They'd gone to do a job and been bushwhacked
in the trying. I was humbled by them all; not just for their
courage, but for the fact they were all so pleasant and
uncomplaining. True heroes, who'd paid an awful price. If
I got anything from Chessington, I realised right then, it
would definitely include the unparalleled honour of having
known and spent time with such men.

Not every man at Chessington was a hero, however, as I was about to find out.

The prospect of being in a predominantly male environment had not really fazed me before coming, and the reality had borne out my confidence. Indeed, I was enjoying it. I'd always liked the company and attention of boys, and though I'd done a fair bit of soul searching since the accident (I couldn't bear the thought that men who'd previously turned their heads as I'd pass would now look at me out of pity or curiosity) I was now as comfortable in my skin around them as ever. But only up to a point. Having expected male interest in me to decline now I was in a wheelchair, I'd been pleased and surprised to discover that it hadn't; I soon learned that men seemed not to mind if a girl was sitting or standing – if they thought she was pretty they seemed perfectly happy. But this in itself was hardly enough. Like any other girl of my age I wanted to be wooed. I still fancied guys and, as an incurable romantic, of course I wanted someone to hold me. But with that desire came the terrifying realisation that someone close enough to me to want to take me in his arms would also be close enough to want to know more about me – including all the bits I really didn't want to share.

My fear of physical intimacy wasn't just about embarrassment. In a male-orientated environment like Chessington I knew that if my situation – my lack of sensation from the chest down – became known, it would be all around the camp in no time. The horrible thought that someone could interfere with me and I wouldn't be able to feel it played on my mind all the time. And it seemed I had good reason to feel vulnerable.

It was a warm summer night and I'd spent an enjoyable evening outside the NAAFI with a group of Welsh Guards. As the light began to fade – it was approaching ten o'clock – I decided to call it a night and head back up the hill to the SMC and bed. By now it was no longer a struggle. As I made my way across from the NAAFI and started up the bottom of the hill, I became conscious of someone behind me. This was nothing particularly unusual, of course, but for some reason I felt slightly uncomfortable. A little further up he drew level with me and asked if I happened to have a light. I turned to see an army private I recognised, a short lad who'd been pestering me on and off all evening, and to whom I'd given not a shred of encouragement. Suddenly he grabbed the front of my wheelchair and pulled it up on to the grass verge.

'What are you doing?' I demanded, but he was quick with his answer. He was just being careful, he said. It was to stop my wheelchair from rolling back down the hill while he lit his cigarette and we had 'a little chat'. I already knew he was a lot the worse for drink, but things suddenly felt scarily sinister. I told him, trying to keep my voice clear and strong, that I didn't want to chat and that I really had to go. I doubted he'd be stupid enough to try anything on because the lights of the SMC were only twenty yards ahead, and I could also hear the chatter floating up from the NAAFI. But he was obviously stupider or drunker than I realised. Seconds later, he'd moved round to the rear of my chair and tipped me out backwards onto the damp grass. Within an instant he was lying on top of me and scrabbling at my clothing, obviously intent on a grope, if not more. I knew I had stronger arms than he did and struggled hard, but with his face right on mine he breathed into my ear: 'Don't waste your time. I know you can't kick me.'

I realised my only recourse was shouting and screaming, and if medals could've been won for sheer volume that night I would definitely have got the gold. Next thing I knew he was lifted bodily off me by a female corporal – one I knew, who was a nurse in the SMC.

'Don't you dare move!' she barked at him – and clearly now poleaxed, he didn't – while she dusted me down, helped me back into my chair and asked whether I was okay to continue to my room. That established, she turned to the hapless miscreant, bellowed, 'You're charged!' and frog-marched him off to the guardroom.

I made a statement, he *was* charged, and that was the end of it – I neither knew nor much cared what the actual charge was. I just thought it very sad and ironic that among so many heroes, this lad, with his relatively minor, off-duty injury, should have been the one to try such a thing.

The Falklands conflict ended on 14 June, but the violence of the Troubles continued. That summer saw two major IRA attacks in London. A nail bomb in Hyde Park killed two soldiers as they made their way from Knightsbridge Barracks to Buckingham Palace, and injured twenty-three other members of the Household Cavalry. Seven horses were either killed outright or maimed so horrifically that they had to be destroyed. Then a second device, under a bandstand at Regent's Park, killed another six soldiers from the Royal Greenjackets Band, and injured a further twenty-four people. The Falklands War might have reached a conclusion, but when would all this ever end?

I stayed (bar the above incident, happily) at Chessington till 10 September 1982. Far from being a sojourn *away* from the real world, the place, its soldiers and everything that surrounded it made me feel very much *in* it. Mr Davies, though right in almost all things, had been wrong. It hadn't felt like Rookwood at all.

chapter 14

Post-RAF Chessington, I felt ready for anything. Ready to put my newly acquired strength to good use, and ready to take on the world.

Indeed, now that I'd had a taste of what was out there I was champing at the bit for more. My eighteenth birthday had fallen in the middle of my time there and Mum and Dad had given me the best surprise imaginable. They'd secretly arranged for me to have two weeks' leave of absence and, in an impressively executed covert operation, had booked for us all to go to Florida. We were to spend five days in Orlando and then five in Clearwater, a resort on the Gulf of Mexico. As trips went, this would be no small adventure. This was the early eighties and flying halfway around the world was not something the majority of people did yet. Though Walt Disney World – a planned highlight, obviously – had been open for just over a decade by now, travelling there was something only very well-heeled Brits could afford. Naturally, I felt incredibly lucky.

As a family, this was a first. None of us had ventured such a distance before. Indeed, Mum and I had only just completed our first trip abroad (to Lourdes), and none of us had ever travelled by air. But Mum and Dad had researched the trip well. America was chosen because it stood head and shoulders above any other destination in the provisions it had in place for the disabled: accessible toilets, ramps, lifts, and everything we needed.

The country, as I'd thought it might, beguiled me. Life as a paraplegic there couldn't have been more different from my experience of living life in a wheelchair at home. Florida, specifically, had been a revelation; it had allowed me, for the first time, to live. It was the most accessible place imaginable; I rarely, if ever, had to stop and think twice about whether I could get where I wanted to go, and, more importantly, go entirely independently. America quickly carved a place in my heart and I knew I'd return there again and again.

Back in the UK, I looked at my situation with fresh eyes and, once I'd left Chessington, learning to drive became my number one goal. As I'd already long since found out for myself, for a paraplegic in eighties' Britain, driving wasn't a privilege – it was an absolute necessity. There was barely any other way to get around.

Buses, for example, were totally inaccessible. Though in today's world there are a few around with low floors and ramps, back then there were none whatsoever in South Wales. Which left me with two options, taxis or trains.

Though many of today's black cabs are equipped to take wheelchair passengers, in the eighties most weren't (and besides, have you ever tried to hail a London cab from a sitting position?). Not that we had black cabs in Port Talbot anyway. Our local mini-cabs were invariably saloon cars. In theory these could manage both me and my chair, but in practice not all did. Though this, of course, wasn't the main point. Who could afford to go everywhere by taxi? Not me, for sure.

Trains were cheaper but, again, complicated for me to access. Though by the time of my accident there had been improvements in disabled provision (we were no longer expected to travel in the guards van, for instance) planning any sort of train trip was complex and frustrating, and not necessarily reliable. I'd already had some experience of this as, not long after I returned from Chessington, we'd bravely attempted to make a trip up to London to visit my cousin Francine.

Back then, disabled passengers were required to book forty-eight hours in advance so that a seat could be removed from a carriage in order to accommodate their wheelchair. (In some cases, as I was later to find out, enthusiastic staff whipped out the table as well, which not only meant you had nothing to hang on to, but also left the idea of getting a coffee from the buffet a decidedly courageous decision – unless you were keen on wearing your beverages, of course.) It was important that we chose our timings carefully to ensure there would be staff to assist. At Port Talbot station this was vital, as the platform was a central island between the two rail tracks and the only way for me to access it – given that I couldn't use the footbridge above it – was to join the road traffic and push across the eastbound line where it crossed the street at the level crossing up the road. That done, a member of staff needed to unlock the platform gate so I could push myself up the steep ramp at the end and, once the train arrived, bring out and set up a portable ramp and so get me on board.

But this was only a prelude to the main event, which was the reality of being on transport that wasn't equipped to deal with me. I couldn't use either the corridors (too narrow) or the toilet (no disabled ones) so the question of coffee was probably academic, but the main stress was whether there'd be anyone at Paddington to reverse the procedure we'd used for getting on. Again, later experience proved that this wasn't something to rely on in a crisis.

All of these problems were ones that wouldn't have crossed my mind for an instant prior to my accident (why would they, for any able-bodied person?) but now they loomed large in my day-to-day life, principally because they were stopping me from living it.

In 1981 we'd moved to a new house in Connaught Street, and the change for me had been transformational. We'd chosen it because it was not only close to the town centre and my new school but also, thankfully, on the flat. Where once I'd looked down at the town far below me, now I looked up to the looming bulk of the mountain. But I didn't mind. The lack of a commanding view was a small price to pay for the chance to be in command of my own life. Transport difficulties notwithstanding, I'd already begun to enjoy a taste of this. The situation of our new home had been a great choice. From Connaught Street I could get to all sorts of places: to the park with my German shepherd dog, Max; to the three local pubs; to Aberavon Rugby Club (just three streets away); and to the paper shop, video store and bakery nearby. Stuck indoors I most definitely wasn't.

Which was just as well, because life was getting busy. The civil legal action suit concerning the accident was being prepared and I was having increasingly regular meetings with my solicitor, in which it seemed I had to answer the same questions time and time again to get the facts absolutely straight. Aldo had admitted liability for the accident from the outset but with spinal injury it can be up to two and a half years before the full medical prognosis is clear and that was partly responsible for the delay. A QC had been appointed and we'd already received an interim payment from Aldo's insurance company to cover the cost of moving house. Once I'd passed my driving test, there would be a further payment to allow me to purchase a small car.

But first I had to learn how to drive one.

One of the highlights at Chessington had been a trip to Wimbledon to go on the driving simulator there. This was a regular feature for personnel being rehabilitated, as a lot of the injuries seen at Chessington involved physical impairments that might have an impact on reaction times and fitness to drive, and a simulator test could assess these. After I told Tadge how keen I was to learn to drive, I was thrilled to be allowed to take such a test, which I thoroughly enjoyed and, most importantly, passed.

Having done so, and in possession of a certificate to confirm it, I had to find a driving school that could cater for my very specific requirements. The car needed to have automatic transmission and hand controls (a lever on the steering column linked to both accelerator and brake – pulling up activates the former, pushing down, the latter), and the instructor needed to be qualified to teach the use of them. Happily I found one, not too far away in Swansea, and my driving instruction was soon underway.

Driving, I soon realised, was going to matter to me hugely. For starters, it was fun. Much better, for example, than riding pillion on a motorbike, with your face being dive-bombed by fast-moving flies and your hair all squished up in a helmet. Behind the wheel of a car I could look pretty. But more important than that was the sense of belonging. Of not being different from everyone else. Behind the wheel of a car I *was* like everyone else. No one knew I couldn't stand or walk. (Although this didn't extend to buying petrol. Many were the times – and it still sometimes happens – that I'd be parked at a petrol pump with Mum, Dad, or whoever, and some seconds would elapse before they'd twig that I couldn't actually leap out and get it. Which, when I thought about it, was really rather nice.)

I took to driving like a duck takes to water, and through the winter of 1982/83 my dozen or so weekly lessons after school were deemed sufficient that I should apply for a test date. In early March, having taken and passed it, I was the proud-as-punch holder of a full UK licence and I was every bit as excited as a child on Christmas morning when they get their first whiff of turkey.

The next step was to hunt down a suitable small car, with a not terribly big budget. It certainly didn't run to the levels of the powder blue BMW a girl in the sixth form had just taken ownership of, but then I really didn't need grand and pricey. I just wanted more wheels than I already had, and (for a change) some engine power to drive them.

Small cars with automatic transmission were, then as now, not that easy to pin down, but eventually our search led us to a Ford Escort Ghia in metallic sky blue, which the local dealer was able to adapt for me. Thus by early May it really *did* feel like Christmas; I was independently mobile for the first time since the accident.

Mobile and raring to go. Like any self-respecting teenager, I had attitude, and here was the means to express it. I was, safe to say, a right poser. I drove with the window down at every opportunity, and was able to serenade my fellow citizens in Port Talbot with the musical delights of the day. My tastes were eclectic and depended on my mood. One day it would be the likes of Meat Loaf, Queen and Jim Steinman, another Neil Diamond and Barry Manilow. But now I had an extra four wheels at my disposal, I didn't just stay in Port Talbot. I went on day trips to Porthcawl and Swansea with my mates and did shopping-and-show jaunts to Cardiff. Basically, if I could drive there, I went there. My car also gave me an opportunity to say thanks to Mum and Dad; I took them far and wide for endless lunches.

But, as was becoming the pattern, it seemed my enjoyment of my car was to come with a price tag. Though my efforts in building up my arms and shoulders had achieved their objectives, my repeated exertions hauling my chair into and out of my car were beginning to take their toll on my left shoulder. As that summer went on, increasing pain and stiffness made me reluctantly concede that things weren't as they should be, and submit to another appointment with Mr Davies at the orthopaedic clinic in Neath General.

I thought he'd have his frown on, but he was really quite nice, congratulating me on how well he could see I'd done at Chessington and sympathising with the less welcome consequences of getting myself so independent.

The solution, too, seemed straightforward. I could go in as a day case and have manipulation of my shoulder under anaesthetic. Together with a big hydrocortisone injection, he thought that would probably do the trick. I was readmitted to Ward Eight one morning soon after and kitted out in one of their familiar operation gowns.

I drifted off quickly and, as usual, before I knew it, I was waking up in the recovery room. I opened my eyes to find my consultant standing by my bed. His previous cheery face had been replaced by his stern one. Yes, he said, he was impressed by my upper body fitness, but it was important that he also made me understand the need to steer a middle course between total indolence (at which I bridled – not my style at all) and aggressive, Miss Universe-type muscle building.

Back on the ward, his words duly digested, I had just got myself dressed and back from bed to wheelchair when he appeared on his post-operative round.

'What on *earth* do you think you're doing?' he demanded crossly, striding towards me with his coat tails all a-flapping.

'I'm a day case,' I replied sweetly, 'so I'm getting ready to go home.'

'How did you get up out of that bed?' he wanted to know, obviously not terribly impressed. 'And did you have any help ...' his eyes began to narrow and he pointed, 'getting yourself into that wheelchair?'

I shook my head. 'No,' I said, sensing the growing rumble of disapproval. 'I managed it quite comfortably myself.'

He glared, and then, in his best Basil Fawlty voice, boomed, 'I thought I'd explained to you in theatre after the procedure that you'd need to treat that shoulder with some *care*!'

'But …' I began.

'Care and *respect*. Not rush straight back to everything like a bull at a gate. Yet, within hours, you're doing triceps extensions, using your whole body as the weight!'

'But I only got up,' I tried. 'I thought you'd be pleased.'

He looked around for moral support from someone else, but there were no nurses or junior doctors to be seen. He sank down on the chair beside the bed I'd just vacated. 'You know what?' he said. 'I'd have thought, *really* thought, that you'd have seen more than enough of me by now.' He looked challengingly at me. 'Well, haven't you?'

I wasn't quite sure how to respond, but I didn't need to. 'Do you,' he continued, 'think you could *please* try to look after things? Not do too much? Not go mad? Not end up back *here* again, basically – for *both* our sakes, Melanie. I do my best, but I cannot work miracles.'

I felt sorry for him by now. He looked a bit desperate. So I flashed him my very best coy sidelong glance. 'If I promise to do as I'm told,' I asked him nicely, 'can we still be friends?'

He stood up and retreated, nodding nervously.

I watched him go, conscious that he felt I'd let him down. Only very slightly – he really didn't need to make *quite* that much fuss – but even so, I took his words on board. I would take care of my shoulder and I wouldn't be coming back.

Or, at that point, so I thought …

chapter 15

In common, I imagine, with any other eighteen-year-old girl, there were lots of things I wanted out of life. As a paraplegic, I knew many of them were closed to me now. I'd done my share of soul searching about all the things I couldn't have or do. But that didn't stop me from dreaming.

I had, as I was quick to remind myself whenever I felt low, achieved a great deal in an incredibly short time. And fundamental to my well-being was my sense of achievement in gaining and maintaining my independence. And fundamental to *that* was the confidence that came from feeling I had control over my body.

Not something the average eighteen-year-old dwells on, obviously, but to me it was all. I knew that medical opinion frowned on my continued reliance on an in-dwelling catheter; how could I not? I'd had it drummed into me at Rookwood often enough. And to be fair, this was perfectly reasonable. I'd succumbed to infection there on more than one occasion, and though I was rigorous about cleanliness and drinking vast quantities of liquid (flushing it through regularly was an important part of the hygiene regime), I knew I was always at risk from serious infection and could even risk shortening my life. But I'd thought long and hard and was comfortable with that. Far more comfortable than with the prospect of returning to sitting in wet nappies. It seemed to me immensely more important to have quality of life than to live a longer one in which I hated every minute.

And I was having quality of life now. A guy called Richard, one of Aldo's biking friends, had been so appalled by my accident that he'd immediately sold his bike and instead bought a car. Richard had been a regular visitor at Rookwood, and had continued to visit me often. And though I doubt the two were exclusively correlated, he also made it clear that, just as soon as I felt ready, he'd be there any time I wanted to be taken out for an evening. Plus he'd do the driving, so I could let my hair down. I don't know if he was hoping that I'd let my hair down so far that I'd suddenly find myself romantically attracted to him – it never happened – but I really valued his friendship. He was kind and thoughtful, and through him my social circle expanded considerably. I'd achieved what I'd hoped for during the dark times at Rookwood – I was once again a part of normal life among friends. With that, very pleasingly, came all of life's normal relationships. I was surprised and flattered to know that among this number were several men who were romantically interested in me. But despite my bravado in public around men, I simply couldn't see this happening. I knew that at the end of every lovely evening out I'd be returning to the very private world of a paraplegic. The catheter and leg bags were for my eyes only, and I couldn't imagine a scenario where that might change.

But the chief obstacle to my enjoying the normality I craved was not my bladder but my bowels. Though it was true that by now the management of my bodily functions felt almost as normal to me as breathing, the reality of attending to the latter would not, I'm sure, be high on anyone's list of 'fun and fulfilling things to do'. The stark truth is that a person's waste management, to be politely euphemistic about it, is not something many of us would willingly want to share with the rest of the world. Yet the threat of this was my constant anxiety.

Dealing with my bowels was straightforward. I would insert a suppository, await the results, deal with them, clear up, and continue with my day – not pleasant, but something that just had to be got on with. But as anyone who has ever suffered a bout of holiday tummy will all too readily imagine, a person's digestive physiology isn't always 100 per cent reliable. Bowels are autonomous, and accidents do sometimes happen.

Given that this is a subject that's perhaps difficult to read about (and, indeed, for me to write about), it takes no small leap of imagination to realise the actuality is a thousand times worse. If you could think of the most embarrassing thing that could ever happen to you and then have that something be a real possibility, not just once but on every single day of your life, then you'll have some idea of the scale of my stress about it all. And if the unthinkable wasn't to happen to me in public, my bowels needed constant policing. Being unable to feel the unmistakable sensation of needing to rush to the toilet, I had only one method of minimising risk and that was to be rigorous about when and what I ate.

As our group was in the habit of going for impromptu Chinese and Indian meals, I was constantly having to make excuses about why I wasn't eating – the truth being that I feared the effects of spicy food on my gut. As a mature woman, such excuses perhaps wouldn't have been needed, but I was eighteen and as self-conscious as any other eighteen-year-old, and could no more make light of such matters as run down the street to catch a bus.

It felt strange that as I entered my fourth year as a paraplegic, my not being able to walk, though excruciatingly limiting, was easier to tolerate than a gut that might function autonomously without warning. Indeed, the indignity of this possibility occurring overwhelmed me. Leaving aside the limitations it placed on my simple social interactions, the crushingly embarrassing effect it might have on any burgeoning romantic situation was unimaginable.

Yet love, quite naturally, was a constant in the air. Juli had recently become engaged to her boyfriend Chris and was busy planning their upcoming wedding. Observing this, and all the other relationships blossoming around me, was exquisitely painful. So, while on the outside I was always lively and bouncy, inside I was desperately lonely.

I knew I needed to find a solution. I just hadn't worked out what it was. By happy coincidence, however, I was thumbing through a women's magazine one morning when I came across an article about colostomy. It featured a number of people, including a member of the royal family and several entertainers, for whom the operation had been a great success. Convinced I'd at last found the means of liberation, I tore out the page and called to Mum and Dad.

'Look,' I said excitedly, 'I want one of those.' It's not every young girl who when questioned about their dreams would say, 'To have my bowel removed, please.' But I knew this was the answer to a much less stressful future. All I had to do was convince a kindly doctor.

I rang our GP the same day. As he was the doctor who'd been prepared to depart from orthodoxy in relation to my catheter, he was, as I'd hoped, sympathetic. Though he told me I'd have to discuss it at some length with an appropriate surgeon – after all, it wasn't like having your wisdom teeth out. He recommended a surgeon called Mr Chare at Neath General and said he'd refer me forthwith.

Things happened quickly after that. I prepared my case well (I was, after all, asking a surgeon to remove a perfectly healthy bowel from a very young woman) and listened carefully to all the possible complications. These were serious and many. The operation was one of considerable magnitude and not one I should undergo lightly. The procedure was not without hazard, either surgically or anaesthetically, and there were a number of potential later complications as well. But having sailed through two major ops under the hands of Mr Davies, I felt confident and ready to confront all the dangers, not least because now I had a solution within reach I was simply not prepared to carry on with my life in the way I had been until now.

After a two-week period in which I was instructed to think long and hard about whether I definitely wanted to go through with it (this was sensibly mandatory, but in my case superfluous) and several meetings to discuss my post-operative anatomy and management with Sister Fay Hastings,

who was a stoma care nurse, my operation was finally scheduled for 1 March 1984. If I'd needed any last reminders about
why this major bout of surgery was the right course of action,
that need was amply satisfied by my pre-op (and final) bowel
evacuation. Oh the joys of that procedure! For the ambulant,
this is bad enough in itself; up go the powerful suppositories
and a short while later on comes the need for an urgent dash
for the loo. I'm not sure anyone thought long and hard about
the fact that I wasn't about to be dashing anywhere, but there
seemed almost a purpose in the purgatory I suffered as a
consequence of mine having been inserted only shortly
before my last posse of pre-op visitors were admitted. Sitting
clutching myself and praying, while pretending all was well,
I knew that even were I to die on the operating table tomorrow, it would be preferable to what I was going through
then.

So it was that, on the morning list on St David's Day, my
life was changed forever once again. I returned from theatre
to the ward, now the proud possessor of a left iliac terminal
colostomy. From this moment on, the results of my digestive process would end up not as an unpleasant daily duty
and cause of major anguish but, via my stoma, instead
empty into a sterile and private and manageable pouch
system, which would finally give me real freedom, of both
the practical and emotional kind.

And not before time. On one of my outings with Richard,
I'd been introduced to his friend Maurice, with whom I
immediately got on very well. We soon became close and at
last I began to feel that I wasn't going to have to live my
romantic life outside looking in after all. Though Maurice

was two decades older than me, he wasn't at all like a father figure. I had one of those already. I soon felt I could confide in Maurice about more of my personal situation than anyone else I'd ever met. He'd been hugely supportive at the time of my surgery and with both of us in celebratory mood afterwards, we made the decision to take our first holiday together – to Florida, which was a big step for us both.

The holiday was duly booked for July, but fate had something else up her sleeve. My long, drawn-out compensation case was finally settled in spring 1984 and, what with that and my wonderful new anatomy, things were looking brighter than ever. I'd been able to organise some modifications to the house to make it more wheelchair-friendly (a lift to the upstairs being principal among them) and my social life was blooming. One of my newer friends – whom I'd got to know via Maurice – was a guy called Alun, who worked as a postman. Given his working hours, I often used to meet up with him for lunch. He was gay, so no threat to my relationship with Maurice, and also fun and flamboyant company.

On this particular day, we'd been out in Port Talbot and were giving Dave, another friend, a lift back home to nearby Baglan in my car. We were travelling on the short, two-lane section of the M4 motorway there, when a black Golf pulled out suddenly from the nearside lane, straight in front of us. Despite a fierce amount of emergency braking, I could see the inevitability of what was about to happen; with no space between us, we ploughed violently straight into the back of it. Knowing Alun habitually refused to wear his seatbelt – as people often did back then, he would only pay lip service to the new law by holding it across his body – I instinctively flung out my left arm to protect him. The gesture, however well meant, was pretty pointless at the speed we were travelling and he catapulted forwards onto the dash. Being legally without a belt myself (I had been exempted because of the potentially serious consequences of whiplash to my neck and upper spine) I too was thrown forward; my head went straight through the windscreen, my chest hit the steering wheel and as my car did a perfect concertina against the Golf, both my legs broke, effectively pinning me in.

While all this was happening, I was overtaken by David, who'd been travelling in the back seat. He became lodged between the front seats, where, milliseconds later (fate having decided to let him off but punish him all the same) he was thumped between the shoulders by my wheelchair, which had been thrown forwards from the boot.

As an illustration of why the current seatbelt laws are in place, it could not have been better. Though my own progress through the windscreen had been arrested by my legs, both Alun and I were incredibly lucky not to have been killed by either David or my chair. As it was, the gods had been kind to us that day, and we spent the next few moments simply staring out in stupefaction while the driver of the Golf got out of his own car and started walking round in circles on the carriageway. At least, I remember thinking, *he* seemed okay.

Dave, his thoughts finally collected, managed to push my chair out on to the road, but before he could address moving himself we were deafened by Alun, who was clearly hysterical. 'Oh, f**king hell, Mel! Oh f**king hell, Mel! Oh f**king hell, Mel!' he screamed, over and over again, while clambering frantically out onto the road, where he immediately started running about, screaming and wildly waving his hands. Dave, by now reasonably composed, and having checked I was too, clambered out and went to try and calm Alun down. Words only seemed to make him worse, though, so in the end Dave just grabbed him and, after apologising politely, slapped him once across the face, which seemed to do the trick. He offered up one last high-pitched shriek to the heavens, then collapsed in an untidy heap.

By this time, a couple of ambulances had arrived and two crew members came and assessed me. I was bleeding freely from a cut on my brow, but in other respects seemed okay. I told them that I'd broken my back and couldn't walk and that I'd need my wheelchair. Puzzled, they looked again at my head and my legs. At this stage I had no idea the latter were broken because I couldn't see or feel them. Consequently I had no idea that my right tibia was sticking out through the skin, nor that my right foot had been turned inwards through a right angle. They, however, *had* seen them, and obviously thought it was this that had prompted me to say what I had. They tried to enlighten me.

'No,' I said, 'you don't understand. I'm paralysed.'

'No, love,' one of them took pains to explain. 'You've had a bump on the head and we're taking you to hospital. We'll have you up on your feet again in no time.'

Too fraught to argue, I was lifted onto a stretcher and carried past Alun towards an ambulance. By this time he was just recovering from his faint, but as soon as he saw the state of my right leg he promptly passed out again. Once in the ambulance I reiterated my need for my wheelchair, but no one seemed to be listening any more and it remained on the carriageway until Dave was able to retrieve it and stow it on the ambulance that was to transport him and Alun.

Meanwhile, my own ambulance crew seemed ever more concerned about my continuing bizarre requests for wheelchairs. As an alternative to blaming my head injury (or perhaps just to pass the time) they now wanted to know if perhaps I'd taken 'substances'.

On arrival at Neath General Hospital A & E, things quickly went from slightly comic to farcical. The nurses, like the ambulance crew, were also at pains to reassure me that they'd (again) 'have me up on my feet in no time'. Were it not so frustrating being so comprehensively not listened to, it would have been hilarious. 'A quick visit to X-ray and something for the pain,' one jauntily informed me, 'and we'll have that leg in plaster and you up on a pair of crutches and you'll be back at home before you know it.' Did they not notice I wasn't screaming in agony?

'No, I won't,' I said, as politely as I could manage. 'I have a broken back, I am a *pa-ra-pleg-ic*, which means I am confined to a *wheel-chair*.'

The nurse smiled brightly and then spoke to another. 'They were right,' she said, presumably referring to the crew. 'She *has* had a bad bang on the head. She's obsessed.'

Fired up now, I decided to unleash my hidden ace. 'Is Mr Davies on duty?' I asked. 'Or Mr Kamal?'

The nurses looked confused now. 'How do you know them?'

'Because they were the surgeons who looked after me. When I broke my back. Back in *nineteen eighty*.'

But the pleasure of finally getting my point across was a short-lived one. The nurses consulted the casualty officer, who confirmed that Mr Davies was on call. Uh-oh, I thought. Now I'm in trouble. Up until this point, though worried about my wheelchair (I didn't at that point know it was safe) I'd been happy and relieved. Pleased that my arms worked, my neck was uninjured and my head (whatever they thought) was going to be all right. But, I suddenly realised, my legs were an issue. All the long conversations about me standing for an hour every day loomed fearfully large in my head. I was still doing so daily – would I now have to give that up? I knew I was about to get a row from him that would hurt way more than any of my physical injuries.

Then there was a whisper – 'Mr Davies is on his way' – and absolutely everyone seemed to freeze. In the silence you could almost hear his coat-tails flapping. He came in clutching my X-ray films. He peered at my legs. He looked cross. 'What,' he asked, 'have you done *this* time?'

But he didn't seem to want a reply, because he immediately started issuing instructions to all and sundry, before sweeping out just as magisterially as he'd entered. Just before he left, though, he turned and frowned at me. 'And,' he said, 'I'll see YOU on the ward.'

* * *

Though the setting and plastering didn't cause my numb legs any pain, I did suffer from my old bedfellow, autonomic dysreflexia, which caused the rise in blood pressure and resultant thumping headache I'd had on previous occasions when there was something wrong below the site of my spinal cord injury. It left me in no fit state to be greeted by a police officer, demanding that I now take a breath test. I knew I'd be clear – I hadn't drunk any alcohol – but the medical staff were incensed. He was bundled away after it had been made clear to him that he was definitely exceeding his duties.

All of which had been quite enough excitement for one day. My parents were on their way (again), I'd been told Alun was safe and well and on his way home and, as David had earlier trotted past me and told me himself that he was fine, I assumed that, bar my poor car and a tedious period in plaster, that was the end of it. It was odd, therefore, when on my way to Ward Eight (again) I was passed by a trolley on which David lay, apparently on his way to X-ray.

'Stop!' I called out. Our trolleys convened. 'What,' I asked, perplexed, 'are you doing on *there*?'

'Ah,' he said, sounding a bit sheepish. 'I was so pleased to come out of such a huge accident unscathed that I had this, erm, sort of adrenaline rush, and, um … karate-kicked the A & E doors.'

I was speechless. He grinned. 'They think I might have broken my ankle.'

They were absolutely right. He had, too.

chapter 16

Just as small children tend to describe all sorts of pain as a headache, so, since my accident, did I. And not without reason: a severe headache was my damaged body's only sure way to let me know about things I couldn't feel via the usual channels. That I still had one now was a clear indication that something, somewhere, was not right. By now it was late and I'd been put to bed back on Ward Eight, where the headache, along with feeling sweaty and shivering, suggested things weren't quite as they should be.

My Uncle Don and Aunt Irene had come to visit, along with Mum and Dad, and it was Uncle Don who spotted what might be the source of the problem. My left foot, which was lying outside the sheet, seemed to be sitting at a rather odd angle. He promptly called Sister Williams, who then called Mr Davies, who (grumbling irritably that he needed to make a return journey) declared himself less than pleased with what he found. He checked the situation by making a couple of exploratory movements, which racked the headache up to such sudden intensity that I actually screamed. This seemed to clinch things. There was no doubt in his mind that I had fractured my left ankle too.

Confirmation by X-ray soon after meant yet another trip down to the plaster room, from where I returned with, happily, an abatement of the pain, but also now both legs in plaster; from the groin to the toes on the right side and from knee to ankle on the left.

In my usual (and, I felt, understandable) hurry to escape the hospital environs, I was not prepared to wait the customary twenty-four hours for an ambulance, so, first thing the following morning, I travelled home in the boot of Maurice's Ford Cortina Estate.

Being home presented its own problems. Then, as in my experience is incredibly still the case today, the majority of wheelchairs provided by the NHS that have elevated footrests to support a long leg plaster come with only four small wheels, and cannot, therefore, be propelled by the patient independently. Having worked so long and hard to regain some independence, this was naturally anathema to me.

Uncle Don, however, had a solution. Ever a practical man, he arrived at our house shortly after we did, armed with a plank, which he proceeded to affix to my own chair, in order to support my long plaster.

Being able to get around on my own after such a potentially serious accident – back to business, as it were – was a massive relief. Despite my gung-ho approach I was still in some shock about what had happened. Indeed, when a policeman came round later that day to take a statement, I realised how lucky our escape from it had been. Memories of my other accident came flooding back to spook me, and I was more shaken up than I realised. This wasn't just because of what had happened. It was also a reminder of how vulnerable I was. How I wasn't, as it turned out, invincible. Indeed, I was soon after charged with driving without due care and attention, and though the other driver hadn't been hurt, and my car was soon patched up, this couldn't help but dent my self-confidence. It didn't matter that the other driver might have been driving like a lunatic; I simply hadn't seen his car soon enough. And though I maintained (and still do) that I'd been driving sensibly and safely, the fact that I had hit his car from behind made the charge mandatory (it always is in such cases) and the facts incontrovertible. Roads were simply hazardous places.

It dawned early on during my first weeks in plaster that potentially I had another, more immediate problem to deal with. Essential though the long leg cast was, it clearly wasn't going to allow me to fly to Florida for our forthcoming holiday. 'But don't worry,' I assured a concerned Maurice. 'I'll speak to Mr Davies and see what we can do.' So it was that when I went back to the hospital for my three-week clinic check-up, I cheerfully set out the dilemma for him, adding that it would be so much more convenient for the journey to have the right plaster converted to a below-the-knee one.

I didn't know if Mr Davies was going to faint or explode. He seemed to struggle to find the words to explain the gravity of developing a deep vein thrombosis, and that my ambition to fly *anywhere* put me at huge risk, but that to attempt to fly long haul was verging on the suicidal. He was also at pains to point out (before I could bring it up) that reducing that plaster to a below-the-knee one would *not* reduce the risk, and additionally, it would compromise the stabilisation of the bones that were now healing in my shin. All in all it was clear that Mr Davies didn't consider my holiday plans to be an especially inspired choice.

Inevitably, however, we arrived at a compromise. He said 'no', and I told him I was going, even if I had to 'modify' the plaster myself. I don't know what images this scenario conjured up for him (they might have involved me brandishing a hacksaw, I imagine) but he at least met me far enough (after all, I had clearly demonstrated I was 100 per cent crazy) to agree to a patella-bearing lower leg cast – as only recently pioneered in sunny California – even though it was being used (and he took pains to point this out) several weeks earlier than ideal.

My success with the good doctor came as a mixed blessing. Much as I'd been looking forward to it, the holiday was memorable mostly for its niggles. In a small way these consisted of being subjected to ten days of well-meaning Americans reassuring me (*à la* my time in Neath A & E) that I'd be back up on my feet in no time. With the first of these I duly explained the reality, but she was so terribly upset that I didn't do so again. Instead, I found myself in all sorts of bizarre conversations with people, for whom I would make up things I looked forward to doing as soon as the casts were removed. I also vomited, shivered and shook throughout the holiday and, for good measure, sunburned all my toes. I felt privileged and relieved to be back safe in Blighty and decided Mr Davies might have been right after all.

But little did I realise that the underlying reason for my deteriorating health (fast becoming a cause for concern once I was home from our holiday) wasn't a combination of the condition of my injured legs, intercurrent urinary infection, or the stress related to my recently completed compensation case. It was, in fact, due to complications arising from my abdominal surgery, and they began taking me back to a very dark place. I was by now, day by day, getting progressively worse, and it was starting to make me feel wretched. What, I kept uncharacteristically wondering, was the point in my carrying on? I'd survived the motorbike accident, survived my time at Rookwood and had done, I felt, everything humanly possible to get my life back on track. Yet it seemed that for every one step I metaphorically took forward, I was promptly knocked two steps back. What was I supposed to do? Just sit staring at a wall, like that poor pathetic soul I'd seen when I first alighted at Rookwood? Just sit and wait to die? Was everything I was trying to do pointless? Was 'it' still going to get me in the end?

Yet despite my black thoughts, another voice could just be heard. It was coming from somewhere in the depths of my being, but even so it was still clear and strong. 'Yes, of course it's worth doing!' it kept on repeating. 'Don't give up! Just keep going, you fool!'

My resolve to do exactly that might have been strong, but it still wasn't enough to save my fledgling relationship with Maurice from an inexorable and terminal decline. It was entirely down to me. I just couldn't bear to be around him – around anyone, really – when I was feeling so low and so sick. It's only been in more recent years that I've been able to understand this trait in myself. I don't know if it's down to my situation or just an integral part of me, but I always like to give of my best around people. Even on good days, that can sometimes be hard, but if I'm struggling to cope and feel I need to deal with the demands of others as well, then I end up, rightly or wrongly, incorporating them into the problem. Which creates the worst kind of vicious circle.

In the end, a resolution to my health problems came in the form of a crisis. By now I'd been in bed for about three weeks, being investigated for various infections, and was in very poor physical shape. I was unable to keep any food down, and latterly – and more seriously – fluids (bar, that is, the thimblefuls of Drambuie Mum regularly administered, which, perversely, might have been my salvation). Nevertheless, I resolutely refused all pleas to allow myself to be admitted to hospital.

But on Saturday 15 September, my resolve finally collapsed. I had been deteriorating rapidly over the previous three days and our family doctor insisted that if I wasn't admitted as a matter of urgency then I'd be lucky to live through the weekend.

By this time I was just too weak to argue. I was therefore admitted back into Neath General, where my now-persistent vomiting and hugely distended belly seemed to indicate something concrete at last – some form of serious gut obstruction. I was initially treated conservatively with a naso-gastric tube to empty my stomach and upper gut and an intravenous drip to correct my dehydration, but I continued to exhibit the same worrying symptoms. On the following Wednesday I was back in theatre for an exploratory laparotomy and here, finally, the culprit was found. A thick band of scar tissue had formed after my colostomy surgery and had effectively sealed off my small intestine, blocking all forward progress of whatever was put in it. In short, everything I ate was backing up and, in doing so, starting to poison me. Dividing this band cleared the blockage and the problem. Within a week I was allowed to come home.

Not that all was once again hunky-dory. Though the lifting of the threat of imminent extinction had done wonders for my psyche, it would take more than just being alive to make me feel properly better. I was, in every respect, so much worse. My lengthy illness had taken a big toll on my physical fitness. All the muscles the Chessington team and I had worked so hard to develop had been wasted away by the long weeks spent lying in bed. I was basically back to square one. And though recovered from the direct effects of the intestinal obstruction, I was extremely weak and my stamina was almost non-existent. Given my Chessington experience I knew exactly what was needed, but where was I going to find somewhere to get me started on the road back to fitness?

I could think of only one source of health and advice. Or rather two, in the form of a brace of paralympic athletes: John Harris, whose discus had so nearly taken out our fruit flan, and his and my other contemporary at Rookwood Chris Hallam. Both were members of and strong advocates for the Welsh Paraplegic/Tetraplegic Sports Club. There was, ironically, a chilling sense of *déjà vu* here: Rookwood Hospital and their number one mantra – the inevitability of salvation via sport.

The whole scenario was obviously something that needed both a deep breath and some serious thought, and I decided that I wanted to take a couple of months out first simply to recuperate and recharge my batteries. However, a couple of weeks' thumb-twiddling soon had me bored rigid and I decided I simply wasn't made for the sit-and-ruminate lifestyle – a clear signal I was ready to get going again. I telephoned John, who suggested a trip up to Cardiff and some sessions to try out my sporting options, as if 'my sporting options' wasn't a contradiction in terms in my case. I spent some time pondering what those options might be. No way could I contemplate racing in wheelchairs – too terrifying and way too uncomfortable – so field events (throwing things; I could do gold medal tantrums) was what it would have to be. The prospect of training for these in what by now was fast becoming a cold winter I sensibly found impractical, so instead, to prepare, I spent much of the time exercising with my dog Max on Aberavon seafront.

Max, who had continued to show steadfastness as a pet in all areas (particularly in the matter of electing to chew the cap and the clipboard of the police officer who'd come round to take my statement following the accident back in the spring), found this very much to his liking.

For me, however, it was no mean feat. Max only had two speeds: 100 miles an hour or stop, and the stopping bit invariably proved hazardous. And potentially unpopular as well. His finest hour at that time was when the stopping was caused by the approach of a perfectly coiffed little *bichon frisé,* whose unnecessarily personal inquisitive actions caused him to take avoiding action. He did this by proceeding to urinate over her, turning her snowy white fur a pleasant shade of yellow.

* * *

With the coming of spring, however, I had no excuse not to turn up at the training sessions John had so thoughtfully suggested and it was agreed, after giving me a 'try out' at some activities, that I'd be coached in discus, shot and javelin. The immediate thought that leapt into my mind (why?) was immediately followed by another (why me?) because I was, even if judged optimistically, hopeless. But at least I was consistent. I was equally hopeless in all three disciplines. Even the quadriplegic who was practising throwing clubs was achieving better distances than I could with any of my various missiles.

Part of the problem with the discus was that though I could hold it perfectly well with my hand underneath it, the moment I turned it over – athletic-hold fashion – it immediately fell to the floor. John was convinced I'd eventually get the knack but I was equally convinced only superglue would solve it – something that would then, of course, present its own problems, as I'd be unable to let the thing go. The shot presented its own predicament. Though controlled magnificently under my chin, as soon as I hinted at any expert-style thrusting, it rolled off my face and straight onto the floor. No one seemed sympathetic to my suggestion that I instead employ a revolutionary 'bowling' technique, citing such dreary things as 'rules' and 'regulations'. Instead it was muttered darkly that if that was my preference, I could instead be banished to the ranks of indoor bowlers. Unthinkable.

As to the last discipline, the spear – sorry, javelin – the less said about it the better. All that mattered was that in the face of apparently incontrovertible evidence to the contrary, John was convinced that practice would make perfect and I was therefore entered for the Stoke Mandeville International Games. In retrospect, I often wonder whether my entry wasn't entirely on the basis of my being the only Welsh female 'athlete' available.

Once again, however outlandish an ambition, I had something concrete to aim for, which felt good. Though I was unprepared for the chill down my spine that happened every time I went to Rookwood for a practice session. It was so intense and unpleasant that, had I had to enter either the hospital itself or the gym, I might have had to abandon my involvement. Happily, however, it wasn't necessary, and though I had a pang of empathy every time I saw a patient wheel past, John repeatedly reminded me what an inspiration I was – how much it mattered that they could plainly see what they themselves could aspire to in time. Not that I felt like much of an inspiration. Certainly not when, time after time, I dropped my discus, with a thud, onto the grass. And certainly not when, after yet another failure, I lit up a Benson & Hedges in order to ease my frustration.

'Do you think that when you're actually competing, you could refrain from bringing along your fags and lighter?' John asked.

I made a note for the competition. I'd clearly need to address this ...

By getting tracksuit bottoms with more capacious pockets, so they wouldn't drop out on the field.

chapter 17

If the summer of 1984 had seen me start to rethink my previous negative attitude to sport, the summer of 1985 saw the transition complete. I was now the very embodiment of a crack athlete.

Well, sort of. Only time would tell if the months of hard work would pay off, but for the moment I was happy to bask in the spotlight of sporting glory. However dodgy my throwing technique continued to be, I had been launched into a career in national competitive sport, which was, all agreed, no mean achievement. Indeed, my hard-working coaches expressed great personal pride at having both discovered and nurtured a Welsh girl to compete in the games for the very first time.

The squad of which I felt so proud to be a part travelled to Stoke Mandeville in a state of confident anticipation, and any private doubts I harboured over the extent of my abilities were soon quashed by the positive atmosphere. And besides, it was exciting just to *be* there. The games were to be held in the grounds of the hospital, in the newly built and grand-sounding Sir Ludwig Guttmann Stadium, which was serviced by its own Olympic Village.

I suppose I was probably a little naïve in such matters, but the latter wasn't quite what I'd expected. Rather than the vaguely hotel-style accommodation I'd anticipated, I was shown into a dormitory-style sleeping area, which looked creepily like a hospital ward, but without even curtains for privacy. I had imagined something a shade more individual, and was, therefore, slightly horrified by this. Not only that, I was with a bunch of total strangers. Being the only girl in the Welsh team, I had no team-mate to bunk down with. Instead I had been billeted with the Northern Irish ladies' bowls squad, for whom the clearly obligatory sporting camaraderie seemed to extend to using the shower area communally – something that reminded me of my school-days and one of the principal reasons I'd always loathed sport. Was a love of group nakedness and team trips to the bathroom hardwired into the psyches of sporting types?

Still, I reminded myself, like a soldier heading steadfastly into battle, I was at a prestigious event and representing my country. I must step up to the plate. Much was expected of me.

I was a total rookie, of course, and this soon became apparent. It had been impressed on me how important it was that I take very great care of my competitor's pass, so I was ever vigilant. Though perhaps shutting it in my locker was overdoing things somewhat. On day one, as a conse-quence, I was denied lunch. In true athletic style, I made an emergency dash back to the village to retrieve it, but by the time I returned, service had finished. This was beginning to feel all too familiar a scenario, but at least I was armed and prepared at dinner-time. Unfortunately, the sense of *déjà vu* only increased. Having proudly presented my pass at the counter, I was promptly presented with a plate of brown stew, which looked and tasted so disgusting I couldn't eat it. Rookwood, Chessington, and now Stoke Mandeville too – did they all employ the same chef? Or was this, in fact, a national catering chain? Muckonatruck Co., UK?

But, staying true to my philosophy of doing my best, I didn't let such small details divert me. My classification group was scheduled for the second day at 2.30 p.m., so I had plenty of time to prepare. Happily, the Ulster Bowlers vacated our dorm early that morning, so I was able to spend sufficient time on the essentials of hair and make-up. In men's competitions, I'd learned, the competitors were generally encouraged, particularly if lacking in proficiency, to apply lashings of liniment. This was in order that they could at least *smell* aggressively competitive, and I'd decided to apply the same logic. Even if I didn't envisage getting a gold medal, I could at least look glamorous enough to compete seriously for one. My tracksuit, in this regard, didn't help at all; it was baggy and made me look fat. The appearance was greatly improved, however, once I pulled on a pair of my tightest jeans – as a sort of corset to streamline my frame and cinch my waist – and pulled the tracksuit bottoms on over those. I couldn't bend, but at least I looked better.

My first event that afternoon was the discus. By now there had already been a succession of track events, and there was an enthusiastic crowd in the stadium. I wheeled into the throwing circle with my discus, whereupon my chair was firmly clamped to the ground to prevent it moving with my exertions. I gripped the rim of the discus with confidence – oh, how I'd improved! – before swinging it to and fro in the approved style of wind-up and releasing it with the obligatory grunt. There was a loud cheer. Then followed a search for the discus; surely not a world-record-breaking 'out of sight'?

Sadly, no. It had fallen on the ground behind me. 'No throw!' the tannoy blasted out. It seemed the cheer hadn't been for my discus attempt at all, but for some other track athletes elsewhere. Undaunted, John Harris, who was coaching me, urged me on for my second attempt. But this time, as I launched myself into the throw, the discus dislodged from my hand prematurely and plopped into the circle, narrowly missing my foot. 'No throw!' the tannoy bellowed again.

I finally achieved success with my third and last throw. This one actually left the circle and was measured. Fair enough, it had only travelled a few inches (not quite up to the fifteen metres or so of my fellow competitors) but it was recorded for posterity nonetheless.

Next up came the shot. This time, I was carefully strapped into my chair so that I didn't fall out as I launched it. Unnecessarily, as it turned out, because there was definitely no danger of that happening. My three rather similar (and similarly ignominious) attempts to propel it any distance were all pretty hopeless, though I was still piqued by what I thought was the rather contemptuous tone of the official as he commented, 'There's not even any point in measuring that.'

My own major concern was different. I noticed that the shot, lying damningly close to where I sat, was smudged with a big streak of my foundation. I just hoped there wasn't a corresponding bare streak tracking down my right cheek. John, by now, had his head in his hands, only lowering them to look in desperation around the stadium – after a tree, I felt sure, from which to go and hang himself.

By now I think we were both in agreement that there were limits to how much humiliation a person could take. But I was destined to endure a little more. Still, the location for the javelin was good, being close to what seemed a most encouraging crowd. Though their cheer as I hefted my javelin aloft might well have been what put me off my stroke. Two swinging warm-ups and, before I knew it, the javelin was stuck fast in the ground behind me. By now, the bark of 'No throw!' was unnecessary.

Throw number two was marginally better, but only in that this time I managed to get the tip of it stuck in *front* of, instead of behind, me. But at least I was getting the idea now. 'No throw!' I shouted with the official.

The third time, as is customary, I actually had success, in that this time I actually managed to launch it – releasing it to fly freely (well, perhaps not very freely) and flop limply to the ground about a foot in front of me. The benighted official was obliged by the rules to go and measure it, of course, and I was at least proud to know I had achieved a world record – for the shortest javelin throw ever in competition.

The crowd must have agreed, because they all rose and cheered me, and then again when I went up to claim my medal a couple of hours later. I was now the proud holder of my very own bronze. The fact that there were only three competitors in my category was, I thought, neither here nor there.

It must be admitted, as a postscript to my moment of glory, that the world record, sadly, is no longer mine. I recently learned that my long-suffering coach, John, has finally snatched it from my grasp. Not the finest of moments for a paralympic medallist and world record holder, but down in history nevertheless. He was competing in a javelin event when the officials stopped to debate a point of the regulations. John leant on his javelin and failed to notice that the tip was sticking into the ground – crucially, in front of the line. This was deemed a valid throw. Of 4 cm.

Stoke Mandeville was, to the consternation of no one, my first and last organised sporting competition. Shortly afterwards, in Port Talbot, I met a girl called Tanni Grey (later to be Grey-Thompson), who was with a group selling flags for 'Sport for the Disabled'. Though one of her fellow athletes was of the opinion that she would never amount to much, I felt an immediate sense that she would be my salvation and could release me from a lifetime of dismal athletic failure. I took pains to let her know how much I looked forward to her taking over as standard-bearer for Welsh Ladies' Sport for those with Disabilities. Moreover I confirmed that I would fully support her, and intended to confirm my retirement forthwith.

I was twenty-one and she was sixteen. I think she's gone on to do quite well.

chapter 18

Having brought down the curtain on my brief athletics career, I decided it was time I got a job. If there was one thing I'd learned about myself since the accident, it was that I really wasn't suited to a life of indolence and introspection.

I had two A levels, a clutch of O levels, and was tolerably well; all I needed was somewhere I could make myself useful and, hopefully, find some job satisfaction.

I knew this might prove something of a challenge. At that time, most employers were not especially keen to take on employees with disabilities, not least because organising an accessible working environment could be costly and difficult to arrange. The only notable exception was Remploy.

Remploy had been established in the mid-forties, under the 1944 Disabled Persons Act. Initially, they set up a furniture and violin factory in nearby Bridgend, employing large numbers of disabled ex-miners. They went on to develop a whole network of factories, and in the late eighties, responding to the downturn in manufacturing, started expanding into the service sector too. Their recruitment arm is now one of the biggest providers of disabled employees in the UK.

In the mid eighties Remploy had two local factories – the one in Bridgend, and also one in Maesteg – providing much-needed employment for disabled workers in South Wales. But working for Remploy felt all wrong for me. Much as I lauded their philosophy and ethos, I didn't personally want to work there. I wanted a job in the general workplace, however hard finding one might be.

With delicious irony, however, a potentially suitable post did come up. The local authority needed a clerical assistant to work in a new venture called 'Care and Repair'. Their job was to arrange for teams of workers to do just that: to repair and maintain properties and gardens that belonged to the elderly and those with disabilities. Naturally, because of the nature of the service, and the various disabilities of their target clientele, the office from which the service was run needed to be accessible to all.

Which, of course, made it accessible for me. I was inter- viewed for the job and really thrilled, once accepted, to start working at my first paid employment in January 1986.

My duties were not terrifically intellectually challenging. I was responsible for maintaining the accuracy of the chart that documented the various types of work undertaken: bricklaying, carpentry, garden maintenance, painting and decorating. As the teams of supervised youngsters completed their tasks (they were all on Youth Opportunities Training Schemes) it was my job to put a tick in the appro- priate box. I also had to act as a part-time receptionist, handle phone calls and book in all the jobs.

Rocket science it wasn't, but I was happy nonetheless. I really enjoyed meeting new people all the time, and also the feeling that at the end of the working day I'd contributed to making a difference to our clients' lives. Being at work had another big bonus – it took my mind off my own situation, and made me look outwards towards the wider world.

This was fortunate as, financially, I was actually worse off than before. Proud as I was to be earning my own money, doing so meant a drop in my disability benefit which, when coupled with now having travelling expenses, meant my income was substantially lowered. So, apart from the personal satisfaction it afforded, there was really no incentive to go to work at all.

The job was initially part-time. I did two days one week and three the next, but, luckily, with a degree of flexibility. So it was that I was able to cobble together sufficient days off that I could treat Mum, Dad and me to a short holiday. I felt they deserved one. They'd had to take a lower than market value offer for the Uplands, and had since spent a great deal on renovation and alterations to make Connaught Street suitable for us. Though the house itself had been paid for by an interim payment on my compensation (before the court case), Mum and Dad's day-to-day expenses were higher because of its much greater size. In addition to this, there had been no guarantee of either what the final payment would be, or the legal costs we'd have to shell out. And with Mum no longer working, and Dad now having taken early retirement, it had been a financially stressful time.

The choice of destination was easy. Having been regaled with its charms by our family solicitor, we plumped for a fortnight in the Gambia, in West Africa. We knew nothing about the continent, much less the country, but it turned out we had chosen really well.

It's difficult to describe adequately just how much independence and dignity meant to me. Just as I'm sure is true for any other disabled person, I wanted my relationships with everyone around me to be the same as for able-bodied people, not tarnished by the ever-present spectres of pity and dependency. The Gambia taught me, on more than one occasion, that this needn't be difficult to achieve.

Our hotel had a beautiful view across the Atlantic and our accommodation took the form of delightful garden chalets; one for Mum and Dad and one for me next door. It was basic but comfortably appointed, as I'd expected, but one small snag was immediately apparent. There was a six-inch step at the entrance. Each chalet had its own appointed member of staff. Mine, who was called Morro, surveyed the offending step, then said, 'You wait here, madam. Don't worry, I'll fix it,' upon which, he promptly disappeared.

Before ten minutes had passed, he was back with another Gambian, this one covered in sawdust and wood shavings. He was carrying a wooden ramp, which he hooked up to the step before inviting me to give it a road test. Happy that it seemed to meet with my approval (it did) he and Morro both shook hands with each other and with me. 'I am your houseman,' said Morro, solemnly. 'I clean and bring you flowers. Come and go as you please now. You are free with the wood, yes?'

Mum and I nodded, too choked up to speak. In six long years we'd never come across anything like this – especially not in the so-called 'developed' world. It was such a little thing but at the same time so enormous. These men had appreciated my need for independence and had gone out of their way to make it possible for me. No fuss, no bother. They just did it. Which meant I could get on with my holiday without constantly needing to ask for help. There was a similar step outside the front of our office in Port Talbot, which never saw a ramp during the whole time I worked there. I usually used the back door, but on the occasions when I had to come in the front I was reliant on someone else to help me.

And it wasn't just Morro who was sensitive to my needs. One day as I lay on my sun-lounger I noticed my wheelchair had a flat tyre. Dad asked the pool attendant, Pa, if he knew anyone who could fix a puncture. Pa came across and wasted no time in removing the offending wheel and, like Morro, disappearing at speed. He returned a while later, minus my wheel, and I'm ashamed to relate that it crossed my mind that it might by now be gracing a local bicycle. But all, as I really should have known, was well. An hour or so later, a grey-haired man arrived at the pool with it, and the two of them proceeded to fix it back to my chair, then requested that I check whether it was satisfactory. Reassured, the older man smiled and shot off again before we could even offer him anything for his trouble.

Pa told us what had happened. 'New tube,' he said. 'Not just repaired. There is now new tube in there.' I asked him where he'd found a new inner tube so quickly, and he explained that he'd flagged the man down on the street. He'd apparently been on his way to market, and my new inner tube had come from the bike he'd been riding. 'But how,' I asked, concerned, 'will he get to market and home again now?'

Pa smiled. 'He's happy. He has legs that work. He can walk. But you *need* the tube. Enjoy,' he finished. 'No problem at all.' I don't think I've ever felt so humbled.

Everything about our holiday was so remarkable that, once home, we immediately booked to go again. It was a place rich not only in natural delights – the vistas, the sunsets, the black velvet, diamond-studded sky – but also home to some of the kindest people I'd ever met in my life.

If being employed gave me a greater sense of self-esteem, it also gave me a taste of something I'd not previously experienced – the structure of a normal working week. Shortly after we returned from the Gambia, the full-time supervisor's post became vacant. Though the opportunity to make the most of the warm summer days was a brief and tempting factor, I didn't have to think too hard before applying. I was comfortable with the work I did, competent and happy, and now I was settled as a member of a workforce, I found that my days at home dragged. I was young and unencumbered and not lacking energy. Plus my financial situation was beginning to grate. Working full-time seemed perfectly reasonable.

As is often the case when you're swept along by enthusiasm, however, the reality was a little tougher than I'd anticipated. Obviously I'd already established a work-day routine, but it was pretty gruelling. Being in the office by 8.30 required a 4 a.m. start, and a system. After waking, I'd surface properly by means of a flask of coffee prepared the night before. Then would come the process of washing. I couldn't skip off to a shower at that time, so my wash took the form of a thorough bed bath, complete with a big bowl of hot water (from another prepared flask) and plenty of soap, towels and flannels. That done, I would get myself half-dressed and proceed to irrigate my colostomy. This activity alone takes a full hour to complete, so it would generally be 6.30 before I could finish dressing and attend to the business of hair and make-up (given the choice between that and having breakfast, there was never, in those days, any contest). That completed, I could at last set off for the office, and, factoring in a half hour for getting myself and my chair both in and out of my car, could be at my desk for 8.30.

All of which I could do with my eyes shut. (Bar the driving and mascara, of course.) What I hadn't fully appreciated, however, was that having to do that five days out of every seven – instead of fourteen – was tiring. I needed a 9 p.m. bedtime just to get sufficient sleep. I'd also now taken on extra responsibilities; as supervisor, I was invariably one of the last to leave the office, which left me precious little time for much more than dinner and bed.

Weekends, however, saw me invariably busy and making up for lost social time. I'd made new friends since starting work, and with both them and my old friends I'd become a regular at a local pub called the Bagle Brook, which ran a popular Sunday lunchtime quiz. The profits from this would be donated to different charities. After one successful session I mentioned a possible beneficiary – the Paraplegic/Quadriplegic Sports Club. I'd been acutely aware how tolerant they'd been of my abysmal showing at the Stoke Mandeville games, and what a great job they were doing to promote disabled sport. They were little known outside Cardiff at that time, but since several of them would once again be representing their country in international competitions I felt it would be nice to give them support and publicity further west.

Though not just via a quiz donation. Instead I suggested that perhaps we could invite them to Port Talbot, and raise money for their cause by means of an event such as a fun sports day at the pub in which all the locals could participate too.

We arranged the 'Wheelie-Walkie Games Day' for August bank holiday 1986, pitting the brawn and skills of the sports club members against the best the Bagle Brook could offer. The disciplines ranged from the wheelchair slalom race in the pub car park (inevitably paraplegics are much more expert than the 'able'-bodied at this), through the usual staples of darts, dominoes and pool to such mad stuff as 'golf tiddlywinks' (with a tabletop fairway) and the perennially popular 'bash-the-rat'. There were also events for the more cerebral amongst us, though the chess competition was a metaphorical walk-over as the sports club was fielding a formidable expert.

The sports club team (which included me, and gave me a chance finally to pull my weight for them; I'd already won my wheelchair slalom) still had their joker left to play in the crowning and final event – the wellie-throwing. Our man was the sports club team's only contender, while the pub side was bristling with confident throwers. The rules naturally insisted – to make things scrupulously fair – that everyone had to throw while sitting in a chair. One after another they sat down and threw, and had the results of their efforts carefully measured. There were indeed some great throwers among Port Talbot's finest, a couple of them managing twenty yards. Finally, our representative wheeled up to the line and considered the task before him. He'd never in his entire life thrown a wellie, and the pub side were confident and noisy. They grew quieter, admittedly, once he took off his jacket and revealed biceps like melons and forearms like Popeye's, but the air was still one of the battle having already been won. But it hadn't. A couple of wind-up swings, and the wellie – a big green one – sailed high overhead (and also dangerously close to the nearby M4 motorway), recording a whopping throw of some thirty yards. There was general consternation. It must have been a fluke. Several from the pub team then insisted on throwing it again, copying our man's distinctive style. They did. They didn't throw the wellie any further. But it *must* have been a fluke, was the general consensus. He surely couldn't repeat it. He did. The wellie was then inspected for hidden weights, the area was inspected for a secret stash of doctored wellies, and it was mooted that were the able-bodied to throw standing, then they'd most probably be able to do better still. They did so. And they didn't. A win was finally announced.

And yes, I *was* almost lynched when I made the announcement that the victor was John Harris, paralympic gold medallist and world record holder in the discus. But I didn't care. I hadn't laughed quite so much in years.

* * *

It was laughter – or more accurately a lack of it – that was key to the next major change in my life. During the wintry start of 1988, my father, by now sixty-one, was taken seriously ill. He'd developed pneumonia so severe that it was decided he was too weak even to be taken to hospital. The subtext was made perfectly clear. He could be treated at home, but we had better be prepared. In all likelihood he'd be lucky to survive.

Yet a miracle happened and he made a full recovery, much to the amazement and relief of all concerned. But not before I'd taken a hard look at my *own* life, and how little I seemed to be getting out of it. I'd by now been in my job for almost two years. Much as I enjoyed some aspects of it, the daily grind of getting up pre-dawn, working a long day and then going to bed long before I'd had a chance to wind down, wasn't living; it was merely existing. Apart from the oasis of enjoyment at the weekends, I had very few moments of joy.

After I'd been forcibly reminded of the finite nature of existence, I decided I must find a different way to live. I hated the thought that I could die at any point and have little to show for my time on the planet apart from an impressive number of hours spent in the office. And if the rewards in terms of personal fulfilment were fairly meagre, the rewards in terms of pay were even worse.

Which made it, in the end, quite an easy decision. I loved being with people, I was outgoing and cheerful, and I had little need of fat salaries or lofty status. I could do so much more of worth with my life if I could take charge of my own destiny and work on my own terms. That decided, it seemed clear there was only one path to follow. To work voluntarily for charity.

I handed in my notice on 16 February 1988 – a week after Dad's sixty-second birthday. My life proper was about to begin.

chapter 19

Much has been written about the nature of love, particularly in reference to those who seek it. It comes, or so the saying goes, when a person least expects it. And so it would turn out for me.

When Chris appeared on my doorstep in the spring of 1988, he was the last person I expected to see. A year or so after he and Juli got married back in 1984, they'd moved up to North Wales with his job, and we'd kept in touch only sporadically since because of the distance involved. He'd come with sad news: Juli had met someone else and left him, and he very much needed a friend.

Which was exactly how I saw him initially. He'd remained in North Wales after the separation because of work, but he started to make regular trips to Port Talbot to see his parents, and meeting up with me when he was down.

I had never been romantically interested in Chris. He was certainly good-looking, with expressive brown eyes, but as the teenager I'd been when we all hung out together, he was manifestly not my type. He had been – and still was – everything Aldo wasn't. He was well-educated, white-collar, went to work in a suit. He was sensible and bright and had prospects. In hindsight, perhaps he hadn't been Juli's type either – what with her being his antithesis in most things – but at the time they had seemed to be a match made in heaven. We were all very sad to hear of their split.

But as far as I was concerned, nothing had changed. As an able-bodied girl, I went for guys like Aldo, not Chris, and that still remained the case all these years on. And by the way the chemistry of these things often works, I assumed the same generally applied in reverse, and that Chris wasn't interested in me.

I was wrong. We became close again quickly – we had a lot of shared history, after all – and I began to look forward to his visits. But it soon became obvious that what *I'd* thought was a strictly platonic relationship was becoming, to Chris, something more. We were sitting in the lounge bar of the local pub one weekend when he suddenly took my hand in his, apropos of absolutely nothing, and told me how beautiful I was. I was immediately rendered speechless, and was even more shocked to hear that his noticing me wasn't a new thing. That it was something that he'd always thought and felt. As a prelude to a seduction, it couldn't have been bettered. I was flabbergasted. I could actually feel my heart skip a beat. When he leaned over and kissed me, it skipped several more, and left me dizzy and tingling with shock. No wonder it felt I was walking on air. I was reeling, and also looking at him with entirely fresh eyes. How on earth had I not seen this coming?

It was difficult to part at the end of the evening. By some strange alchemy, Chris suddenly seemed so desirable and I wondered if my previous romantic indifference had been, on some level, because he was out of bounds. But now everything had changed. And the emotional intensity of the following weeks was so great that I couldn't deny it. I was twenty-three years old and suddenly, inexplicably, I was falling in love. Not only something I'd barely ever dared to hope might one day happen, but also with a man for whom my disability didn't matter, because he already knew me so well.

Chris knew me, knew my history, knew everything about my situation. He knew about my catheter, my leg bag, my colostomy; he and Juli had even visited before I'd had the op. He not only knew – he'd been involved in it all. After their marriage, I often used to visit him and Juli at their house in Ammanford, where the only toilet had been upstairs. On the first occasion after they'd moved in, when we'd spent an evening drinking lager, he'd even carried me upstairs so I could deal with my catheter, and so Juli could give me a tour of the bedrooms at the same time. But this was neither practical nor good for his back so, after that, Juli would generally find me a bottle while Chris, ever the gentleman, would retreat from the room, returning only to collect and dispose of the contents, which he always laughingly referred to as 'taking the piss'.

What was happening now, however, was a whole new situation. Despite our closeness as friends, we were approaching new territory: a physical relationship. Which excited but also terrified me. Once we began the process of exploring each other's bodies, the fear was beginning to feel overwhelming.

It would have been all too easy to call a halt at that point; to run away and shut down that whole side of my life. But Chris understood. He knew exactly how my mind worked. 'It's *you* I've fallen in love with,' he said. 'You as a person. You are beautiful,' he told me. 'And funny and intelligent. And the way you manage your life is a part of who you are. Nothing bothers me, Mel. Nothing is a problem unless we make it one.'

That, to put it tritely, was it. If I hadn't been entirely swept off my feet by Chris already, that would have been the point when it happened. And he was true to his word. When we did get properly physical, he was so sensitive and considerate about my hang-ups with my body, that, little by little, I began to feel free with him. It felt amazing to be able to share myself with someone, to enjoy romantic love with a man without my 'secret bits' becoming a huge issue.

Which isn't to say it wasn't one initially.

Like any other woman, I'd had a scenario sorted. Despite my very obviously unusual situation, I'd thought things through sufficiently to have an idea. I could easily – and often did – picture the moment. I would be his siren, the focus of all his attention, and he the ardent swain, utterly besotted. The air would be charged. We would be completely absorbed in one another and what we were about to do. We'd face one another in the bedroom. He'd approach, breathing heavily, while my heart fluttered in eager anticipation. Slowly, we'd begin to undress one another and I'd feel his hot breath on my neck as his hands moved all over me. My skin glistening, I'd soon be in my underwear. Then, as he planted soft kisses on my neck, his hands would reach behind me to unclasp my bra.

I wouldn't have been idle with my own hands either; by now I'd have removed his shirt also. The atmosphere would crackle as skin touched skin. I'd lie back on the bed as his hands continued to move over me, his fingers caressing my breasts and running down to my hips where he would gently but deftly slide off my panties. We'd kiss again, passionately, as he moved on top of me and entered me …

Except, naturally, it didn't happen anything like that.

Being a successful paraplegic requires lots of adjustments, particularly the growth of a robust sense of humour, and, boy, did I need one the first time we made love. Because the reality was that we made for the bedroom and he put me on the bed fully clothed. We then achieved Nirvana as far as my waist, but my skin-tight jeans posed a serious challenge. I couldn't lift my bottom to help with their removal and, in any case, the act itself required serious caution to avoid compromising my catheter. As between us we contrived to slide them as far as my knees, I produced a leg spasm of such record-breaking proportions that it actually threatened to kick his head off. We hadn't really contemplated and certainly hadn't discussed venturing into the realms of sado-masochism, but even so …

I began fretting then. Had the moment been lost? Fortunately not quite, for his nose, I saw, wasn't actually bleeding. Sore but apparently undeterred by the assault, he pressed on and the jeans were successfully discarded.

A pause occurred here while he undressed himself, and I grabbed the opportunity to sort out my catheter. 'Who said romance was dead?' I wondered as I did so. Surely our mutually glistening bodies made a definitive statement of carnal joy. But no, the steam rising from us both by now was the result of the exertion, not lust.

At this point, for a short while, we returned to my script, lying close and indulging our romantic inclinations. Desperately and bravely, he sought then to part my knees, which refused to budge because of another involuntary spasm. Wisely, he kept his head (and all other important bits of his anatomy) clear of all potentially uncontrollably dangerous parts of me. Eventually he was on top of me and my knees, which at first had seemed to doggedly repulse his advances, now spasmed around his hips in a grasp so resolute that he had no prospect of escape. I opened my eyes and saw he was purple in the face; was this paradise, I wondered anxiously, or asphyxia? Sadly, in all of this frenzied activity, I was not aware of what exactly was going on below mid-chest level, and my mind wandered back to the tampon in the wrong orifice; definitely not the best thought to enter my head. Resolutely, and slightly desperately, I cleared away the memory and tried to look as if I was a totally involved participant in the immediate erotic activity (something I've since learned that able-bodied women do too …). After much huffing and puffing there was a long moaning sigh – was this release or relief because my leg spasms had abated and I was lying legs akimbo looking like a porn star? I wasn't quite sure, but clearly something significant had happened as he promptly collapsed onto the floor.

I thought that when he got his breath back he'd make a bolt for the door anyway, but it turned out that things were quite the opposite. He said he felt that our lovemaking had brought us closer together because of the trust I had – of necessity – put in him. I believed what he said; I believed in *him*.

Chris's weekend visits thereafter became the focus of my life. I would hate it when he left to return to North Wales on a Sunday, and ache for him till he returned the following Friday night.

They say that loving and being loved brings the best out in a person, and every pore of my body could see that was so. True love – which is precisely how it felt, how it was – did incredible things for my psyche. I felt stronger and lovelier. I held my head higher. My body language must have oozed confidence and pride. And I *felt* proud. I wanted to shout it out loud: look at me, folks! I might be stuck in a wheelchair, but I've got an able-bodied fella – so there!

My new-found confidence spilled over into all areas of my life. I'd started working on a voluntary basis for the Spinal Injuries Association. As a patient at Rookwood, I'd become a member of the SIA almost by default. Though I always read the quarterly magazine they sent me, I hadn't had much to do with them up until then, as they were based in London and didn't have much representation in Wales. But they'd recently set up a new scheme in which volunteers gave 'Awareness and Prevention' talks to children in schools, which seemed to be exactly the sort of work I thought I could do.

The talks were arranged through the local SIA representative – herself a former teacher – and I would travel all over the area, regaling pupils with all the grisly details of my accident, which they, particularly the boys, seemed to love hearing, and chatting to them about the need to wear helmets when cycling. Back then almost nobody bothered. It was a job I loved and I soon developed my own style. I found that humour could sell a safety message much more effectively than sermonising, and that a bit of light mocking of authority figures generally went down well too. More than once I told the children about my relationship with my grumpy orthopaedic surgeon (I never did as I was told; he mostly wanted to throttle me) and they always seemed to find that hilarious. The only downside was something that I hadn't been prepared for: that a few children (and there seemed to be a few in every school) would ask the sort of intimate personal questions that, had I been of a less robust disposition, would have made my hair curl.

But while I was changing for the better on the outside, inside it was an entirely different matter.

I had always suffered a few troublesome symptoms post the accident, most notable among them being a tendency to sweat down the right side of my body, and an embarrassing flushing of the right side of my face. Both of these had always defied diagnosis and I simply assumed I must get on and live with them, and just apply my foundation with a trowel. But as the decade drew to a close I had started feeling increasing pain and a disturbance of the sensation in my right hand and arm. In addition to this I was beginning to find it difficult to distinguish between heat and cold, as a result of which I suffered the odd burn. All of these symptoms were scary. When you relied as much as I did on the functioning half of a body that largely didn't, the prospect of that failing too was terrifying indeed. Which was probably why I kept talking myself out of the idea that something was seriously wrong.

But you can only remain in denial up to a point. Though these new symptoms defied any sort of definitive diagnosis – and I hadn't been rushing to seek one, operating on the 'if I put my hands in front of my eyes you can't see me' approach – by the autumn of 1989 the changes had increased in severity so much that I was becoming properly concerned. For one thing, the pain was nigh on intolerable. Something bad was happening to me and I needed to find out what and why.

My local neurologist was a Dr Weiser. I'd initially been referred to him by Mr Davies some years back to see if he could shed any light on my bizarre neurological symptoms, and I'd seen him several times over the years. With these new symptoms proving equally mysterious, he referred me to a consultant neurosurgeon called Mr Teddy, who worked at the Radcliffe Infirmary in Oxford. Mr Teddy was an internationally acknowledged expert in his field, so when he told us he suspected my symptoms were being caused by a serious neurological complication of my original injury, I began to feel decidedly anxious.

The MRI scan he ordered seemed to confirm it, showing a cyst-like abnormality within the substance of my spinal

cord. And my fears were not allayed when Mr Teddy
decided to arrange for me to be admitted as an in-patient at
the Radcliffe, in order that he could undertake some more
tests.

With a sense of foreboding that wasn't at all quieted by
the fact that I was now having difficulty operating the hand
controls of my car, I drove Mum, Dad and myself up to
Oxford on the day of my planned admission. We booked
them into the nearby Randolph Hotel, while Chris, who
drove himself separately from North Wales to be with us,
booked into a B & B just outside the city.

When we presented ourselves at the hospital admissions
desk, however, it appeared there was no record of my scheduled arrival. Not only that, but no one seemed much interested in obtaining any details. No forms were produced and
no details were requested. Instead I was shown to the ward's
day room and promptly ignored for the next hour and a
half.

I had just reached the point where I'd run out of justifi-
cations for this (they were busy/short-staffed/had forgotten
where they'd put me) when Mr Teddy, sporting his usual
bow tie, strode purposefully in our direction. Efficiency
personified, he told me he had a room prepared for me elsewhere and immediately escorted us to it. This done, he left
Mum to help me settle in and promised to return again soon.

And he didn't disappoint. After the protracted absence of
staff that had been my initial experience, it seemed Mr
Teddy was about to make good the lack, because he
returned with a cohort of students so large that they filled
every inch of my cubicle. He then proceeded to address his

awed-looking retinue with every single detail of my clinical situation without so much as a glance in my direction, behaviour I'd only ever seen in the movies before. I had, he told them, in authoritative tones, a complex neurological condition. Given this, he proposed that his next course of action would be to carry out a similarly complex neurosurgical operation which would apparently do something called 'top and tail' me. I didn't have the first clue what he meant by that statement, only that it didn't sound great. Wasn't topping and tailing what you did to runner beans? But there was no chance to ask him to elucidate for me, as he immediately ushered out his white-coated coterie, turning only to inform me that the following morning I'd be transferred to the Churchill Hospital, a few miles away, to undergo urodynamic studies.

Slightly stunned, Mum and I pondered all this for some moments. Even my new-found and ever-growing confidence was clearly not a match for the imperious Mr Teddy. Three things concerned me. One was that I had prior experience of urodynamic studies (in which the bladder is filled with fluid through a catheter and various measurements are taken) and the continuing existence of the radiologist who performed them on that occasion was largely a matter of luck: they hurt so much I very nearly killed him. The second, all the gaps in my medical knowledge accepted, was that I couldn't understand why I needed to endure them again. It was my upper limb neurological problem that needed sorting. What purpose could such a procedure have? Thirdly – and most importantly, given my mood by this time – I myself appeared largely peripheral to proceedings.

That being the case, I had no intention of spending the rest of the day pointlessly holed up in a hospital room. Mum, Dad and I returned to the hotel.

Like the good patient I (mostly) was, however, I knew I must accept my clinician's decision, and after Chris and I had spent a little time together in the hotel bar, I returned to the hospital to spend the night. This was necessary, I knew, to ensure that I'd be there and ready for my transfer to the Churchill the following morning. On waking, however, and asking the nurse about it, I was told that they had no record or knowledge of any transfer.

Baffled and cross, I made a decision of my own. I packed my small bag and left.

Making a stand has its plus points obviously. I didn't have to undergo any further hateful (yet so benignly named) urodynamic 'studies', and I didn't have to subject myself to any further horrors at the hands of Mr Teddy, but, sure though I was that he could do nothing for me, I didn't know quite what to do instead. I had little choice but to plunge myself into a personal quest to find more information about my condition. Having adjusted to being an independent paraplegic, the thought that my right arm was under threat terrified me. I felt almost as if I was under attack. Where the accident itself had paralysed me in an instant, it seemed I now harboured some sort of alien *something* that was creeping inexorably up my spine to my neck. How long before my right arm was lost to me? I needed to know more about what was happening inside me before committing to a drastic plan of action. I wasn't stupid. I knew enough to know that spinal nerves, once damaged, could not be repaired. So I could not accept the prospect of surgery on them lightly; the cyst was *in* my spine. It was incredibly risky. If there was any other course, then I needed to know about it.

Coincidentally, one of Dad's friends had recently suffered a massive heart attack while on holiday in Fort Lauderdale in Florida, and had talked at length about the stunning medical treatment he'd received from the cardiologist there. Working on the possibly shaky but intuitively sound theory that one great doctor might well know another great doctor, I asked if perhaps I could have her number.

It may have been clutching at straws, but given that my ability to clutch *anything* was under threat it didn't seem in the least batty. In fact, it turned out to be a very good move. Dr Chavez, who was charming and couldn't have been more helpful, suggested I speak with her neurosurgical colleague Dr Feeley who, to my utter astonishment and delight, called me himself the very same night all the way from Florida.

Dr Feeley, who should be knighted for services to desperate and gabbling paraplegics (okay – me, then), listened patiently while I described all my symptoms – at length – and even came up with a possible diagnosis: a condition called syringomyelia.

Syringomyelia is essentially a destructive and progressive cavitation of the substance of the spinal cord by a collection of fluid, which is driven to 'slosh' upwards by such ordinary activities as straining or sneezing, and which then behaves, as I was later to hear it described, like 'a boring insect, destroying the spinal cord from inside'. ('Syringo-', incidentally, derives from the word 'syrinx' – a mythical nymph who, tiring of the unwanted attentions of Pan, asked the gods to transform her into a hollow reed. Hence pan pipes. Hence the term for my potentially hollow and useless spine.) This grisly news notwithstanding, I was so excited to find someone who thought they knew what was wrong that I almost slammed the phone down and booked the next flight to Florida. I didn't care how many arms or legs it would cost; my own arms were too precious for me to lose. Could he see me? I asked him. Could he treat me? I entreated. Could he please do so now, this very minute? Dr Feeley, however, had other ideas. Yes, he said, he could certainly see me to undertake investigations to confirm his tentative diagnosis, but much better, he suggested, would be to see someone else.

'Who?' I wanted to know.

'Bernard Williams,' he answered. 'The world expert in syringomyelia. He's the man for you to see. He's based in Birmingham.'

'Birmingham, Alabama?' I asked, scribbling everything down.

Dr Feeley laughed. 'Not quite that far,' he answered. 'Closer to you than me, in fact. He's based in Birmingham, *England*.'

I put the phone down, elated. There was someone who might be able to sort out my problems less than 150 miles up the road. Little did I realise that what was soon to follow would mark a change in direction only slightly less major than the accident that had brought me to this point.

chapter 20

On a chilly day in February 1990, Chris and I got engaged. It was a Saturday, and we were out shopping in Swansea when he suddenly guided me towards the window of a jeweller's and pointed out a ring in the window.

'Do you like that?' he asked me. I studied it more closely. It was a broad gold band with a single diamond set into it. I was a girl and a romantic. What was there not to like? I told him I did, and minutes later it was mine. Not yet on my finger – it had to go and be re-sized – but even so, the deed was done. We were from that moment official. I belonged to Chris now. For keeps.

If my memory of that day is now sketchy, however, there's a reason. Chris's gesture (this was an engagement but not a proposal – no knees were involved at any point) had come not only out of the blue but also at a time when my mind was almost fully occupied with the potential consequences of my steadily worsening condition.

Though I wasn't without hope. Just as I'd anticipated from speaking to Dr Feeley, Mr Bernard Williams, world expert on syringomyelia, was about to loom large in my life. To say that he now felt more important to me than the man who'd just put a ring on my finger sounds harsh, but in many respects was simply the truth.

Everything had happened very quickly. My initial phone call to his secretary, Anne, had resulted in an appointment in Birmingham the following week. It was still very wintry and bitterly cold, with snow lying prettily all around. Chris had come down specially, as befitted his new status as my fiancé, and drove Mum, Dad and me up there.

I was to be seen at the Priory, a private hospital, which I would pay for out of my compensation money. Though costly, I knew it would be money well spent. This was my first experience of such a place, as up until now I'd been treated – perfectly competently – by the NHS. This place, in stark contrast, didn't feel much like a hospital at all; it was more like a five-star hotel.

We were shown into a comfortable waiting room, with a view over the snow-covered hospital garden, and my first sight of the doctor who was to save me from potential quadriplegia was when a very tall man, with grey hair and dark-rimmed glasses, appeared suddenly from a doorway just behind me. I judged him to be in his mid to late fifties, and his presence and charisma were immediately arresting. He looked straight at me without speaking and then retreated again. Moments later (after checking my name, I suspected) he appeared again, called out 'Melanie Bowen, please!' and then ushered me into an adjacent office. Chris followed behind and held the door.

I couldn't help but warm to Bernard Williams after his next utterance, a gratifying 'Hello! You're a very sexy lady.' He introduced himself then turned to Chris: 'And *you* are?'

Chris didn't look terribly impressed.

We had taken my MRI scans up to Birmingham with us and Bernard Williams now put these up on his viewing box.

'So,' he said, 'tell me what's been happening to you.'

I ran through the course of events that I'd retold on so many occasions. I also explained my global route to find him, which he seemed to find highly amusing. 'So you've come from Wales, via an Irishman from Cork who's based in Florida, to see me right here in Birmingham!' But for the most part he was serious. He asked searching questions about my symptoms and their progression, which filled me with confidence and hope. It almost felt as though he'd lived the last ten years with me.

After explaining the procedure he intended to perform, he agreed that he'd book me in at the first opportunity. He then looked hard at the vertical scar down my back that was testament to the two operations Mr Davies had done. 'Who was responsible for that?' he enquired. I told him.

'Well,' he said, frowning, 'I'm afraid I can't guarantee to make it that neat again.' On the matter of looks, he was adamant that I shouldn't have unrealistic expectations.

To which the correct response, surely, would have been something along the lines of 'I don't care a jot – please just make me well.'

But, me being me, I said no such thing. Instead I said, 'I like to wear backless tops, so you better had. Tell you what, you could always give Mr Davies a ring for tips. He won't mind. I'm his favourite patient.'

My youthful tongue-in-cheek flippancy didn't bother Bernard Williams a jot. It marked the start of an enduring friendship.

My operation was scheduled for Monday 17 April. During the intervening weeks I started to question my original unquestioning acceptance of Chris's ring. Foremost in my mind was one incontrovertible fact: that had he actually asked the question 'Will you marry me?', my answer, without a doubt, would have been 'no'. I simply couldn't see us married and living together, and I wasn't sure he could either. Which made it something of a nonsense that I had accepted an engagement ring from him, however romantic the gesture had seemed. I knew lots of people got engaged without any clear plans to marry but the more I thought about it, the more wrong it felt.

It had come at a particularly testing time. In some ways, I was forced to admit to myself, the potentially disastrous nature of my new symptoms had caused me privately to question the validity of our relationship. Simply put, my major focus right now was my health. Though I had every confidence in the skill and ability of my surgeon, I still had to face the fact that surgery might not mean salvation. It might actually make things much worse for me. It might make life barely worth living.

How would Chris and I manage then? Suppose I became even more disabled, with one useless arm as well as two useless legs, and was forced to cede so much of my cherished independence? Specifically, forced to accept becoming dependent on Chris to do all the personal, private things I'd worked so hard to do for myself over the last decade? Could I bear that? Could *he*?

Just thinking about it made me feel angry and frustrated. It seemed so unfair that, just as I'd reached a state of physical and emotional strength – enough to go through life's journey alone, without needing a man to justify my existence (something having a man, ironically, had brought about) – it felt as if fate was in some way punishing me for getting such lofty ideas. Could any relationship survive what might happen if things worked out for the worse?

Yet Chris was completely unfazed. He'd stuck with me through thick and thin and he was clear that he intended to continue to do so. He understood the risks. He knew I could end up a great deal worse. And he still wanted to put a ring on my finger to show the world I was his. How many men would love someone enough to do that?

Little by little, I thought it all through and tried to cast aside my fears. What I needed to do, I kept telling myself sternly, was stop trying to analyse Chris's motives for loving me and simply accept that he did. I decided to be grateful and to stop being so bloody selfish. I was twenty-five, after all. I should be ready to settle down, shouldn't I?

But there was no settling of any sort to be done in the short term. On 16 April we all travelled back to Birmingham, again driven by Chris. I later learned that, despite my protestations that it was unnecessary, he had taken unauthorised leave so he could be at my bedside for the duration.

By now, I felt strangely calm. As the day of the operation approached, I made a decision. This did not involve Chris, but my mother. After a long and emotional conversation she agreed that, should the operation fail, she'd support me in making the choice not to continue with my life.

It was the most appalling burden to place on anyone, but Mum accepted it, just as she'd accepted everything that preceded it. She (and Dad) understood me better than anyone and knew I simply couldn't contemplate a life in which I couldn't feed myself, dress myself or put on my make-up, in which I would be completely and wholly dependent on other people. Like me, she still recalled the quadriplegic boy in Rookwood who had needed her to scratch his nose for him. It was an image that wouldn't go away.

So she said she would support me if I wanted to die in that eventuality.

It's hard to imagine the emotional toll the conversation took on her. Once we had spoken about it, I had to push any thoughts of failure from my mind. I had absolute faith in my doctor's skill and wisdom. If I was fixable, I knew he would fix me.

The swanky hotel-style nature of the Priory Hospital extended beyond the outpatients department. After Mum and Dad had gone to get settled into a local B & B, I was shown into a spacious en-suite room, with a remote-control telly and a wonderful electric bed which seemed capable of going into any position my imagination could suggest. My window once again gave me a wonderful view of the now-verdant garden.

Once I'd unpacked, Mr Williams appeared to run through the details of the procedure he was going to carry out on my back. I'd be asleep, it would be opened up, he would perform his magic, then he'd close me up again – as neatly, he assured me, as was possible. As I had already been through it in my head several times, it all sounded fairly straightforward.

The only jarring note was when the anaesthetist came in later and explained his own part in the proceedings. He told me that I would be be awake from start to finish, my hair would be shaved off and an incision would be made in the back of my head. I dare say I'd have been re-packed and on my way at that point, were it not for the fact that Bernard Williams returned and enquired why I was looking so pale.

Several anxious minutes later, the muddle was resolved. Though what the lady in the next room thought of the news that they were to open up her spine in order to sort out her head injury is anyone's guess.

As it was, everything went like clockwork. Or, at least, I assumed so, as I knew nothing about it. The first thing I saw when I came round in the ITU was a pair of black biker's boots, at which point I might have been forgiven for thinking that I'd died on the operating table and gone straight to hell.

As I came round properly, I realised I wasn't dreaming; the boots were real and attached to a bona fide human – a very tall one in a dark pinstripe suit, with a red tie and those distinctive dark-rimmed glasses. Mr Williams, it seemed, had come to check on his patient. He stroked my brow and wanted to know how I was feeling. It was impossible to find words to convey my emotions as, one by one, I flexed and unflexed all my fingers. Left and right. Every single glorious one. I felt a lump grow huge in my throat. I managed a watery smile as he placed his hand in my right one. He smiled back. 'Let's do it, Mel, shall we?' He asked me to squeeze his fingers as hard as I could. 'I'll be happy if you hurt me,' he added. I did so and he winced, delighted at the power of my grasp. All was well. Mum was freed from her onerous burden. I couldn't wait to see her and show her.

Of course when I was allowed out of ITU, I had to take it easy for a bit – not something I was terribly good at. Doubly hard when all I really wanted to do was to shout and sing and rejoin the world. A week in my enforced imprisonment felt like more than enough, particularly as Chris, doggedly true to his word, had taken up residence on a camp bed in my room and was refusing to leave my side. Even Bernard, on one of his post-operative ward rounds, had commented, 'Don't you ever leave the room?' I knew my parents were also finding it difficult to adjust to the proprietorial nature of my fiancé's behaviour. He seemed ever-more anxious to exclude them. So much so that they were beginning to feel they had to ask his permission to visit me. They didn't say anything; they were much too sensitive to his new role in my life, and patient with his evident insecurities. But *I* minded. It seemed so over the top and controlling. I kept reminding myself how much I loved my fiancé, but I was beginning to feel stifled by his constant presence and domineering ways, which came as a shock in a relationship in which for most of the time we had only seen one another at weekends. Once more I began to fret about how robust my feelings for him were.

Naturally, my claustrophobia meant that when Bernard Williams popped in to see how I was doing, with his usual cheery greeting of 'Hi, Dizzy!' (he called all women 'Dizzy', especially if they were young and decorative), my reply was a polite 'Fine' quickly followed with a plaintive 'When can I get out and go home?'

Not yet, was his instant reply. I must stay in hospital for a minimum of ten days, not because he was some sort of sadist but because of the very real risk of meningitis; succumb to that and I wouldn't want to be anywhere else. 'You need to be here,' he pointed out, looking stern, 'so that if anything bad happens I can treat you.'

He turned to Chris at this point, clearly keen to enlist an ally. 'Is she always like this?' he wanted to know. 'Can't she relax for a few days without nagging?'

Chris's response – a resigned shrug – spoke volumes. 'Tell you what, though,' Bernard said, his expression changing. 'I have a proposition for you. Something to think about while you're stuck in here. How do you fancy flying to Nashville, Tennessee? There's a convention in June on syringomyelia and I've been invited to be the main speaker. It's been organised by ASAP – the American Syringomyelia Alliance Project – and if I could bring you along as a demonstration case, it would obviously have a strong impact. There's just the one snag; they pay my travelling expenses, but I'm afraid you would have to fund yourself. Anyway, you might want to give it some –'

'Yes!' I replied instantly, already in Graceland. 'Yes, yes and absolutely yes.'

Bernard turned to Chris and in his best John McEnroe voice said, 'Just like that? Is she seeerious???!'

Of course I was serious. How could I possibly say no? I had absolutely no intention of getting any complications and this sounded like a brilliant adventure. As I tried to point out to Chris, it's not every day you are given the opportunity to travel halfway around the world to be the focal point of a presentation given by an eminent, world-renowned neurosurgeon. Stuff settling down! I was twenty-five years old and on a high again. Life had just begun. The money wasn't an issue. I had been careful with what I'd been awarded by the courts, and this felt like a good way to spend some of it. Something meaningful. Something in which I could actively help others – being presented as proof of Bernard's success.

Chris, however, wasn't impressed. 'So just like that we're off to Nashville, then, are we?' He was looking at his feet as he spoke. 'You know it will mean me taking more time off of work – and I've already used up all my leave for your operation.'

This made me feel both stunned and cross. In the first place, I hadn't actually asked him to come with me – he'd be bored by it all, surely? And second, I hadn't wanted him to take time off for my operation – certainly not the whole ten days. I hated to think of his colleagues hearing how he had to take leave in order to look after me and I also questioned his reasons for doing so. It felt as much about staking his claim and separating me from my parents as anything else.

Once again, I berated myself. Why shouldn't he feel he had first claim on me? He was my fiancé, after all. He should come first. And yes, I knew my closeness with my parents was more than Chris obviously considered was usual, but my life since the age of fifteen hadn't *been* usual, had it? And I certainly wasn't about to cut them out of my life. They'd supported me through hell and back, and I loved them. Why did he always act as if it had to be him or them?

Round and round my thoughts went, endlessly circling. Was I right to feel this? Was he right to think that? Only one thing was crystal clear in my mind: I was going to Nashville, with or without him. Ideally, I thought, to my dismay, without him. Surely he wouldn't be allowed further time off work?

It was with this uncomfortable thought nestling in my mind that I prepared to leave the Priory on 27 April. I couldn't wait to get back to my own home and bed and to start looking into flights to Tennessee.

Bernard Williams, I knew, would be such fun to be with. Now I'd got to know him better I liked and respected him even more; what an honour it would be to give something back to someone who'd done so much for me.

He popped in to see me on the eve of my departure and confirmed he'd be in touch regarding dates. As he left, he gave me one final instruction: to look out of the window in fifteen minutes' time, when I'd get a glimpse of something 'big, red and impressive'.

Naturally, I did so, but I heard it before I saw it: a strangely familiar growling rumble. What came into view was exactly as billed. A powerful red motorbike, gleaming in the setting sun, its rider in head-to-toe leathers. I recognised the biker boots I'd seen in ITU and, beneath the visor, the same dark-rimmed glasses. Bernard Williams raised a hand and waved a farewell. I waved back.

A strange mode of transport for a man in his line of work but, at the same time, it absolutely figured.

It was with a fair degree of excitement that I settled back into a routine at home. The weather was kind and once I'd organised the flights that would take Mum, Dad, Chris and me (yes, he definitely wanted to come) to the States in June I would spend my afternoons enjoying the sunshine in the garden. But my state of happy anticipation was soon to be quashed.

About a week after coming home, I was sitting on the patio, soaking up the last rays of the afternoon sun, when I was struck by a crashing headache, the likes of which I had never experienced before. The pain was so appalling that I started screaming and very soon I was violently sick. Mum managed to get me inside and up to my bedroom in the lift we'd had installed, and then called the emergency doctor. He had never heard of syringomyelia and I was obliged to deliver a short tutorial on my condition between continuing bouts of agony and vomiting. An injection of cyclimorph failed to stop either and an ambulance was called. Once again – this was by now becoming tediously familiar – I was gripped by a sense of absolute terror. I knew Bernard Williams had left the country the previous day and wouldn't be back for a fortnight. He and his family had gone to Tehran to stay with his in-laws for a holiday.

Which left me, to my dismay, in the hands of the hospital that had been unable to diagnose my problem in the first place. Not a terrifically encouraging state of affairs. How could they possibly know what to do now?

But as I waited for the ambulance, with every blinding thump of my head I considered my situation. It didn't much matter if I went there or not, did it? This was it. My time was up. I really was about to die.

chapter 21

My arrival at Morriston Hospital in Swansea was a blur. By now I was drifting in and out of consciousness, though I did surface sufficiently to register that the date was 10 May 1990, exactly ten years to the day since the original accident. After this had sunk in, I retreated to the comfort of oblivion, pausing only to make one quick mental note: should I by some miracle survive (and I was convinced that I wouldn't) I must somehow endeavour to avoid all subsequent May 10ths.

Everyone got busy. A whole barrage of tests was ordered, including a lumbar puncture, which seemed to me pointless. I wasn't a doctor, but even I knew how difficult it would be to get any fluid from beneath my operation site. No one seemed to take on board my diagnosis of syringomyelia, or my conviction that the sudden and catastrophic headache might have been caused by displacement of the shunt that had been put in. Instead, there was much talk of my having meningitis (hence the lumbar puncture), and discussions took place about what should be done next.

As the hours passed and it began to seem that I wasn't about to expire imminently, I had no choice but to lose myself in the morass of pain and frustration that seemed to be my lot for as long as I hung on. I was being nursed as a paraplegic so, while slight relief could be gained only by lying on my left, I was being turned, as was normal, two-hourly so I only got this relief for two hours out of every six. The lumbar puncture failed. I couldn't cry because it hurt to. I didn't know quite what to do with myself, other than lie there and wonder 'Why me?' I decided I must have done something terribly heinous in a past life to have so much bloody wretchedness heaped upon me now. Eventually I decided I'd return to my fallback of praying: 'Our Father who art in heaven …', 'Hail Mary, full of grace …'. Look, I told God. If I'm going to die anyway, at least get on with it, will you? And please, if you feel inclined to grant me one wish, let me be reunited with my gran and my cat.

It was slap bang in the middle of one of these entreaties that Chris arrived from North Wales, prompting me to realise that it didn't have to be this way. I wasn't necessarily going to die. It wasn't a given. So why didn't I just do the obvious thing and get Chris to ring Bernard Williams in Tehran, for goodness' sake? He'd given me a contact number for that very purpose, after all.

Chris went back to Connaught Street and made the call for me, and Bernard Williams's advice was straightforward: don't let either of the neurosurgeons at Morriston Hospital even contemplate operating on me. With meningitis ruled out and my pain now at least bearable, I should simply hang on in there and await his return. I knew little of hospital politics, obviously; only, in keeping with much of the general public, that neurosurgeons – often dubbed brain surgeons by the non-medical – were both deified and held slightly in awe. No wonder, then, that they tended to have a reputation for huge egos. I later found out that both of the esteemed neurosurgeons at Morriston had other appellations around the hospital: one was known as 'God', the other as 'God Almighty'. So, despite all the usual diplomacy that was brought to bear on the situation, it was perhaps understandable that neither was terrifically impressed at essentially being told what (or, rather, what *not*) to do.

But it was Bernard Williams in whose skill and expertise I'd placed my trust, and if Bernard Williams said I must not be operated on, then I was content to do as instructed. This meant my spending my final few days as the black sheep of the hospital, with only the ward sister for a friend, but, given the pain I was in and also my fierce loyalty to my consultant, I really didn't much care.

After ten days in Morriston, they let me go home to wait for Bernard's return and readmission to the Priory. By now I'd been sent to another hospital for an MRI scan, which had been forwarded directly to the Priory Hospital, and all I could do was hang on as best I could. We had at least established that my pain could be managed for the most part simply by my remaining almost absolutely still. Mum phoned and cancelled the flights to the States, Chris went back to North Wales and returned to work, and I tried not to feel sorry for myself.

I was back in the Priory by the end of that week, where the sight of Bernard Williams's concerned face reminded me that not dying was a plus. Or would have been if only living didn't hurt quite so much.

'What's been happening to you?' he asked gently.

'It feels for all the world,' I said, without too much animation, 'as if the shunt has slipped and is sucking all the fluid out of my head. It feels like my eyes could cave in.'

'Oh, that's typical,' he said, smiling. 'I ask what's been happening, and you come out with a bloody diagnosis! Well, it's easily proved or disproved with an X-ray, in any case. Can you cope with an X-ray, Dizzy? I'll get you some decent pain relief first. You shouldn't be in pain. How's that sound?'

My relief knew no bounds.

The X-ray and MRI did indeed prove that the shunt had slipped, but any smug satisfaction I might have felt about my clinical acumen was soon displaced when he announced he'd have to operate again. 'The shunt's done its job and the syrinx is flat, so it looks as though I'll have to open up old what's-his-face's scar and pull it out.'

'And stitch me up *care*fully,' I pointed out, grinning back (the pain relief had worked wonders). 'Old what's-his-face had to open me up twice, remember, and he still managed to do a neat job.'

Bernard seemed to take this as the ultimate challenge. There was obviously male pride at work here. Ridiculous. Two gladiators, both big, both imposing, both savers of lives, both competing over who did the best sewing.

He operated on me the following day, bringing an instant improvement in my headache. However, a strange thing happened. Where previously I'd flushed on the right side of my face, now I had flushes on my left. Physiology was absolutely clueless, and Bernard too. So he asked me. 'You got a hypothesis for this one, Dizzy?'

Sadly, I didn't. 'No matter,' he said. 'Be something to add to your case presentation at the convention. It's such a shame you won't be coming after all.'

A *great* shame, I thought. Then I had another thought. Now he'd removed the wandering shunt, I felt fine. I felt wonderful, in fact. I felt for all the world as if there wasn't a single reason why I shouldn't re-book and go with him.

I said so and, having considered, Bernard Williams agreed that there was no medical reason why I couldn't. 'But it'll hit you in the pocket,' he added, ' Re-booking flights so late.'

I didn't care. I simply wanted to go. So, fourteen days after my second operation, the four of us were on a plane on the way to Tennessee: Mum, Dad, me and, of course, Chris.

Being at the convention in Nashville was like having a light switched on in my brain. Although I'd previously been averse to spending heaps of time with people similarly afflicted to myself, this was different and new and exciting.

It was completely different from going on holiday. The Americans I met there were such interesting company, and I looked forward to hearing their stories all about their diverse backgrounds and how they coped with their problems. As well as being a medical conference (I felt quite the celebrity during Bernard's main lecture), it was also a massive networking opportunity. However overused the buzzword, the networking was a key part of what was happening here. There were all sorts of workshops, some for syringomyelia sufferers and separate ones for their partners, which I unsuccessfully urged Chris to go to.

The main highlight, however, was being in another country for a more meaningful reason than just lying around getting a suntan. And being around Bernard, of course. He was such a character and a life force, it was easy to see why he commanded so much respect. And he lived life to the full in all ways. Now fifty-eight, he was soon to become a father for the seventh time. After his first marriage had failed, he'd married a young Iranian radiographer from the Midland Neurological Centre, the beautiful Suzi, who was now pregnant with their second child. I'd met their first, Georgie, when I'd been staying at the Priory Hospital, as well as one of Bernard's daughters from his first marriage, who was a junior doctor there.

My time in Nashville was so unlike anything else I'd ever experienced before that I was mostly in a state of mild bedazzlement. I wasn't entertaining any wild ideas about launching myself off on some sort of medical career, but it was still exciting to be a part of the global science community and to feel such a strong sense of camaraderie and support, and of really worthwhile things being achieved. I was also happy to be back in America. It had never lost its charm. The more I saw of it, the more it seemed to me that this was somewhere I wanted to be.

* * *

Though I didn't necessarily want to be there with Chris. Having paid such a lot for our flights, we'd already decided that once the conference was over (and Bernard had decamped to the Bahamas to visit his brother) we'd take an internal flight and head for some sunshine in Florida. Nashville, by now, was experiencing pretty grim, wet weather, whereas the Sunshine State would hopefully do as described and deliver.

Which it did. Though we were slightly anxious to be greeted on the tarmac at Orlando by torrential rain, lightning storms and predictions that both were set in for the duration, the following day dawned as hot and sunny as anyone could wish for. We made the most of it, winding down after all the excitement of the conference by spending the next two days camped by the pool.

By day three, however, I was anxious to be active, and was keen to go and visit the newly opened Universal Studios. Mum and Dad were also keen. Chris was not. He was more interested in improving his tan.

This didn't worry me in the slightest. We'd been cooped up together for so many long stretches just lately that I thought it would do us good to spend some time apart. I told him that I'd go with Mum and Dad and we'd tell him all about it on our return.

To my complete consternation, however, Chris thought my decision was the wrong one. If he was staying by the pool, then *I* should stay by the pool. He didn't seem able to advance a reason for this, other than whatever he was doing, I should be doing also. In short, I must not entertain any notion of ever being out of his sight.

We'd had these conversations before, several times. I was used to the drill of his phone calls on weekdays, demanding to know what I was doing at all times, and, most importantly, who I was doing it with. At first I'd been flattered that he missed me so much, but in time it began to get just a little irritating. I trusted him. Why couldn't he trust me?

I put up with it, however, because I didn't know any different. I'd not been in a serious relationship before and I didn't know what the rules were. Yes, I knew Chris had always had slightly possessive tendencies, but they were understandable, weren't they? It must be hard for him, after all, being so far away. But we'd been living in each other's pockets, it seemed, for weeks now. I needed some space. *He* needed some space. This was getting ridiculous. I rounded on him. I told him I would do exactly as I liked. If he didn't want to come, that was up to him. But equally, what I did was up to *me*. We were supposed to be equals. He didn't *own* me.

In the end, though, I didn't go to Universal Studios. We were much too busy rowing. I packed Mum and Dad off – they were happy to go, I think – and we went at each other for a horrible, exhausting and ultimately pointless two hours.

Had I known that this would soon become a pattern, perhaps I'd have had the sense to act differently in future. But as it was, the row eventually ended. He felt awful, he said. He apologised. He told me he couldn't help it. It was just because he loved me. He didn't mean to be so possessive and controlling. And so I forgave him, as I'd continue to do.

After all, I told myself, it was better than being alone.

chapter 22

When I returned from the States I felt energised. I knew I'd found my vocation at last. And I also wanted to say thank you. I was still doing 'Awareness and Prevention' talks for the Spinal Injuries Association, but in the weeks and months following Nashville I also threw myself into fund-raising for the charity in the UK that supported Bernard's work and research. ANTS (Anne's Neurological Trust Society – now renamed the Anne Conroy Trust) had been founded by one of Bernard's patients. As well as being a fund-raising organisation, ANTS was also an information provider and self-help group, in which I began to take an active part.

The people of Port Talbot were incredibly generous with both their time and their money, and between us we were able to raise thousands of pounds. I organised anything I could think of where people would have fun, from well-attended pub quizzes to twenty-four-hour pool-playing marathons – one of which Bernard and his family even came down to take part in.

My life, in short, had become both full and meaningful. There was always something new to be doing, new places to go and new people to meet. I travelled to Birmingham on a regular basis, sometimes for meetings, sometimes for cheque presentations, and, as my involvement with the charity's work grew, to spend time with other paraplegic syringomyelia patients, at both the Priory Hospital and the Midland Centre for Neurosurgery and Neurology – work that I particularly enjoyed.

Chris, by this time, was living two streets away. He was sacked from his job in North Wales shortly after we returned from Nashville. He'd done exactly what I'd feared he might – taken unauthorised leave to accompany me there. I wasn't sure quite how to feel about this. On the one hand, his commitment to me was touching, but on the other hand – and this thought was constantly in the forefront of my mind – why would Chris do something so reckless? It seemed completely out of character. It surely couldn't have been just because he was desperate for the holiday. Was his job really worth losing for a fortnight in the sun?

I couldn't help thinking it was more to precipitate what had been on his mind for some time: he wanted to come back to South Wales for good. But if that was the case then why not talk to me about it? Plan it? Why lose his job and his chance of a good reference?

Once again, I made myself accept it as par for the course. Perhaps this new me – the person with the feisty, independent, go-getting spirit that I liked to think was simply my natural personality resurfacing – was someone he felt uncertain and insecure around. After all, he was used to being in charge, being in control. Once again I pushed aside my sense of things not being quite right between us. Nowa-

days I'd be more inclined to call it inertia – or even fear –
but back then I ascribed things to the normal amount of
compromise adult relationships required. Either way, Chris
and I trundled on.

The USA, however, was never far from my thoughts,
together with all the new friends I'd made there. We'd been
given an open invitation by Don and Barbara White, the
founders of ASAP, to go and visit them in Texas. Since my
own surgery I had set up a network for syringomyelia
sufferers in South Wales, and an important part of that was
to disseminate information on what was happening of interest to us elsewhere in the world. I was keen to get back and
get an update on ASAP and what was happening over in the
States.

Mum and Dad needed no such excuse. Dad had always
wanted to visit the Lone Star State and was anxious to start
making plans. But in the usual Bowen way, we were over-
due a hiccup, which Dad duly supplied in the April of 1991.
While chatting at the bar at his beloved Aberavon Rugby
Club, just before kick-off one Saturday afternoon, he
collapsed like a pile of potatoes on the floor right in front of
my terrified eyes.

After all the years we'd spent worrying about his chest,
he'd branched out. He had had, it turned out, a mini-
stroke. Watching your sixty-four-year-old father collapse
unconscious on the floor is a singularly arresting sight. I
simply couldn't imagine my world without Dad in it, and
though he recovered quickly and with minimal fuss and

drama, it dawned on me, in ways that perhaps up to then it hadn't, that my parents had been nothing short of wonderful. The epitome of tireless and unconditional love. I put all thoughts of globe-trotting out of my head. My wonderful life of travel and adventure was, I decided, as nothing compared to the reality of Mum and Dad's health.

All of which Dad thought ridiculous. He wasn't about to let some mere neurological event stand in the way of his trip to the Alamo – after all, *I* hadn't, had I? So it was that we re-made our latest travel plans. Chris had by now started working in Port Talbot. He was doing what he'd been doing before the move to North Wales – selling advertising space in a local newspaper. He was adamant he had amassed sufficient paid holiday that he could come to Texas without jeopardising his career prospects.

Again I felt ambivalent about where things were headed between us. I was no longer sure I still loved him the way I once had, yet I'd become so used to us as a couple – to *him* – that I couldn't seem to find the will to give him up. But things were clearly far from right. I obviously didn't feel sufficiently strongly about him that the pull of living life on *my* terms wasn't equally compelling. I was particularly looking forward to visiting the charity headquarters and finding out what else, in real terms, I could do. I knew Chris wasn't interested in any of this, but if he was happy to come along on the understanding that I *was*, then so be it. Perhaps it would all work out between us in the end.

But if it didn't, in the planning, feel quite right for either of us, the trip itself was a great success. I even made my very first TV appearance, interviewed as one of Bernard's success stories.

By now I'd got the bug and was only too pleased to be asked to accompany Bernard on his next ASAP conference, which took place in early 1992 in Washington, DC. This time we decided to treat ourselves to some luxury and so tacked on three days at the Fontainebleau Hilton on Miami Beach. Here the gods smiled on us. A mistake over our booking for a disabled-access room was deemed by the hotel manager to be an error of sufficient gravity that we were upgraded to two of the hotel's finest suites – completely *gratis* – with complimentary champagne, fruit and flowers every day for the length of our stay.

The Fontainebleau itself was very much of the moment. It had recently acted as the backdrop to the feature film *The Bodyguard* and, just as it had for Whitney Houston and Kevin Costner, the luxurious surroundings would provide the backdrop to Chris's and my last romantic gasp.

Mum and Dad had seen Sunday brunch advertised and on the final day suggested we treat ourselves. The hotel's Sunday brunch was a legendary affair, involving champagne on tap, elaborate ice sculptures, and world-class cuisine prepared by world-renowned chefs. It was expensive and somewhat formal (you had to dress appropriately), but it was just what we fancied to finish off our trip. A chance to escape the unforgiving Floridian sun and also to splurge the money we'd saved by being given our wonderful free rooms.

Chris, however, didn't fancy it and, as so often happened, told me to inform Dad that he and I wouldn't be going because we would be sunbathing on the beach. I told him I'd already done more than enough sunbathing, and went off to plan what I'd wear.

Sunday morning came and we all trooped down in our glad rags while Chris trudged off grumpily, in flip-flops and shorts, to the beach. But we'd only just had time to take in the bubbly, the fresh flowers and our place at the buffet, when we were startled by his sudden arrival. As were the staff – he was still in his swim shorts and vest, having obviously had a change of mind and rushed up straight from the beach. The horrified *maitre d'* sped over in seconds. 'I'm so sorry, sir,' he mouthed, 'but jackets and ties *must* be worn.' Chris affected irritation and said he didn't have them, and a tweedy brown jacket was eventually found. I was pink with embarrassment and fuming with my fiancé. How difficult would it have been for him simply to go up and change first? I couldn't believe he could be so bolshy and childish in order to make such an unimportant point.

Looking back, I can see the signs and reasons for our demise so clearly. We were only in our twenties: young and, in many respects, carefree, yet we were locked into the worst kind of power struggle. Years later, I'd find out from Juli that a similar pattern had ended her marriage to Chris. In me, he had taken on someone who he felt needed a carer and, as such, someone over whom he could maintain some control. Many relationships thrive on such inequalities. Few romantic partnerships are equal in all ways, and successful unions often depend on the right fit.

So it had been for Chris and me in the beginning. But every step I subsequently took towards making my life full and worthwhile and exciting meant one less reason to need him. I dare say he'd have his own take on what happened, but for me, on that day, it seemed perfectly clear. We'd run our course. There was never going to be any marriage. We wanted entirely different things from life.

We finally split up three weeks after our return to the UK. I obviously hadn't found the man of my dreams yet. If I did, I was convinced I would know it. I just didn't imagine I ever would.

With Chris out of my life I felt disorientated and strange for a bit, but I was also visited by a growing feeling of release – so much so that it soon became obvious that it had been right to part. I felt unfettered and free to embrace anything that came my way. This was in part down, once again, to my parents.

They'd been brilliant all my life, obviously, but since my accident they'd been tested way beyond what was usual and, in my eyes, they'd never once faltered. They were both supportive and positive about my need for independence, but always made it clear that they were there for me.

I was constantly aware that the nature of my relationship with my parents post the accident differed markedly from that of almost all my contemporaries – how could it not? – and also acutely aware what a debt of gratitude I owed them. Now they were getting older, and suffering various health problems, I was proud to be in a position to give something back: from seeking out the very best medical care for them to spoiling them whenever the

opportunity arose. They were nothing short of my very
best friends.

And, as best friends do, they wanted me to be happy. So,
far from dissuading me from travelling and making my way
in the States, Mum and Dad were all for it. They'd been
bitten by the travel bug themselves when they were young,
and had gone almost all the way down the path to emigrat-
ing to New Zealand in the fifties. Their plans were only
scuppered because Dad wasn't eligible for assisted passage
and the £200 cost was beyond his reach. They were all too
aware of their own mortality and anxious to see me settled
and contented. If that meant in America then they were
behind me all the way. The frequent winter visits were also
good for Dad's chest. For a while we even entertained the
idea of us all moving there permanently and setting up some
sort of business – we rather fancied the idea of a Welsh
restaurant and bar. But reason prevailed. When we began to
discuss it seriously, our solicitor (by now a family friend)
pointed out that for Mum and Dad this would be somewhat
reckless. Should the business fail, they'd have nothing to
come back to.

But still it felt the place where I was destined to be. I was
as keen as ever to be involved in the syringomyelia charity,
but had also hatched a plan to do travel journalism out
there, writing about my travelling experiences from the
point of view of a disabled person, which, at that point, was
a relatively new thing.

In the meantime, the travelling continued. I was not quite
yet thirty. I had the world at my feet. All the bad times, I felt
sure, were behind me.

chapter 23

There's a saying that everyone reaches a point when life stops giving you things and instead starts taking them away. A slightly maudlin sentiment, but nevertheless often true.

For me, by 1994 life was still good. Not by any means perfect – the man of my dreams had yet to appear – but in most respects I was happy and busy and, most importantly, well. I was definitely not fulfilling the prediction made at Rookwood that I would most likely be dead by the age of thirty.

As well as my travels and charity work, I was by now a regular at my old school, St Joseph's, continuing my work on Awareness and Prevention in a local and very personal way. I'd also joined Swansea gun club, having first convinced the board that no, I didn't have a particular ex's face in mind every time I raised and aimed a pistol. It was a good gun club, too. The son of the founders, Adrian Morris, had already competed in the Commonwealth Games in Canada that year. My own ambitions were less lofty. I was happy enough to become a pretty good shot. It's not every girl who can say she can handle a Smith & Wesson .38 revolver.

Life had, however, been flexing her muscles around me. In late 1993 Dad had another health scare. He'd been having symptoms of lumbago and sciatica, which Morriston Hospital, after conducting some tests, had decided were the result of wear and tear. Yet Dad was in pain and didn't feel right; surely something more was going on here? I paid for him to have a private MRI scan in Cardiff but, once again, we were told there was nothing obviously wrong. A week later, however, his symptoms started worsening, and I decided to ask Bernard what he thought. He organised a CT scan for Dad, which finally revealed what the problem was. There was a mass pressing on the nerve roots in his lower back – in other words, a tumour. By this time Bernard and his family had become firm friends, but it never occurred to any of us to expect favours. Nevertheless, Dad was taken into the Priory Hospital immediately, got the best care imaginable, and Bernard refused to accept a fee. Happily, the tumour turned out to be benign, and Dad made a speedy recovery. We were all hugely grateful, and also felt blessed. This wonderful man had come into our lives and, although Dad's tumour hadn't been malignant, it still felt as though he'd managed to save him.

But the tide of good luck wasn't to last.

Dad wasn't the only person involved in Aberavon Rugby Club. My original saviour and much-cherished adversary Mike Davies was a major figure there too. Indeed, he had been their team surgeon for some years. Mike's love of rugby kept him pretty busy. As well as his role at Aberavon, and his surgical commitments to the rugby players of almost all the surrounding areas, he was also surgeon to the under-19 squad of the Welsh Youth Rugby Union, travelling with them all over the world.

It was through the rugby connection that Dad, now recovered, learned that Mike had fallen victim to cancer. He'd apparently found a lump in his groin the previous Christmas that he rather strongly hoped was a hernia. It turned out it wasn't. Having tried and failed to find any benign reason for its existence, he began to suspect a lymphoma. So he took himself off to see one of his general surgical colleagues, who'd suffered from the same thing a few years back. Tests proved him right and he'd immediately been started on a course of chemotherapy in Cardiff.

The news of his ill health affected me deeply. He must still be so young. I didn't know his exact age but it seemed to be so cruel that this titan – this man who'd always seemed so invulnerable to me – might be struck down by this horrible disease. It made me feel vulnerable myself. Ridiculous really, as I'd not seen or spoken to him in over a decade, but so great had been his importance in my life and well-being that just knowing he was there made me feel strong. Thinking he might not be was scary.

Though I was surrounded by less than edifying events, life was unkind to me personally that year in only a small way. At the end of October, I managed to break my heel getting from my chair to my sofa. Not normally something noted for being a hazardous manoeuvre, but my talent for such mishaps was becoming legendary, so no one was terribly surprised.

I made the familiar trip to Neath General Hospital where the fracture clinic sister, Delyth, told me our favourite surgeon would be in to see me and my heel shortly. 'He'll have a shock,' she said. 'Seeing you here after so long.' I just hoped he wouldn't consider it a bad one.

I was pleased to see him looking so well, and told him so, even though his hair, mostly lost as a result of the chemo, still had a little way to go. 'Hmm,' he answered, ruefully, clearly less impressed than I was, 'I look just like a Balkan terrorist.'

Seeing people you love and care about going though bad times is the best reminder you could ever be given that you need to make the most of your time on the planet. I was determined to press on with my plans for my own life, and by the end of that year I was back in Florida again, on the one hand to protect Dad's chest from the damp winters of Port Talbot, and on the other to do some fact-finding for myself. One of the ideas I'd had for employment (given that I couldn't stay in the States for more than 90 days without it) was the by then massive Walt Disney machine. The Disney Empire was growing all the time and was well known for having a very enthusiastic and proactive approach to employment of disabled staff.

During our pre-Christmas visit I'd applied for a job there and been for an initial screening interview. When we returned in January I had a second interview, where it was suggested that I might be suitable for Epcot. The Epcot Center, which was at that time one of the three big attractions at Walt Disney World, was a leisure park whose theme *was* the world. Most of the major countries you could think of were represented, their famous monuments scaled down to fit. Within this, they had a Welsh section, complete with a Welsh gift and souvenir shop, and though their souvenir T-shirts bore the mis-spelt legend 'LLanelly' (instead of Llanelli), it sounded like a fun place to be.

Less fun, however, was the reality of becoming one of Disney's 'cast members'. Accommodation was shared between staff (many of them students) from all over Europe, the working days were routinely twelve hours in length, and there was a hyper-strict code regarding clothing and jewellery. For perhaps the first time in my life, I actually felt old – too old to be a cog in such an inflexible wheel, too old to rough it, too old, particularly, to lose my individuality.

Still, the trip proved of benefit in other ways. I needed to prove to myself that I was truly independent, and this was the first time I'd stayed and lived there alone. Mum and Dad headed back to the UK once I was settled and I remained, without drama or incident, till May.

By then, though I had ruled out the idea of working for Disney, I was committed to making a new life for myself over there, albeit with frequent trips home to see my parents. When I returned to the US in the summer, it was with the firm intention of finding myself work.

On my most recent ASAP conference trip to Chicago (one that Bernard had had to miss due to pressure of work but requested that I report back to him about) I'd met a man called Rusty, who worked for the Disability Rights Movement. We had already met before, in a fleeting sort of way, back in Washington when I'd been to an ASAP conference with Chris. Unbeknown to me, because of Chris's reluctance to socialise and what looked, as a consequence, like our frosty aloofness, we'd been dubbed the Prince and Princess of Wales. I was mightily pleased to have a chance to put things straight.

Based in York, Pennsylvania, Rusty was in his mid-thirties, and quadriplegic as a result of his syringomyelia. Before the condition had taken hold and done its hateful work, he'd been a track athlete. Ironically, he'd been given the nickname of Rusty – his real name was Ralph – when his performances started falling away. Little did anyone know at the time about the devastating nature of the condition that was the cause.

Rusty's work with the Disability Rights Movement involved lobbying politicians, giving talks on equality, organising and co-ordinating protests and events, and running a busy and dynamic office. Happily for me, it seemed there might be an opening coming up soon, for someone to do secretarial and administrative work.

Rusty and I really hit it off, and here was the prospect of a perfect-sounding job. Crucially, a paid one. And it wasn't just a matter of getting a Green Card; outside the UK I couldn't claim disability benefit and my compensation money was not a bottomless pit. I also needed a good wage in order to get medical insurance, and this one even had insurance as a part of the package. This, however, was for the long term. In the short term I was still acclimatising and fact-finding, and looking for a suitable apartment in Florida. Ideally I wanted somewhere outside the main tourist areas so I wouldn't be fleeced for rent.

With the prospect of an interesting job on the horizon, everything, it seemed, was going well. *Too* well, clearly, because on 29 July, the day before my thirtieth birthday, Mum telephoned me with terrible news. Bernard Williams had had a motorcycle accident. He was critically injured and things didn't look good.

It was as if all the stuffing had been ripped from inside me. Dad's tumour. Mike's tumour. And now Bernard close to death. How *could* he be? I'd thought he was invincible. The horrible thoughts tumbled thick and fast around me. What about his wife Suzi? What about his children? I prayed for the best but expected the worst.

My thirtieth birthday saw me desperately trying to get a flight back to the UK. Mired in anxiety and gloom, it didn't escape my notice that there was the cruellest-possible irony in all this. The three men who had meant the most to me – the father who'd cared for me, the surgeon who'd saved me, the neurosurgeon who'd saved me a second time – had all had a major brush with mortality in the year I'd been told *I* was scheduled to die. If this was fate's joke, I decided, it was a sick one.

Then Mum called again. Bernard had gone.

chapter 24

Despite the best efforts of Hurricane Felix, we arrived in Birmingham in good time to attend Bernard Williams's funeral.

It hadn't looked as though I'd make it. Mum's terrible news had come at a time when the airspace above Florida was buzzing with traffic – ferrying happy travellers to their holiday destinations, to live out, albeit briefly, the American Dream.

For me it was a dream that I was hoping would become reality. I'd been back in the States for the best part of three months this time and was beginning to feel very much at home. A big part of this – which was now to prove crucial – was that I'd begun to make friends.

One of the highlights of my trip on this occasion had been a visit from a woman called Mary Catherine, who'd driven down from her home in Massachusetts earlier in the summer to spend her vacation in Florida with me. I'd first met her the previous February in Orlando, at a conference organised by the American Spinal Injuries Association. We'd hit it off straight away but, with a packed conference agenda, had had little time just to hang out as friends.

Mary Catherine had been born with spina bifida and had been largely wheelchair-dependent all her life. She'd also had her right leg amputated below the knee when she was ten, following septicaemia as a result of an infected pressure sore. Not that it seemed to stop her doing anything. We'd had a brilliant two weeks taking in every theme park we could manage, culminating in a thrilling helicopter ride – my very first – which was her treat for my being 'such a good hostess'. I was touched and happy to receive this compliment; not only was I living entirely independently, but I was even entertaining house guests!

Mary wasn't just a vacation thrill-seeker, however. She was a powerhouse of energy who had spent much of her adult life campaigning on disability issues, and had also got a degree in counselling. In what was left of her time she'd managed to get herself a private pilot's licence, the open biplane being her aeronautic machine of choice.

Though I didn't share her confidence once above terra firma, I certainly enjoyed the helicopter experience, and, hyped-up and excited, we decided to finish the last day of her trip in fine style by heading down to the Mercado. The Mercado was one of Orlando's highlights, and one of the main tourist attractions on International Drive. It was an open square surrounded by brightly lit and coloured shops, bars, restaurants and nightclubs. After a meal and a few beers we swerved our way into the centre of the square, with live music – a nightly staple – throbbing all around us.

We'd just spotted a vacant table and were making our way towards it when we heard a male voice obviously directed our way call out, 'Hey, a good-looking broad in a wheelchair!' We'd just registered that when it was followed by 'Holy shit, TWO good lookers! Look out, ladies, here we come!' I couldn't quite work out what I was seeing at first; I was looking at the back of a very wide wheelchair, in which sat a very wide guy. One who seemed to be closing on us fast. And 'back' was, in this case, the operative word – because he was actually approaching in reverse, at some speed.

Just as it reached us, the wheelchair spun around with a flourish and we were greeted by the sight of a broad toothy grin set in a huge bushy beard, beneath eyes that were full of wicked-looking mischief. All this was set amid a curly brown mane.

My eyes travelled down over a generous expanse of stomach and the reason for the wheelchair became obvious. Where his right leg should have been was an empty and rolled jeans leg – his amputation had been almost at the hip joint. Still grinning, he introduced us to Greg, his able-bodied friend, while mopping his brow with a handkerchief. He then extended his free hand in greeting. 'My name is Martin,' he said brightly. 'I sure hope you girls like sweaty guys!'

I grinned back at him, delighted. I was about to make another, rather wonderful, new friend.

Before long, I was to find out just how good a friend Martin was. By the end of the day following Mum's second call, I finally managed to secure a flight back to the UK. Not from Orlando – there was nothing available from there for another seven days – but from Miami, at four in the after-noon the following day. Though even if I could make the 300-mile journey to get down there, the airline weren't at all happy about taking me. Last-minute seats weren't easy to come by, particularly in the middle of high season, and they certainly weren't cheap. Determined to get there by hook or by crook, I'd pulled out all the stops to get one. Their response, understandably, was to attach the condition that as they didn't want to have to manage a distraught paraplegic they'd only take me as long as I wasn't travelling alone.

I'd been in conversation with Martin and told him my tragic news and when I explained my problems getting back to the UK he'd produced a solution just like a magician pulls a rabbit from a hat. 'Simple,' he said. 'I'll come with you. I've always wanted to go to the UK.'

And it wouldn't be just the two of us travelling either. Two years divorced, Martin currently had his twelve-year-old son Lee staying for a month, and saw no difficulty in combining helping me out with an impromptu trip across the Atlantic for him and Lee. Lee was a sweet boy, who I got along really well with, and I was pleased for the distraction of his engaging company. He was, as expected, seriously excited.

Within the day Martin had got organised, packed and sorted for the journey, including what would have to be an extra stop in Miami to get his hands on two equally impromptu passports. The travel plan to get there was complex too. As there was no room in his tiny Nissan for a third passenger, let alone one who travelled with a conti-nent's worth of luggage, we arranged that we'd travel to the

city separately. He and Lee had left Orlando six hours ahead
of me, to give them time to locate the passport office in
downtown Miami – a place with one of those daunting
American addresses: something like '301 Northwest First
South 53rd Street East'. It felt a real possibility that he'd
never find it and be trapped in Miami's road grid in perpe-
tuity.

In the event, though, he did, and our rendezvous was
seamless. Despite spending a four-hour hurricane delay
stranded miserably on the tarmac, we arrived in the UK as
scheduled, and after a night in Port Talbot to dump luggage
and pick up suitable funeral attire we were on our way to
Birmingham the following morning.

By now we had managed to book rooms at the Birmingham Hyatt Hotel, where we'd stayed many times in the past.
The Hyatt had always been superb at accommodating us
and had never found difficulty in meeting my specific needs,
so we knew they wouldn't fail us now. And they didn't. As
soon as we arrived I spoke to the concierge about hiring a
suitably accessible and appropriately coloured car that could
transport the five of us to the church and the cemetery. This
would not be simple. Not only did we have a brace of wheelchairs, but there was also Martin's size to consider. Nevertheless, the hotel got it sorted, as I'd hoped, and when we
arrived in the lobby at the appointed time we were assured
it would be waiting outside.

It turned out to be a busy day at the Birmingham Hyatt.
This was around the time of the hugely successful TV show
Gladiators, which was filmed every week at Birmingham's
National Indoor Arena, just across the road. So it probably

wasn't noteworthy for us to come down to find the lobby
full of the gladiators themselves: Saracen, Jet and Wolf, to
name just a few. No surprise either that when a navy stretch
limo drew up outside, they all headed, in a gaggle, towards
it. Then came a voice: 'Bowen party, please!' I'm not sure
which party was more stunned to hear this. The gladiators
certainly looked pretty non-plussed as we passed them – me
sweeping past in my wheelchair, Martin hobbling, one-
legged, on his crutches, and two tiny older people and a
young boy trailing behind. Showbizzy celebs we were not.

But if we thought we'd made an impressive exit, it was as
nothing compared to our entrance at the church. As if we
weren't making quite enough of an impression by turning
up in a stretch limo, our driver, clearly anxious to take care
of his disabled cargo, was keen to ensure our experience was
a smooth one. Such was his determination to secure parking
close to the disabled rank in front of the church that he shot
off after the hearse, cutting off one of the family funeral cars.
And his zeal didn't end there. He was so concerned that the
ramp might be blocked by another vehicle that he parked
right up so close behind the hearse that the coffin could not
be pulled out until I was safely deposited on the pavement.

I just hoped Bernard, in death, had retained his sense of
humour. Somehow, I felt sure that he would have.

It was only once we arrived at the cemetery that the loss
of this brilliant doctor and wonderful friend began to sink
in. We stayed in the limo during the burial itself to let the
family have time together in private at the graveside. It was
a hot August afternoon and we were grateful for the cool
of the car in which to be quiet with our thoughts. Other

mourners sought shade from the sun under trees. Once the family had left, Mum, Dad and I went to the grave. We'd each brought white roses, which we laid in silence, but soon the still of the afternoon was broken as scores of other mourners began appearing around us, many of them obviously current and former patients; some 'walking wounded', and some in wheelchairs. My gaze was drawn by a woman who I judged to be in her seventies, supporting a young man – her son, I imagined – who was walking unsteadily.

'Are you a patient of Dr Williams?' she asked me as they drew near. I nodded, the lump in my throat too big for me to speak.

'Him too,' she said, indicating the silent young man beside her. 'Mr Williams removed his brain tumours. No one else would touch him.' She gazed down at the coffin, as if, like me, she still couldn't quite accept that within it lay the man who'd transformed so many lives. Then she turned back to me and there was anxiety in her features. 'It feels,' she said softly, 'as if we're tightrope walkers. And now our safety net has gone.'

In hindsight, I think perhaps my own American Dream was buried along with Bernard on that sultry summer afternoon. I returned to the US, as planned, in the middle of September, where my flat in Florida was now organised. I even made a trip up to Pennsylvania to see Rusty, to take further my application to move there and work for Disability Rights. But when I returned to the UK for another visit in the October of that year, it was to find my father's health very poor. His chest had become a matter of serious concern, and, in my absence, he'd been admitted to hospital as an emergency patient and had been through a sticky few days.

Much as I loved America, its pull on me was weakening. In December I made the decision to cancel my impending interview and put all thoughts of a permanent move there right out of my head. Bernard had died, Dad was seriously ill, and if there was one thing I knew that I simply couldn't contemplate, it was the thought of losing another of my nearest and dearest while I sat in the sun 4,000 miles away.

It was time to implement Plan B.

chapter 25

Implementing major life plans is a fine idea, for sure, but I didn't have any in my head. In the months following my return to the UK I felt lost and demotivated. Though I was obviously relieved to be with Mum and Dad, and anxious to support Dad through his health problems, I felt sad that the goal I'd carried with me for so many years was no longer with me – was over. Plus being back in the UK brought it home to me forcibly that Bernard Williams was no longer at the end of a phone. No longer anywhere, in fact. I felt lonely. I had always said, and believed, that I wouldn't live out my life just existing in Port Talbot. If it was true that my accident had happened for a reason and that all the things I had done since were as a result of my misfortune, then it was equally true that what I'd been through could not, would not, be for nothing. But all the opportunities and challenges that I'd so much relished being able to take on in America were no longer available to me. My engine was still running but I had no direction. What I really needed was a push.

And happily, I got one. Almost literally. Because I'd been a patient at Rookwood with Chris Hallam, and had been coached for my (mercifully short) sporting career by John

Harris, it made perfect sense for these two paralympic champion athletes to get in touch with me when planning their 'Push around Wales'.

This was the second of their ambitious fundraisers. They had completed their first 'Push around Wales' in 1987 to raise money to build a new sports centre for the disabled on the Cyncoed campus of the University of Wales Institute in Cardiff (UWIC). It had opened in 1994, and now their goal was to raise even more money to help keep the fledgling centre going. As the push was scheduled to pass through Port Talbot, they wondered if I'd like to get involved.

Though the push itself didn't appeal to me – I had absolutely no intention of joining in with their testosterone-fuelled brand of manic wheelchair pushing, thanks all the same – I was certainly keen to join the support team behind them, and happy to use my estate car (the big red bus, I called it) to help out with some of the stages.

The push energised me. Keen to capitalise on the presence of such titans in our midst, I slotted in a visit for them both to St Joseph's. Their presence dovetailed nicely with my 'Awareness and Prevention' sessions, and the kids were both enthused and inspired. And though the event itself was marred towards the end by Chris developing kidney problems (which would eventually lead to a transplant from his dad), everything about it felt so good and right that I began at last to see where my future might lie.

'Melanie Bowen, trustee, Wales Sports Centre for the Disabled'. Nope. I couldn't quite believe it either.

*　*　*

Even so, that's what I was invited to be and, after some thought, in 1998 that's what I became. My love of sport hadn't increased an iota, obviously, so the whole sporting ethos didn't much appeal to me personally. However, the concept of a fitness and well-being centre with special provision for users with disabilities did, and I felt honoured to take on the role.

It turned out to be a busy one. Once appointed, I threw myself into my responsibilities with gusto. I even – perish the thought – helped with fitness instruction, my special strength being that I was good at supporting uninitiated new users, particularly those who found the whole thing intimidating – in other words, the elderly, the overweight and the disabled. Despite its name, the centre was used by people from all walks of life, with or without disability. The university students had access to it at all times, and it was used by Welsh International squads in all sports: rugby, ladies' hockey, power lifting and so on. The legendary Olympic long-jump gold medallist Lyn 'the leap' Davies held his sports science classes there as well. As an unthreatening female in a wheelchair in this company, I was much less intimidating than most.

It also gave me an idea. It occurred to me that there was one important group of potential beneficiaries of the Wales Sports Centre for the Disabled (WSCD) who had not, at this point, been considered.

The patients at Rookwood were only based five miles or so away and could, I knew, benefit hugely from being given the chance to come here. It would not only give them an opportunity to experience state-of-the-art equipment designed specifically with disability in mind (instead of the rusting heaps of apparatus I felt quite sure were still in use at Rookwood) but, even more importantly in my book, it would also give them a regular opportunity to be a part of the outside world. It might have been a long time since I'd been banged up there but the sense of incarceration I'd felt had never left me. Here was something useful and valuable I could instigate to help ensure those that came after me didn't feel that way too.

I brought it up at a trust meeting and it was instantly adopted, with me, unsurprisingly, charged with the task of approaching the hospital to see what they thought.

Though I had vowed I would never willingly return to Rookwood, it was with a sense of great purpose and pride (as well as a dry-mouthed *déjà vu*) that I drove back through their gates a few weeks later. I had initially arranged a meeting with the doctor in charge, but he felt it was a matter for the superintendent physiotherapist, so I was duly sent off to address her. Happily, she wasn't in full physio-terrorist garb, but was nevertheless somewhat forbidding. She did hear me out, but her initial response was anything but encouraging. The facilities at Rookwood, she was quick to point out, were coping perfectly adequately with the rehabilitation of their patients. Sensing I was tiptoeing across uncertain, and possibly enemy, territory, I steered clear of the obvious response – that the gym and the equipment there were almost antediluvian. They'd been ancient when I was there twenty years previously and it looked to my eye as if they'd not changed much since.

Instead, I played my other card – that of social rehabilitation. This was something on which she had few grounds to argue and, clearly realising that, she sat patiently and listened while I pointed out that at Rookwood the patients were isolated; they had no contact with anyone bar the hospital staff and other patients. There were no members of the outside world available to interact with, no one to stare at them – something they would soon have to learn to cope with – and, more pressingly, little chance of making spontaneous friendships with people other than the scant few they saw regularly 'inside'.

And all the while, I finished, they'd still be getting fit. She finally agreed that it was worth a trial period and so, a few Wednesdays later, a weekly Rookwood contingent started coming to the WSCD.

The first session wasn't terribly encouraging. The Rookwood group arrived looking like a team of refugees recently evicted from an encampment somewhere grim. Which, in a sense, I suppose they were. They were mostly wearing shorts, as they would usually do inside Rookwood, with their urinary leg bags in full view. Clearly they'd not been given any opportunity to prepare themselves for interacting with the outside world before being bussed here. I was brought up short. No wonder people stared. How hard it must be to develop a sense of dignity and confidence while adjusting to your new situation when you looked as though you belonged in an institution. There was no doubt they felt likewise. My overriding impression on meeting them all was that they looked like rabbits caught in particularly bright headlights.

Happily, a quick word with the physiotherapist accompanying them seemed to do the trick. The following week things were entirely different. Long track pants (velour not compulsory) covered up the leg bags that so clearly marked them out, and the girls had brushed hair and, for some, make-up. Little things, maybe, to the non-interested observer, but to me this transformation really mattered.

Rookwood's association with the WSCD continued past its trial period and is still going to this day. But for me, a new Plan B was brewing.

Not to mention a Plan C.

It was March 2000 and I'd just come into the house after a day at the WSCD. I'd picked up the phone expecting it to be for Mum or Dad, but it wasn't. It was for me. A man called Max Gold, who was a friend of my cousin Francine, who lived in London.

'How do you fancy being in the movies?' he asked.

Max explained to me that he was currently working with a casting director, Leo Davis, who was an industry bigwig, by all accounts. They were currently in talks about a prospective new British movie. It was going to be called *Kiss Kiss (Bang Bang)* and was apparently going to star Martine McCutcheon, latterly a big name through *EastEnders*. I knew Max moved in those sorts of circles, but still wondered quite what all this had to do with me.

A character called Polythene Pam was the answer: a wheelchair-bound hit-woman who murdered her victims by suffocating them with a polythene bag, and who (unsurprisingly) they were having trouble casting. They were after a genuinely disabled woman in her thirties, who had a distinctive accent. Max, it seemed, had suggested me instantly – he well knew that I'd have a go at anything. And, yes, to a Londoner I *did* have an accent, I supposed. And he'd been right. I said yes straight away. Even if the name Polythene Pam did sound like a character in a porn film, it seemed that a better part for me couldn't have been written; I even had the requisite talent with a handgun.

In true movie-world style the script was FedExed to me two days later, and before the week was out I was whisked up to London (first class) and Max was there to meet me at Paddington. We were very soon barrelling along in a taxi to Soho for the first read-through of my bit of the script.

The building was enormous, with a grand and spacious lobby, and an elevator (we were in movie-land – one couldn't possibly call it a lift) that took us up to the first-floor auditioning suites. I was greeted by Leo and a man called Stuart Sugg (who was the writer) plus a producer who had the bad luck to be the last one to greet me – there were so many stars twinkling in my eyes by this time that I was in a daze and forgot his name as soon as he uttered it.

The walls were lined with ranks of glossy movie star photos: Mel Gibson, Michelle Pfeiffer … a whole cornucopia of film idols. It was about now that the reality of where I was really hit me. Worse still, the reality of what I was about to do. My mouth went dry and I began to shake so much that it's a wonder I didn't set off vibrating around the room. I thought calming thoughts. This was just a bit of fun, after all.

Happily, we got underway without delay, and they seemed pleasingly impressed that I'd already learned my lines. In fact, I was just warming to my new role as Major Film Actress when Stuart, for reasons best known to himself, felt the need to prick my bubble of confidence by announcing without warning that I'd be much improved once 'over the abject terror'. Cheek!

Despite the slur, Leo, it seemed, rather liked me, and thought I'd be perfect in the role. Principally, it appeared, because I really looked the part, which was no surprise because I had dressed for it. With my waist-length black hair (this was during a Morticia Adams life phase) and my black leather trousers and waistcoat, I was inhabiting my character as well as I knew how.

A screen test was arranged for the following day, so Max and I spent the evening working on developing my fledgling acting skills. A year at RADA might have been the better option but we made the best of the short time we had available to hone me, and by lunchtime the following day it was all over. The screen test went by in such a blur that I can barely recall any of the details.

I returned to Wales elated and with my head full of dreams. How exciting it would be to be An Actor! The only niggle on the sunny landscape was the reality of it all, and I tried to push all of that away. Yes, the travelling would be hard and the hours would be punishing, but I'd cope – I coped with everything, didn't I? And yes, the thought of doing my own stunts *was* rather scary, but how hard could rolling down a steep ramp at speed leaving my wheelchair to direct itself while I was busy attempting to murder my

assigned victim involving the use of both hands and a polythene bag actually be? I could practise it, couldn't I? I probably wouldn't crash *that* much. And anyway, I had a
fortnight to wait till they came back to me – perhaps I could
find a slope and start practising now.

In the event, the film-makers had the same concerns as I
did, and when the fortnight was up I was greeted with the
news that they'd decided to take the potentially less risky
option and had cast an able-bodied actress instead. I was
disappointed and relieved in roughly equal measure, except
in the matter of the major disappointment of not now
getting the chance to have the whirlwind romance with the
lead actor – the gorgeous Stellan Skarsgård – that I'd
already half plotted in my head.

I neither saw the finished movie, nor pursued any further
brushes with stardom. I had less spangly but more pressing
things still on my mind.

Much as I enjoyed my work in Cardiff, there was no getting
away from the fact that the three days a week round trip to
the UWIC campus in Cardiff was in excess of 70 miles.
Despite my car and my relative independence, this was still
a tedious length of journey. For some disabled people it
would be totally prohibitive, even more so for those from
further west.

Why, I asked myself, should there not be a similar facility serving the people of south-west Wales too? It might
even, my thoughts continued, be built in Port Talbot –
Heaven knew, the area could do with the kudos. Yes, I

thought, *we* needed a WSCD, and I would be the one who was going to build it.

Like Rome, fully formed fitness and rehabilitation centres don't generally get built in a day, so once my plan had become less of a whim and more of an actuality, I knew I was in for the long haul.

My years with the WSCD now proved invaluable. I needed to resign from my post there, obviously, but in doing so I knew I was taking them all with me in spirit. If I could do half the good they were already doing then I'd have done something very worthwhile. I resigned from the WSCD in the autumn of 2000 and set about making my plan happen.

Happily, my many years' association with charities meant I knew I first needed to get people on side. To this end I gave an interview to my local paper in Port Talbot, setting out the details of my intended campaign to get a treatment and rehabilitation centre built there.

As with any self-respecting campaign, what I next had to do was to put on some sort of high-profile event in order to help raise awareness. For reasons that were, and remain, close to my heart, I decided to make this a fashion show. After all, stage, rather than celluloid, was my more natural home.

I knew it was a whole different ball game, so I began recruiting willing friends to help out: friends in Port Talbot, University of Wales Institute fitness instructors, my friend Robin, who'd not long been discharged from Rookwood, staff from the David Evans store in Swansea – who would be providing the fashions – and a bunch of volunteers from the staff of Swansea College. We'd decided our venue would be the historic Brangwyn Hall, part of the Guildhall in the centre of Swansea, and set the date for 2 November. I recruited half a dozen disabled models through my WSCD connections plus a handful of young female and (rather gorgeous) male models from Swansea College.

Logistically, things would be a challenge. The catwalk itself would need to be carefully designed. It needed a ramp with a kind enough gradient to allow those in wheelchairs (me included; I didn't intend to miss out on that limelight) an elegant ascent and descent.

Then there was the matter of changing. Outfits needed to be carefully planned as the paraplegics among us – again, myself included – were incapable of making speedy changes. Trousers of any description were out – to get them on and off I, for example, needed to lie flat, which was just not possible in a busy changing area. The solution for me was to wear some skin-tight ones underneath and only model tops and skirts. Knee-length boots meant that I could model different skirt lengths, though obviously baby-dolls were, this time round, a no-no.

As the countdown to the big day drew nearer, I began, in a small way, to get excited. But also, inexplicably, very nervous. Much as I was determined to enjoy every moment, nerves were threatening to completely engulf me. Where on earth had my confidence gone?

Luckily, my male partner, a very gorgeous young thing, seemed to sense the extent of my unspoken terror. We were mid-rehearsal, running through the evening-wear section, and I was having difficulty keeping the shakes at bay. The piece was choreographed so we arrived on the catwalk together, splitting up halfway down it to take our own routes and then coming together at the end, before exiting, once again, as a couple. We were just being reunited when he stuck out his hand for me to clasp; something we'd not rehearsed before. I automatically took it, and he suddenly twirled me full circle in my chair, before bending and planting a kiss on my cheek and whispering, 'You've done this before, haven't you?'

It wasn't the most earth-shattering utterance in the universe, but it was as if he'd given me the sun, moon and stars. After that I felt I could do anything. My nerves disappeared and they never returned, and the show, on the day, went like clockwork. No, it wasn't quite the same as the first time – how could it be? – but one constant remained. I was proud and I was confident of the way that I looked. The teenage model had grown into a woman; the only difference was that now I was on wheels.

Even so, as the event finished, I felt tired. And continued to do so for days. I put it down to the sheer effort involved in running such a thing, not least in managing a gaggle of young prima donnas. More than once I'd reflected on what those Dorothy Perkins ladies had had to deal with when I'd been a prima donna myself. Perhaps, in hindsight, I'd done a bit too much. Organising it was one thing, modelling it, yet another. Perhaps in doing both I had overstretched myself.

Still, it had been an enormous success and had resulted in masses of press coverage. My picture had even appeared next to Claudia Schiffer's in one paper. While I was chuffed, though, I was also well aware that there was a point to all this – that I now had to crack on and get a proposal written up for the authorities.

It was while pondering this – while exercising on a lateral pull-down machine at the WSCD, where I still regularly went to work out – that something even more pressing struck me. Every time I pulled downwards I was feeling a sharp pain in the left side of my chest. Exploring the area, I found a hard lump in my breast, and though I was only thirty-six years old I knew such things shouldn't be ignored.

I headed home to Port Talbot and made an appointment with my doctor, who saw me promptly but reassured me that, at my age, it was unlikely to be sinister. Even so, he referred me to the breast clinic at Neath, where Mike Chare, the surgeon who'd agreed to my colostomy, arranged for me to go and have a biopsy.

It was Christmas Eve – seven weeks since my fashion-show high – when I received the anxiously awaited result. However unlikely it might be, I had breast cancer.

chapter 26

When Mike Chare entered the room with my test results, I immediately knew what he was going to tell me just by looking at the expression on his face. It seemed an inappropriate day to receive bad news. As well as being Christmas Eve, a day generally reserved for happy anticipation, it was also bright and sunny with a cloudless blue sky. His office was hot from where the sun struck the window, which he now turned to open before clearing his throat to administer the words I'd expected and dreaded.

I had dressed that morning in clothes that made me feel confident and strong, almost as if by doing so I could ward off, or at least outface, whatever was coming my way. Red jeans and red jacket. Knee-high black boots. I'd pulled my hair into a ponytail, which I fixed with a pretty red hair clip, and made up my face with grim precision. I looked every inch the fashion model I'd been seven weeks before. If I was going down, I was going down fighting.

I naturally hoped for good news, as one does, but inside I knew I was clutching at straws. Since I'd discovered it, my lump, as if lonely without a friend to call its own, had been joined by a new one. They both felt like marbles. One big one, one smaller one. Cancerous marbles, as Mike Chare's voice now confirmed. I could feel my heart thumping beneath them.

All at once the fact of my adoption came to mind. I knew absolutely nothing of my biological mother. Did she too have breast cancer? Was she now dead because of it? Would it now kill me? And if it didn't kill me quickly, would I now lose my breast? Would it spread to my other one? Would I have to lose them both?

The questions tumbled over one another, terrifying yet silent. And hard behind the 'What ifs?' came a phalanx of 'Whys?' Or rather, just the one: 'Why *me*?' My breasts were the one thing I had going for me. Twenty years ago, of course, I'd had a bottom as well – a bottom that attracted comment, garnered wolf whistles and attention – not to mention a pair of long, shapely legs. But for the past twenty years I'd had to sit on my bottom, and my legs were just things that sat lifeless, out front. All I had left were my face and my breasts. And now one of my breasts had gone and grown a cancerous tumour.

I seethed inside at the injustice of it all. I was yet to find true love with a man who would cherish me for the woman I was; paralysed, yes, but a woman none the less. And now the remaining manifestation of my femininity had become diseased. For God's sake, I thought desperately, the accident had spared them, hadn't it? Hadn't robbed them of sensation. And in sparing them, at least, had allowed me to develop a sense of physical sexuality. Had allowed me to become a woman. As had the syringomyelia surgery later. How could this one thing be taken from me now? More scary still, what man could be expected to be physically attracted to, let alone fall in love with, a cancerous cripple who was past her sell-by date and whose already damaged body was turning rotten? 'Not fair!' a voice inside my head screamed. 'NOT FAIR!!'

Even so, I sat impassively, my guard firmly in place, until the pressure in my head grew too powerful and a single tear fell onto my cheek, where it tracked a straight line through my flawless foundation.

Mike Chare wordlessly proffered a hankie. I took it. 'Could I,' I wondered, 'tell my mother?'

She was duly ushered in and found a chair, and then I told her.

She looked at me, clear-eyed, radiating strength. She took my hand in hers. 'We'll get over this again, love.'

Being told they have cancer is something many, many people have to face, and I doubt my reaction differed much from anyone else's. Not so much doom and despair – not immediately, anyway – more a sense of infuriation and of the unfairness of it all. It was like the bullies from school coming back into my life, only this time the bully was my own private one, manifesting itself inside my own body. This was nothing to do with my paraplegia. This was a woman thing. Something that happened all the time, to women everywhere. Nothing unique, just an absolute bloody nuisance.

Because of the ever-present worst-case scenario, however, I was constantly visited by thoughts I wished I didn't have to think. Unlike some, I suppose, I was used to the spectre of untimely death; but even so, having beaten the odds for so long, there was always the thought that my time had come at last. That I'd been lucky up to now, and that I might beat them no more. I grew adept, day by day, at pushing such thoughts away. Mum was right. We would get over this again. We had to. I'd be damned if I'd let it beat me after what I'd been through. What right did cancer have to finish me off? To hell with it, I thought. I was going to give it the fight of my life. Not just beat it, but beat it on my terms.

I was prescribed a drug called tamoxifen, which I was instructed to start taking immediately. Whilst an effective anti-cancer drug, it was not without side effects, the worst being that it would in all likelihood bring about an early menopause. To begin with this felt like a definite plus. Hooray! No more periods for me! Then all at once my mind created a similar minus. This could prevent me having children. At this point I was convinced I'd gone mad. I had never wanted children. I had never felt maternal pangs when confronted with other people's babies. I didn't know if this was some sort of subconscious response to my physical condition or the unusual nature of my life since the accident, but even before it I'd found the whole idea of pregnancy and childbirth a bit grim. Too messy, too painful, too much like trying to pass a Christmas turkey. Hence I'd always tended to adopt the 'rather you than me' approach to it all. My dogs were my babies. Human kids? No, thank you very much. So what, in God's name, was happening to me now? Besides that, I also reasoned, you needed a man to have babies; something I believed I was never going to have, not now all this had happened to me.

But I gritted my teeth. I told the feelings to go away. Enough about babies; I had a cancer to banish, not to mention an important project to get off the ground.

I knew I would have to have surgery on the tumour, but was disappointed to find out it wouldn't happen for three weeks. Christmas and New Year accounted for one of those, obviously, but the remaining two stretched like the worst kind of desert. Featureless, inhospitable, with no distracting features. I resolved to fill the time by pushing forward with my plans for a rehab centre in south-west Wales. By the day of my surgery I'd drawn up an initial plan, and spent time considering how best to deliver it.

By now my project had a name. I'd decided to call it the TREAT Trust. TREAT, which would eventually be the name of my new centre, stood for Treatment, Rehabilitation, Exercise And Therapy – an acronym I felt rather proud of.

I was guided through all this by a man called Ewart Parkinson, who, as a retired Chief Planning Officer, had a wealth of experience in such initiatives, and who'd been chair of the Trust Board at WSCD. Following Ewart's advice, I approached the family solicitor, John Spender, who agreed at once to be the Trust's legal advisor and who graciously promised to take the project forward in the event of something happening to me.

Now on something of a roll, I made the further decision that the trust should a) become a charity and a limited company, in order to protect its trustees, and b) I'd better get out there and find some.

Some names came immediately to mind. The first of these was my old stalwart, Mike Davies, but as I was scheduled, in any case, to visit my gastroenterologist, Professor John Williams, it was him I nabbed first, in his clinic. He was kind enough to describe my new venture as brilliant, and I exited his office on a very welcome high.

Almost immediately, and with immaculate timing, I collided with Mike Davies in the corridor outside. After he'd brushed himself down I showed him my TREAT draft proposal document, which he perused and pronounced to be extremely worthwhile.

He agreed TREAT addressed a major gap in provision in our area, but when I asked him if he'd consider coming in with us as a trustee he shook his head firmly and handed the papers back.

'I can't,' he explained. 'I'm retiring in five months and I intend to spend the time with my wife and family.' He went on to explain that, as with any busy doctor, his family had been very much short-changed by his commitment to the health service over the years. Now it was time to give *his* time to them. I could see straight away that he wasn't to be shifted, but still wondered at his retiring quite so young. I watched him as he walked off. He'd changed a lot since we last met; he'd grown a beard and his post-cancer Balkan terrorist hairstyle had changed into a thick silvery mop. He seemed too young, too important, to be leaving Neath General, though I could well understand the sentiments behind his doing so. There was more to life than work, after all.

But chair of my trustees he wasn't going to be, so I went back to John Williams and asked if he'd take on the role, and was genuinely pleased when he agreed.

I underwent a lumpectomy and removal of my lymph nodes on 15 January 2001. I had been firm that I couldn't begin to contemplate a full mastectomy, so I was hugely relieved to receive the fabulous news that the lymph nodes were clear of any cancer. Next up was a visit to Singleton Hospital in Swansea to discuss my ongoing treatment options. I say 'discuss' but, in the event, there wasn't much discussion. I was told that the next thing would be courses of both radio-therapy and chemotherapy. I'd already accepted that the former was necessary, but I had serious doubts about the latter. I'd been told that my hair would fall out, and was prepared for this, obviously. Indeed I'd already shorn my long locks in preparation. But I could also apparently expect nausea, vomiting and diarrhoea – and about this I was seri-ously concerned. My kidneys were precious to me, and I feared the noxious cocktail would jeopardise their health. Given the compromised nature of my general health anyway, it wasn't something I was prepared to risk without an absolute trade-off in terms of justifiable benefit. The oncologist, however, was less than forthcoming and, frus-trated, I left before making a decision; I felt I needed more time to think everything through. I was less than inspired then, speaking to the nurse outside, to find that I'd appar-ently been included in a chemotherapy 'trial'. Less still when, on hearing that my lymph nodes were clear, she said she couldn't understand why I was having chemo at all. The nurse wasn't qualified to make that decision herself, obviously, but her words sowed yet another seed of doubt in my mind.

By now I'd already decided that I wanted to seek a second opinion in any case, and, with no personal knowledge of any experts in the field, I asked the long-suffering Mike Chare if he did. He spoke highly of an oncologist in Cardiff, based at a specialist cancer hospital called Velindre. A couple of phone calls later and an appointment was fixed for me to see Dr Peter Barrett-Lee.

Dr Barrett-Lee turned out to be an excellent listener and took on all my concerns about the risks of chemotherapy for someone in my paraplegic state. He was of the opinion that excision of the tumour plus radiotherapy would give me a 75 per cent chance of eliminating my cancer, and that adding chemotherapy into the mix would only increase that percentage very slightly. Chemotherapy, he explained, could be seen more as an insurance cover, designed to prevent the cancer from returning. Nothing was or is guaranteed in such matters, of course, but armed with my clutch of estimates I felt able to make the decision to spare my kidneys and my gut and stop at radiotherapy alone.

A course was duly mapped out at Velindre hospital and I was back to making daily journeys up to Cardiff, using much the same route as to the WSCD. Funny how life sometimes goes.

Though my body was exhausted by the journeys and the treatment, my mind, by this time, was in overdrive. My plan for a rehabilitation facility largely for those with mobility problems had begun to expand radically. After the removal of my lump and lymph nodes I'd become aware how vital it was that I mobilise my shoulder and arm; after all, my arms *were* my mobility. I'd also been in a ward with several other breast cancer patients, where the response to the bouncy post-surgery physiotherapist had ranged from the apathetic to the frankly unprintable. It must be hard to get motivated to move a painful arm, I realised, when you had another one available to use instead. I immediately realised that there were all sorts of useful applications for the treatment centre I had in my mind.

I looked back to the point when my cancer had been diagnosed and felt a surge of optimism well up inside. By now it was spring, already shaping up for summer, and though I knew I was far from being out of the woods I felt I could start to look forward again at last.

Little did I know that, as I was doing just that, a tragedy was about to be played out elsewhere.

part three

chapter 27

Just as I was getting into the routine of making daily trips up the M4 motorway for my radiotherapy sessions in Cardiff, my long-suffering surgeon, Mike Davies, was preparing for a rather different kind of journey. The Welsh Rugby under-19 squad were soon to be competing in the Junior World Cup competition in Chile and, as team surgeon, together with his physician colleague, Dr Gareth Jones, he was gathering items for the sizeable skip of medical equipment that would accompany them all.

The two doctors set off from Mike's house on a sunny day two weeks before Easter; the long weekend would be a break that would provide some of the welcome family time that he was looking forward to on his return.

As Mike kissed his wife Karin goodbye he knew she'd be unlikely to miss him much. She was used to his being away. Apart from the inevitable housework, and a little cooking for their elder son Phil, who still lived at home, he knew she'd be busy fulfilling her role as Chair of Governors at their local comprehensive school.

The journey to Santiago was uneventful, if long, and the squad were soon settled in a comfortable hotel, anticipating the run of matches ahead. Though woken by the rumble of mild earthquakes on a couple of nights, they commenced their campaign on top form, winning against both Chile and Uruguay.

It was, therefore, in a happy frame of mind that Mike returned to his hotel on 9 April to find a message from home. He was to contact his son Phil urgently. The initial news wasn't good; the message – or so Mike understood it – was that his mum had had a stroke. This was bad news, certainly, but not unexpected. Mike's elderly mother had already suffered one a few years earlier. But within moments, the full horror of the situation became apparent. It wasn't Mike's mum Phil had been talking about – it was *his* mother – Mike's wife, Karin.

Mike was dumbstruck. He'd only spoken to her two days previously and she'd seemed in perfect health then. But no longer, it seemed. On his return from work Phil had found her conscious but helpless on the living-room floor, having had what appeared to be a massive stroke. She had no idea how long she'd been there, but it soon became clear that it must have happened three hours or so earlier, after her return from a governors' meeting. She was now at Morriston Hospital and in a serious condition. Mike needed to get home, and fast.

Phil had mobilised Mike's colleagues and they'd all rallied round, so he knew Karin was in the best hands possible, but he needed to get home to be with her – not easy when you're on the other side of the world. His principal reaction was one of shock and disbelief, closely followed by one of blessed relief that his son still lived at home. Had he moved out, as they'd been encouraging him to do, Karin might have lain there without help for God only knew how long. As it was, the situation seemed serious enough. Might she die before he could make it to her side? If she lived would she be horribly disabled? The Welsh Rugby Union leapt straight into action to sort out flights and he arrived back in London on the morning of the 11th, where his brother Richard, who'd driven down from Milton Keynes to collect him, was waiting.

Forty-two hours after receiving the phone call, Mike was finally at his wife's bedside in Morriston Hospital, where things were looking every bit as bleak as he'd feared. It was confirmed that she'd had a severe stroke. Karin could recall much of what had happened – the growing headache, the collapse, the sensation that her left side was 'missing' – but she was paralysed down the whole of the left side of her body and was suffering from recurring headaches and nausea. She was also – perhaps due to the medication – sometimes confused. With his medical knowledge crowding out reasons to feel hopeful, Mike prepared for the worst, as, over the next three days, the medical team strove to control Karin's soaring blood pressure. But their efforts were in vain. On the evening of Saturday 14 April she died, aged just sixty years old. She and Mike had been married a little short of thirty-six years.

Now that his future had been rewritten so tragically and suddenly, when Mike returned to work after the funeral his colleagues asked if he wished to reconsider his decision to

retire. He was due to leave around the time of his own sixti-
eth birthday, which was in June – now just a scant few
weeks hence.

Mike considered this option – he could, after all, have
continued for another five years – but in the end his decision
was easy. Although the future had altered for him now, he
resolved that he would stick to his plan. He had always
planned – and made provision for – retirement at age sixty,
not least because the fact was that medics who retired at that
age had much better survival rates than those who soldiered
on till sixty-five. He'd long looked forward to it, too. His
children were all grown – two of them now based in
London – and he couldn't see that dragging on for another
five years at work would help any of them to cope with their
collective grief. And though it might have been a good
distraction for him personally, in the end he felt better able
to live with his thoughts and memories with a measure of
autonomy and solitude. He would retire as he'd planned,
even if the retirement itself would be far removed from the
one he envisaged.

The first I knew of what had happened was when Dad
returned from Aberavon Rugby Club a couple of Saturdays
later and relayed the tragic news. Mike, characteristically,
had come across to speak to him to find out how things were
going with my trust.

I was stunned by the news. And also angry. I recalled our
conversation about his retirement plans earlier in the year,
and how very much he was looking forward to spending

time with the wife who'd supported him so steadfastly and patiently for so long. How could fate do something so unspeakably cruel to someone who'd spent his life doing so much good?

I judged the time he'd need to travel home to where he lived in Pontardawe, and then I called him. I didn't think, I didn't stop to ponder propriety. I just phoned. It felt the most natural thing in the world.

Even so, I was relieved that he sounded genuinely pleased to hear from me, so much so that I then did what seemed more natural still. I asked if we could perhaps meet up. I knew he and his wife had been happily married for over three decades, and I couldn't begin to imagine how he must be feeling without her. I didn't have much of a plan at that point. I just had this strong sense that I ought to do *something* – at the very least offer a hand of friendship, of support. He'd supported me so very well over the years, after all. If I could offer something in return then I'd be glad to.

When I arrived in his fracture clinic a few days later, Mike was just entering the busy corridor leading to his office. As usual, it was crammed to bursting with orthopaedic patients, some in wheelchairs, some on crutches, others with various limbs plastered – a bit like a spent battlefield minus the blood. On this particular day there were lots of children in the clinic and my first sight of him was as he nearly fell over a small boy whilst trying to make it through the throng to come and greet me. He smiled ruefully, and I was struck by how different he looked. His hair had fully regrown after the chemo. It was now grey, with a distinctive Mallen streak of white, and his newly grown beard and moustache really suited him; but what really struck me that day were his bright blue eyes, which I'd never really noticed before. They smiled as he approached.

'Hi,' he said, pecking me lightly on the cheek. 'Let's go into my office, shall we? Coffee or tea?'

Mike sat and told me everything that had happened over coffee, and I listened, feeling sad but also privileged and slightly awed that he should feel comfortable relating such personal things to me. It was as if a relationship shift of seismic proportions had taken place, and it occurred to me that in his job, and in a hospital hierarchy, it was usually him – at the top of the pile – who did most of the worrying about other people, expecting very little of the same in return. It was, I imagined, quite a lonely place to be. I felt so glad I'd decided to come and see him.

Typically, he soon wanted to talk about me, and asked how my treatment for breast cancer had been going. 'Are they poisoning you, frying you, or both?' he wanted to know. He was warm and very funny and his demeanour was relaxed, but every so often his eyes, those windows to the soul, exposed the depth of the grief welling just beneath.

After our lengthy health catch-up – he also talked frankly about his own experience of cancer – he asked me how TREAT was getting on. I told him I'd roped in a whole bunch of consultants and that Professor Williams had agreed to be chairman. Then, as his interest seemed not just polite but quite genuine, I took the plunge and asked him if he'd change his mind about joining us now his own circumstances had changed so radically. His 'yes' was both firm and immediate, though he was keen to point out that he'd soon be retired, and perhaps wouldn't be so much use to me as a has-been.

'Nonsense,' I told him, and, ever quick to seize the moment, I decided to plough on and go for the double whammy. Since he was now less committed time-wise, I suggested that perhaps he'd consider being vice-chair, as well.

His response was to smile, but also to confirm another yes. He'd be grateful, he said, his voice growing quieter, to have something to occupy his mind.

This to me was like a double-edged sword. I was delighted that he'd agreed to come on board with the project, but at the same time terribly sad about the circumstances that had precipitated it. Still, I decided, fate might have been hideously cruel to him and Karin and their family, but it had also given me an opportunity to help my former consultant during a bleak and wretched time. If keeping him busy through his retirement was what he needed, I resolved that I would do exactly that. Indeed, I would do whatever I could for him, as he'd done for me for almost twenty-one years.

This time, however, the roles had shifted somewhat. Although to me he was still the heroic young doctor who'd been charged with the care of a frightened and damaged teenage girl, the girl herself was now a fully grown woman. And, I hoped, by now also some kind of friend. It would be good to work together as equals with a common goal.

As I left, I noticed for the first time his cauliflower ears, which he wore, I suspected, with some pride. Not only did he spend half his professional life treating rugby players, he'd also been one, and he would always be proud to be 'one of the boys'.

And now, to my joy, he was playing on *my* team.

chapter 28

Twenty-one years to the day after my accident, on 10 May 2001, the inaugural meeting of the charity I had founded took place and straight away I knew I'd found my reason for being. The project made everything that had happened to me feel almost worthwhile.

While no one would try to make a case for the delights of a life of paraplegia – least of all me – there seemed something particularly right and appropriate in the realisation that the accident had set in motion the chain of events that brought this gathering about.

Even more appropriate, perhaps, was that it also brought me and my fellow trustee – Mike Davies, my former surgeon and hero – right back to the place that had brought us together. For it turned out that Neath General Hospital looked like being the very best place for TREAT's building to be sited.

Not that the plan was for it to be sited *there*, exactly, because Neath General Hospital was itself soon to move to a brand new state-of-the-art site on the southern edge of the town. The land there provided ample room for an equally state-of-the-art rehabilitation and well-being establishment. What better location could there be?

At the meeting, everyone seemed to be in agreement with the concept and, most importantly, with our thoughts about siting it adjacent to the hospital's new home. What was needed, it was decided, was some sort of concrete confirmation of our intentions; in short, TREAT needed to justify its existence with a positive feasibility study before the hospital would consider moving on to the next stage.

I didn't know a great deal about feasibility studies. I had heard the term, obviously, but no more than that. What did it involve? How did you arrange one? What did they cost to carry out? As our charity's coffers contained the grand sum of nothing, the last of these questions was, for the moment, academic, but I certainly needed answers to the first two if we were to get going on sorting out the third.

The person who I knew could best help me lived in Cardiff, where I was coincidentally headed straight after the meeting in order to have that day's radiotherapy. I resolved that as soon as I'd finished my treatment I'd call him and ask him what to do.

Ewart Parkinson, my chairman from the Wales Sports Centre for the Disabled, was a former chief planning officer for South Glamorgan. He'd played a key part in the transformation of Cardiff from just another provincial city into what had now become a worthy capital for Wales. He'd also established several successful charities in South Wales, almost every one of them from scratch.

Ewart wasted no time in bursting my happy bubble, with the news that the cost of a feasibility study started at around the £30,000 mark. Where on earth would my embryonic charity find that kind of money? 'But don't you worry,' he said calmly, once I'd scraped my jaw up from the floor. 'You leave it with me, Mel. I'll get back to you.'

I don't know if it was fate having a particularly good day, or just further confirmation that my new life plan was a sound one, but Ewart was back on the phone to me within the hour. He'd spoken to someone with strong Neath connections who by some miracle had agreed to fund half the cost. A whole £15,000. Just like that!

I rang our chair, John Williams, and also Mike (now officially vice-chair, of course) to tell them the good news. All we needed now, I enthused, was a huge fundraising drive in order to raise the other half. I couldn't be happier. Or so I thought. Perhaps I could. For when I finally put the phone down it rang almost immediately. It was Ewart again, enquiring why my line had been engaged for so long. When I told him, he laughed. 'You won't have to do any of that, as it happens.'

It seemed our anonymous donor had had a rethink. They were happy, they'd now decided, to donate the entire £30,000.

Suddenly things were in overdrive. With funding in place and the project up and running, it was important that we make moves to establish ourselves properly; not in Trust terms – we'd already covered that aspect – but as a credible, viable, professional organisation and, crucially, one that was recognised as such. I felt almost dizzy with excitement about it all. This wasn't a pipe dream. It was *real*.

* * * *

As is the way of such things, another meeting was called – this time in an air of celebration. We were keen to involve both local politicians and our family solicitor, John Spender, who we hoped would agree to be legal advisor to the trust.

The sensible plan seemed to be to meet informally over a meal, and a Neath-based country hotel was chosen for the location, on the grounds that Mike had been to a function there a few weeks earlier and considered it ideal in every way.

The participants were informed, and on the allotted day we all gathered, as arranged, in the car park. Ewart and I had been chauffered there by Dad, who dropped us off and smartly drove off.

The two of us made our way into the hotel and enquired about our table, where we were promptly informed that we hadn't *booked* a table, and also that, regrettably, they weren't serving food. I was taken aback. Mike had booked it, hadn't he? And besides, this was a hotel and it was dinnertime – were they a part of some curious non-dining sect? Mike arrived at this point and we had quick exchange of facts. *Hadn't* he booked it? No, he hadn't. He'd thought *I* had. In any case, he added, the no dinner thing was nonsense. He'd had dinner here only four weeks back. His protestations were met with looks of disbelief and the chef was duly summoned from the kitchen. No one on the staff seemed to see anything vaguely funny in the fact that he was standing there, pinny liberally splattered with food, telling us, 'No, we don't do food in the evenings – only on special occasions.' Mike's prior evening, it seemed, had been one such.

And whoever it seemed they were feeding tonight, it obviously wasn't the guests.

John Spender, our solicitor, had arrived by this time, so it didn't seem sensible to stand there huffing and puffing about details at a point where we were trying to appear professional and organised. Instead, I suggested we try and find another restaurant, and take up the meeting from there. We were just making our way back outside when Gwenda Thomas, the Assembly Member for Neath, arrived. She had been driven by her husband, so we suggested that Mike run outside immediately and stop him driving off. Unfortunately she was keen to clasp Mike in a bear hug first, and by the time she released him her husband was long gone back down the lane.

By now we only required our chairman to have a quorum, but as he'd yet to arrive we couldn't actually leave. Buoyed by the stellar nature of our gathering (an Assembly Member, a solicitor, a hospital consultant, a high-ranking local government official, a professor of gastroenterology and, er, me) I killed time by approaching the staff once again about the possibility of finding us some food.

My request was met, as expected, by an unimpressed Gallic shrug, which left us with Plan B – to go somewhere else. We left messages with the staff for the still-absent John Williams and duly trooped back out to the car park. As Ewart, Gwenda and I were without transport, John Spender graciously suggested Ewart and I travel in his rugged Range Rover, leaving our esteemed Assembly Member to travel more decorously with Mike. I considered it. It looked fearfully high for me to pull myself up into, and was in any case cluttered (for reasons never properly explained) with a large number of parasol-less parasol poles. Mike, who seemed to be enjoying the whole débâcle immensely, studied the car and then the poles and then me, and he frowned.

'Tell you what,' he said to John. 'Even with the improvised pole vault you've organised, I don't think she'll make it in there, John.'

I laughed, as we all did. I even offered to make a stab at it. In the end, though, I travelled in fine style with Mike, and we kept laughing all the way to the delightfully named (and also delightful) Bagle Brook Beefeater at Baglan. The parasol poles remain a mystery to this day.

Laughter, I soon realised, was entirely non-negotiable, and became a central part of whatever we were doing. Not just because Mike's sense of humour was so acute, but simply because we couldn't seem to help it.

With our second formal trust meeting, we hoped for great things. At the very least we hoped we wouldn't spend any of our time ferrying important government ministers around on wild quests for such implausible items as plates of food. To this end, we decided upon Port Talbot's civic centre as the venue, and the company was all assembled in the (very formal) boardroom. Mike, in the meantime, had been busy. He'd been talking with a local millionaire farmer (as you do), and telling him all about our plans for TREAT. Somewhat advanced in years now, Joe was well known in the area and considered by all to be a bit of a character –

exactly the sort of supporter we wanted on side. Mike felt that inviting him to our second meeting could well be in all of our interests.

Assuming, that was, that we actually *had* the meeting. 'Excuse me, Mister Chairman,' farmer Joe announced at the off. 'I'm afraid I'm at a bit of a disadvantage here. I can't hear you.'

'Can't you?' queried Mike. 'Sorry. CAN'T YOU?'

'No,' said farmer Joe. Then, by way of explanation, 'Dog's gone and eaten my hearing aid.'

The chairman and the rest of the committee did their best to suppress their emotions with varying degrees of success. Mike motioned for calm. 'IT'S ALL RIGHT!' he boomed at him. 'DON'T WORRY ABOUT THAT. I CAN WRITE EVERYTHING DOWN FOR YOU!'

Farmer Joe shook his head. 'There's no point doing that,' he went on to explain. 'Even if you do, Mike, I'm afraid I won't be able to see it.'

Mike frowned, at something of a loss. 'Why's that?'

Farmer Joe shook his head again, as if dealing with ninnies. 'Because,' he said, 'I haven't brought my *glasses*.'

It was a credit to everyone attending that meeting that we managed to get through the agenda.

Within a year, life had become busier than ever. Mike and I were the only two members of TREAT's committee without full-time jobs, so it fell to us to run almost all of the day-to-day business. The front room of my home had been all but given up to its role as the charity's nerve centre, and when we weren't in there, sending letters, making phone calls, designing publicity material and so on, we were out on the road. In the early days this mostly involved long rounds of meetings, both to get the charity's aims more widely known and to seek advice from similar and politically interested groups. Later on, it meant venturing further afield, as we travelled to similar centres on visits, to see what ideas we could garner from them. I hadn't woken each day with such a powerful sense of purpose since during the dark weeks at Rookwood two decades previously, when dogged determination to survive and to cope was the only way to stave off the massive waves of despair.

This was different. This was brilliant. This was what I'd been born for. Not only was I fronting such a worthwhile endeavour (not to mention spending time with such wonderful people) but I was also answerable to no one, completely independent, bursting with energy and looking forward to the future. I was properly in control of my life at long last.

It would be less than a year, though, before another truth would dawn. That, boy, was I wrong about that last bit!

chapter 29

I was, and remain, an incurable romantic. But what is romance exactly? For the adolescent me, it was clear-cut. It was walking through cornfields, holding hands, laughing, sharing secrets and kisses beneath a panoramic sky. And, with the coming of maturity, it was also, inescapably, about sex as well. About being lowered gently onto warm grass in an urgent embrace. Of being caressed. Of anticipating sensual nirvana. Of sharing yourself physically with another human being. Back then, I still liked to fantasise about it; in my perfect world, there'd be no horse flies, no cow pats, no grass stains permitted. Just glorious, cinematic, *al fresco* lovemaking, with a happy-ever-after thrown in.

All of which, I came to realise, was rubbish. What might have seemed natural for the young able-bodied me had, since my accident, been rendered null and void, and I could see all such whimsy as the nonsense that it was.

It was 2003. I was thirty-eight years old. And I had put all thoughts of romantic love behind me. I had thought, with Chris, that the miracle had happened. That despite my doubts, the chance of romantic love might exist for me. But I'd got it wrong and I wasn't about to go there again. Not least because I now had another scar to add to the list of things I didn't want anyone to see.

I could picture the scene all too easily: 'Hi, I'm Mel. As you can see, I'm sitting in a wheelchair, which is because I've been paralysed from the chest down for twenty years. Yes, you're absolutely right. I made such a good job of breaking my back that I can't stand up, even for a second, let alone walk. Oh, and I've also got a neurological condition that I can hardly pronounce, let alone spell for you. And guess what? The surgeon who sorted that out for me has died, so if it comes back I'm buggered. Good news though – my breast cancer is at least in remission. Shame about the scars, but there you go. Such is life … hang on a minute. Where are you going?'

The cancer had been the last straw. Since the initial injury, my sexual self had struggled so long and so fitfully to emerge, and now the cancer had completely knocked it flat. Why spend any more time dwelling on what wasn't going to be? Spinsterhood was what beckoned for me now, with lots of lovely male friends amongst the female, and no more angst about things I couldn't have. I was much too busy anyway. Busy and largely happy. TREAT was the driving force in my life now.

All of which was thrown into absolute chaos on a dull after-noon in early autumn.

When Mike had taken himself off to Prague for a ten-day holiday a fortnight previously, I knew I would miss him both on a personal level and in regard to TREAT. Over the previous eighteen months or so we'd become something of a double act where the latter was concerned. We invariably gave TREAT presentations together, and worked closely on all things related. I wondered how I'd cope without his calming presence beside me if, in his absence, I was called to put flying solo to the test.

As it was, I wasn't, so mostly I looked forward to his return and hoped he was having a good time. I hoped he was moving forwards from a very dark place. He'd become a good friend along the way. I hoped he was enjoying himself, getting a well-deserved break, having fun and appreciating good music as well – he had some serious operas lined up. I even wondered, as one might, if he missed me.

But no. As it turned out, he hadn't. Hadn't seemed to, anyway. He arrived on my doorstep looking rested and refreshed and ready to get straight back to work. Though not right away – he first wanted to show me his photos and regale me with details of his trip, which he did enthusiastically, particularly in regard to his pretty Czech tour guide, who went by the name of Marina.

Prague looked lovely, and sounded it too, so I was perfectly happy to hear all about it, and how it had picked itself up after the previous year's floods. I was pleased to know how much he'd enjoyed his visit, obviously, and glad that the operas had been such a success. But looking at a photo in which Marina grinned out at me, I was suddenly overwhelmed by an inexplicable sensation. Indeed, I realised I was feeling decidedly strange.

Mike rattled on. This view. That monument. The other statue. *Marina*. What on earth *was* this feeling that had assaulted me so suddenly? Oh, yes. Oh, no. OhmyGod – I was *jealous*.

There is obviously no legislation in place with regard to the reining in of unruly emotions. And, in the wider world, that's probably a good thing. But this feeling, in this person, at this time, for *that* person, was decidedly not a good thing.

But feelings have a way of asserting themselves, and before I knew it – before the week was out – I had impetuously put it to Mike that he might take me to my first opera. This was not as ridiculous as might be supposed. Though my in-car musical diet was generally more Meat Loaf than Verdi or Puccini, my tastes were eclectic and my mind pretty broad. Once exposed to some opera I didn't doubt for a moment that I would soon start to share his enthusiasm. Besides, he was always going to operas alone – he would surely enjoy a bit of company.

In my head, therefore, it was all quite straightforward. Mike would take me to the Swansea Grand and introduce me to opera and we'd have a pleasant evening of social engagement.

Or so I convinced myself anyway. In my heart, it was a different matter. Mike had now become Richard Gere sweeping Julia Roberts off in her red frock and jewels, as so beautifully portrayed in *Pretty Woman*.

Of course, the minute I opened my mouth and uttered the words, I almost expired in a cloud of my own embarrassment. How cringe-makingly forward I'd been! How rude!

Happily, Mike didn't seem to notice. He was used to me speaking first and engaging my brain later, so to him it felt not in the least unusual. He'd be happy to, he told me, though given my opera-virgin status, he said he'd try and choose something 'undemanding'.

This turned out to be *Tosca*, and he took the trouble to tell me the story: political prisoner escapes and seeks sanctuary with an artist friend who is painting a picture of the Madonna, which has some likeness to the prisoner's sister. Jealous girlfriend (singer, the Tosca of the title) turns up and suggests at least an alteration of eye colour. Police chief then discovers painter's complicity with political prisoner and has him tortured. Distraught girlfriend gives away political prisoner's hiding place but police chief offers to organise a faked execution of painter and safe passage for the couple in exchange for sexual favours from Tosca. Tells lackey, with nod and wink, 'Just like Palmieri,' and signs passport. As lackey leaves, police chief closes in lasciviously on Tosca, only to be met with a letter-opener through the heart.

Last act: painter gloomily awaiting death gets visit from Tosca. 'All fixed,' she says, 'but make faked death look convincing.' Firing squad do their duty, very convincing fall of victim. But turns out 'faked' execution is double cross (exactly like Palmieri, who went the same way). Police chief's body has been discovered, angry mob can be heard approaching, painter's now terminally distraught girlfriend throws herself off battlements to death. All good, light-hearted, undemanding fun …

That, I was assured, was what would happen *on* stage. What happened off stage was not without drama either.

Namely: hero (Mike) sets off from home in Pontardawe. Whisks fair damsel (me) into silver chariot (Skoda Octavia). They sweep up into amphitheatre in good time for leisurely refreshments (house red), whereupon hero discovers a flaw in his planning (OHMYGOD I'VE LEFT THE TICKETS ON THE MANTELPIECE). Hero's mumbled explanations fail to reach fair damsel's ears (particularly in the matter of the distant location of missing tickets) and she is thus bemused by hero's sudden disappearance. Opera begins. Usherette takes pity on lone damsel in bar and shows to seat in back row of auditorium. Hero eventually arrives breathless and panting with by now unnecessary tickets.

Back on stage, it was all kicking off, of course. The opera, as operas often are, was sung in Italian, but Mike had cleverly booked seats in a position that would enable me to read from the surtitles. Sadly, the seats in which the usherette had placed us were at the back of the stalls, which meant the surtitles were obscured by the balcony. As was Cavaradossi, the Madonna-painting artist, as he launched into his first signature aria. Perched on the painterly scaffolding, as he was, all we could see were his boots. Still, everything worked out, three persons died as scheduled, and the audience could go to bed happy.

All in all, I decided, as I drifted off that night, the opera 'The Singing Boots' had been a roaring success.

The night at the opera was the first social outing Mike and I had ever been on. We were used to being seen out together as business colleagues, obviously, because he'd been working with TREAT for a good length of time now, but this was different and slightly unsettling. During the interval, two women from Neath Hospital spotted us and came over, whereupon there were introductions all round. Mike introduced me as 'my friend Mel' and I suddenly felt on strange ground. I was all too aware that they might have known Karin, and though over a year and a half had passed since her death, I still desperately hoped that Mike wasn't embarrassed about being seen out with me in this capacity. If he was, he made no mention of the fact, but just the thought that people might put two and two together and consider me a love interest made me want to blush to my roots.

Pink though I was, my emotions persisted in shaky mental arithmetic, namely adding two and two to make five. Mike had given me not the slightest indication that he noticed or was anxious or uncomfortable about it, but neither did he give me the slightest indication that his feelings remotely mirrored mine. I resolved to stop all my ridiculous mooning and accept that I was very lucky to be able to consider us very good friends.

Apart from anything else, it *was* ridiculous. I harboured no sexual fantasies about him simply because it was unthinkable to do so. Much as I found him very physically attractive, there was the small matter of our large age difference: I was only three years older than his daughter, effectively putting us in different generations. Then there was the matter of his having been my consultant surgeon all these years, which had long ago put him loosely on a par with a deity. Add to that his general eminence, not to mention his lofty status in the wider community, and it was obvious any notions a girl like me could entertain were far off the mark.

Despite this, I couldn't seem to stop my brain from whirring. Much as I chided myself for allowing it to happen, I found I was thinking about him pretty much all the time. I would wake, I would think of him, then ring him and talk to him. Then we'd plan and carry out the work to be done that morning, have our lunch, and continue long into the afternoon. Then he'd go, and I'd spend half the evening thinking about him, before going to bed and thinking about him there too. It was only in the wee hours, as I drifted off to sleep, that I allowed myself the luxury of another secret thought. Was he, I used to wonder, thinking about me too?

As Christmas 2003 approached, I was beginning to concede that despite my best intentions I was falling in love with Mike. How crazy and masochistic could an otherwise sane woman be? He had shown me the sum total of zero indications that he felt even remotely the same about me. In fact, I suspected that if I so much as hinted at my feelings, he'd be mortified, embarrassed, tongue-tied and floored. Anxious not to bring about that state of affairs, I kept my counsel and my mouth firmly shut.

One of the Christmas traditions I always looked forward to was a visit from my friend Tim, who was a medical rep I'd first met in the early nineties at one of Bernard Williams's Spinal Injuries Association talks. He often travelled to our part of the world on business, and I tended to be the lucky recipient of all-expenses paid dinners whenever his chat-up lines with the local nurses didn't work.

He'd been particularly supportive the previous Christmas and had been with me the day after the breast care nurse had drained a bag full of fluid from my then Dolly Parton left boob. Disconcertingly, we were sitting in the pub (the Bagle Brook again) when the damn thing re-inflated before his very eyes, as operation sites which seep fluid are wont to do.

The plan for our festivities was simple and unchanging: a lovely long lunch, followed by copious quantities of alcohol, followed by supper and a festive sing-song at home, followed by total collapse. Similarly unchanging was the hangover that followed, but this was Christmas. It was time to let our hair down.

This Christmas, however, the whole idea felt unappealing if I couldn't persuade Mike to come with us. Tim didn't mind; indeed, he and Mike got on well. So the only objection was from Mike himself – he felt sure his being there would be an intrusion.

After much persuading, however, he agreed to join us later in the day, and it was decided that we'd all go and have a curry. Mike arrived to meet us and we piled into his car – me up front with him and Tim in the back – to set off for the restaurant in Pontardawe. Fate, as it has a mind to, stepped in once again. Minutes later, as Mike negotiated a roundabout, I lost my balance and toppled to my right into him. I instinctively steadied myself with my hand, which landed on his leg. As it seemed prudent, given my tipsy condition, to maintain my balance for the remainder of the journey, I asked him politely if he minded if I let my hand stay where it was.

Mike raised no objection, so I kept it in mind – and made a note in my head that I should sensibly do likewise on the journey back home.

We were joined for the meal by Mike's son Phil, whom I'd got to know over the past couple of years, and with whom I had built up a good rapport. We dropped him off so that he could head out with a bunch of friends, and the remaining three of us arrived back at Connaught Street sufficiently early that Mum and Dad could join in with a fulsome round of traditional choral exchanges, which could quite possibly have been heard for some miles. It was during one of these that, seeing some glasses empty, I took myself off to the kitchen to fetch a fresh bottle of wine.

They always say that accidents happen mostly in the home but, distracted by the general air of merriment, that fact completely slipped my mind. Almost as if a Christmas without a crisis was too boring to contemplate, I reached for the wine bottle with manic abandon and promptly found myself sprawled flat out on the kitchen floor.

I also heard a very loud crack as I landed, which inspection revealed hadn't been the bottle.

Oh dear. Nothing for it. 'Erm …' I called. 'HELP!'

chapter 30

Mike and Tim responded to my SOS promptly and soon had me back in my chair. Was all well, they enquired? Was I hurt in any way? I gave the matter all of a half second's serious thought. Absolutely not. Not a bit of it, I assured them. We all returned to partying in the living room.

Mike – who was driving – left us at about midnight, and Mum, Dad and I settled down with Tim for a chin-wag; they'd not had a chance to chat to him properly earlier in the day. A bed was eventually made up for him in the living room, and we took ourselves off to our own beds at two. It was only once up in my bedroom and undressed that I noticed that things were in fact far from well. I was lifting my legs to try and clamber into bed when I noticed considerable swelling in my right leg, and realised I was unable to straighten it. It was obvious there was a great deal of damage, and, even as I thought this, my dysreflexia kicked in, the pounding headache confirming what I already knew: that the cracking sound had in fact come from me.

Mercifully, my bedside phone was within reach so I did what seemed the best thing – I called Mike. He sounded

sleepy, but once I described the situation he began to sound
very awake. He told me I must call out an emergency ambulance; this wasn't something that could safely be left. That
agreed, I then had to rouse the rest of the house – two of
whose inmates were partially deaf, and the other as much
the worse for wear as I was. Eventually however, my shouts
roused Tim, and we gathered to await the paramedics.

It wasn't long before I was strapped into a carry-chair and
delivered into the back of the ambulance. Tim was to travel
with me – Mum and Dad would sort out the dog and join
us later – and we were soon on the road to the A & E at
Morriston Hospital in Swansea.

As I lay on a trolley in my A & E cubicle, I was absolutely
livid with myself. One careless moment and all this had
happened, causing everyone else so much stress and inconvenience, and committing myself to a jolly Christmas in
hospital. I was furious. Hadn't we had enough heartache last
year? I felt ashamed. I really should have known better.

I was just considering new and interesting ways in which
to curse myself for my stupidity, when I became aware of a
figure approaching. Even though I saw him through a fog
of self-admonition, I would have recognised the walk and
bearing anywhere. Mike had come all the way down to
Swansea in the middle of the night to be with me. Twenty-
three years after he'd arrived at A & E at Neath Hospital to
face that horrendously damaged teenager, he was back by
my side to assess the situation. Though this time he wasn't
there as a doctor with a job to do, but because he was my
friend, and – my spirits soared at the realisation – because
he cared. He must do, mustn't he? He was *here*.

Time passed slowly as we waited in A & E that night. The casualty doctor was busy with a sick child and I – with my stupidly self-inflicted injury – would simply have to be patient and wait my turn. Paradoxically, I was in a fair degree of pain. Though my accident and Bernard Williams's subsequent attentions should have guaranteed numbness below the site of my spinal fracture, some freak of human electrical engineering meant I was conscious of pain in my thigh. Mike sat by my bedside as the hours crept by, talking soothingly, trying to assuage both my pain and my frustration. He took my hand in his and he sat there and stroked it – and there couldn't have been any better analgesic.

My parents arrived, bleary-eyed, but after it was clear that I was okay and in safe hands, both they and Tim were soon dispatched. Mike promised he'd stay with me till I was taken to the ward. Mum and Dad needed their sleep and their strength, and Tim had to get back to Peterborough in the morning – which we all realised was fast approaching.

And that's exactly what Mike did: not leaving my side for a moment (bar my X rays), even holding my hand as they wheeled me to Ward A – the very same ward on which he'd had patients of his own before his retirement. I was admitted under the care of his successor, Paul Williams, who confirmed I had fractured the upper end of my femur. It would need to be fixed by means of an operation in which they'd put a long metal rod inside the bone. I didn't ask whether this type of rod had a name, but I did confide to Mike my slight anxiety about my surgeon being so young; he was younger than I was. Was he old enough? Mike laughingly reassured me that Paul was a big boy now, and that he was leaving me in excellent hands.

I didn't argue the point, but something struck me all at once. I really didn't want him to leave, period. But it was now eleven o'clock on the morning of 23 December. He'd been with me for eight long hours and we were both exhausted. Despite his reluctance I chivvied him off home. He kissed my brow then, and left me to my morphine.

The operation was scheduled for the following morning, Christmas Eve, and everything went without a hitch. I was returned, plus my rod (which remains to this day), to my bed on Ward A, where Mum, Dad and Mike were all waiting. I might be in hospital, but I had the three people I loved most around me. Perhaps Christmas wouldn't be quite as bad as I thought. I was pleasantly drugged up and remember little of the visit, though I'm told I spent most of it apologising to everyone for causing so much fuss and disruption. One thing, however, was pin sharp. Mike, who was the last of the three to leave my bedside, bent down towards me and smiled. 'You poor thing,' he said. 'You're being assaulted from all directions. Time to let you get back to sleep.' With that, he leaned closer and kissed me on the lips.

I lay there stunned and speechless while I let it sink in. This hadn't been a peck. This had been a proper kiss, lingering just long enough to make my heart skip a beat. This was it, I thought. This was the sign I needed. I could feel it long after he'd gone.

As I knew Mike would be spending Christmas Day with his family in Cowbridge, I resolved not to lie in my bed feeling soppy and distracted but to get up and get fit, so I could get back to normal as soon as possible. That same morning I got myself up into my wheelchair so that I wouldn't have to eat my Christmas dinner in bed. In doing so, I unfortunately terrified the junior doctor on call; I'd apparently become quite anaemic overnight, and would need treatment for that as well. So, between the unscheduled blood transfusion and Mum and Dad's visit, I had plenty to occupy my mind. Even so, it kept returning to the only burning question. What was happening now? Where was this going?

Boxing Day wasn't about to provide any answers – just another tantalising glimpse of what might be. It was a busy one; as well as Mum and Dad and my cousin Francine, I had a visit from my quadriplegic friend Mike Ward and his assistant, and then – oh relief – also from Mike. It was such a social whirl, there was no time to be alone – nor would I have wanted to drive family and friends away – but as visiting time ended, Mike found some unexpected tidying to do, meaning he, once again, was last to leave.

As before, no words of any meaning passed between us but, as on Christmas Eve, our lips met.

Being a paraplegic does have some unexpected compensations. Freed from the pesky need to prove to anyone that I had become proficient in the use of a walking frame or pair of NHS-issue crutches, I was announced good to go the next morning. Mike once again stepped in and offered to collect me and drive me back home to my parents. So far so good – I was positively tingling with anticipation – but nothing was said, and I didn't want to broach it. I had no clues or ideas about the reasons for his reticence. Was he shy? Undecided? Or – worst-case scenario – horribly assaulted by remorse or regret?

Don't be ridiculous, I told myself; it was only a case of two kisses. But even so, I felt entirely unable to speak out. For all our ease with one another over the many, many months of our friendship, it suddenly felt as if there was an elephant in the room. Or, at least, riding in the back of Mike's Skoda.

They tend to say 'third time lucky', don't they? But in my case, it was actually fifth. For on both that day and the one following, when Mike came to visit, he kissed me goodbye on the lips. Looking back, I think I felt a little like a Jane Austen heroine, which is so far removed from my usual persona that I was beginning to fear for my sanity.

This would not do. This could not continue. So when Mike said he'd be over again on the 29th, I told myself I would gather my courage in both hands and confess how I felt about him. Now that he'd kissed me, perhaps he *needed* telling. Perhaps he'd been equally nervous and uncertain. Perhaps he'd worried that *I* was the one having doubts.

I made soup for lunch – always a handy distraction – but even as I stirred it, down the phone came the message that his car was playing up and that he wasn't going to make it. He'd have to call out the local garage instead. 'Oh, well,' said Mum, oblivious, as she sniffed appreciatively at my efforts. 'These things happen. We can always save some for him to have tomorrow.' Arrgh! Stuff the soup. I couldn't keep this in till tomorrow! The thought of postponing what I'd girded my loins for all morning was almost too much for me to bear.

Happily, the phone rang again. The car was mended. If it didn't disrupt things too much, Mike wondered, could he still come over as originally planned? I managed, with some effort, to contain my emotions, and when he duly arrived we all sat down to lunch. After that, Mum and Dad went out for the afternoon, and the two of us got down – as had been the intention – to catching up with all the Trust business currently piled up as a result of Christmas and my impromptu hospital stay. He seemed so set on business, I didn't know quite what to do. No single moment seemed right.

All too soon it was time for him to head home, and my stock of suitable moments to speak out was dwindling. Now or never, I decided. We were out in the hall. I cleared my throat. I hadn't quite decided exactly what I would say, and what came out eventually was the rather nervous enquiry: 'Do you feel ready for another relationship?'

His 'no' was tossed back in the blink of an eye, leaving me almost as speechless and desolate as the day when he'd told me I'd never walk again. But this time, also stupid and embarrassed to boot. Perhaps seeing this was what prompted him to walk the two steps to kiss me goodbye.

There's lots said about time standing still at such moments, but for me it was racing altogether too fast. I had a scant half a second to persuade him he was wrong; that he was absolutely ready to start a relationship, and that the person he should start it with was me. Nothing in my life had ever felt so right and perfect. I knew in that instant that if I had my time again I'd want everything that had happened to happen exactly as it did the first time, just as long as it brought me to the man in front of me. Without the accident, chances were that I would never have met him. Without it I wouldn't have what I had at that moment. The man that I loved, standing captive in my hallway, too polite – for the moment – to make a bolt for it and escape.

I was firm on one thing: that I wasn't going to waste it. Fate had cruelly taken one woman he loved from him. I wasn't about to let go of the reins and give fate the space and time to interfere with either of us again. I put my arms around him and I kissed him like I meant it. Seconds passed. It appeared that perhaps he'd reconsidered. We drew apart finally, the deal very much sealed.

Our eyes met, and my heart skipped a whole handful of beats. 'On the other hand,' he said softly, 'perhaps I am.'

epilogue

M e. Married. As if. At no point since the 10th of May 1980 had I ever really believed – deep down, at any rate – that falling in love and marrying the man of my dreams was anything I could seriously hope for. Yet it happened, on 2nd of October 2004, and we honeymooned, without mishap, in Barbados. Now in partnership as both a couple and campaigners, Mike and I have continued to devote much of our time to making TREAT Trust Wales a reality. After all, in a life in which so much has already happened, it would be a shame if the process stopped now.

Finally a footnote. No account of my life would be complete without mention of my meeting the Queen. How nice to be able to relate an encounter commensurate with respect for the Crown, due observance of protocol and a cordial and mutually enjoyable exchange. Nice, but, unfortunately, not possible. My 'moment' came about during Her Majesty's Golden Jubilee state visit to Margam Park, near Port Talbot. TREAT was invited to participate in the event and one representative – me – would have the honour of meeting the Queen herself.

The day was cold and wet and we were dressed for setting up our exhibition on muddy grass – mud-spattered track-suit and trainers. My identity-badge ribbon had snapped and was held together with hairy string, completing the scruffy picture, while my smart clothes were stashed to change into for the formal part of the visit later.

On presenting myself at the door of the Orangery where I was to be presented to the Queen, I noticed that just inside was someone with whom I'd crossed swords on a number of occasions. I couldn't face being incarcerated with them while waiting for the Royal arrival so I pleaded with the secret service agent to be allowed to wait elsewhere and he agreed.

Though happy to have been excused the wait inside the Orangery, I realised that I couldn't get back to the car park for my smart clothes, leaving me surrounded by those attired in their finery – frills, hats, tail coats, chains-of-office – there I was, in my muddy tracksuit, ready to regale Her Majesty with my vision for TREAT, while looking like an extra from Emmerdale.

On her arrival and eventual approach, undaunted – and I could be embarrassed no further – I launched into a full explanation of TREAT's aspirations, despite the Herculean efforts of her entourage to release her from my diatribe. She stepped away, I wheeled nearer. Another step back, another push and so on until I had finished my lecture. Unendeared to my neighbours, who had missed out on their introductions by my lack of brevity, but completely unrepentant, when called to account for my actions, I sniffily retorted "Well, she did ask!".

As I recall commenting to Mike at the time, at least I knew I'd made an impression.

Which is what, ultimately, I hope has been done in writing this book of my life. If it goes any way towards helping those struggling with life as a paraplegic, then it will have done a valuable job.

And, on a practical level, if it helps get South Wales the rehabilitation centre it deserves then one of my and Mike's dearest wishes will have come true.

No-one could ask more than that, could they?

Melanie Davies
October 2009

Thank you for reading this book; it is a labour of love for TREAT Trust Wales, the charity Mel founded nearly seven years ago.

Working in partnership with ABM University NHS Trust, TREAT is dedicated to providing a purpose-built, world-class centre of excellence on land adjacent to the exciting redevelopment of Morriston Hospital. With accessible, modern gymnasium equipment and a heated, ramped-access swimming-pool, together with alternative therapies, TREAT will provide a welcoming atmosphere encouraging the development of personal health and well-being in all its aspects. It is for all ages and all levels of ability or incapacity and will encourage everyone to participate together.

I am proud to remind you that Mel's share of the proceeds from book sales will be used to help finance the running of the TREAT building and that in supporting us, you will be supporting others. Thank you.

Mike Davies
October 2009

treat|trust
WALES

www.treattrust.org.uk
Company registration number: 04328884
Registered Charity number: 1090939